One

Response
Paper #2
Nov. 12

Week 12 Moderation

ADVANCE PRAISE FOR

Nov. 19

Curriculum and the Cultural Body

"Stephanie Springgay and Debra Freedman have created an engaging text that is both introspective and performative. The authors challenge our assumptions about embodiment by suggesting fresh ways to understand the location and (dis)location of the body in contemporary culture. This brilliant text moves the field beyond the pedagogical discussions and curriculum debates of recent decades. The diverse authors assembled in this collection provide a richly textured investigation of complex notions of the body that inspires aesthetic sensibilities and demands heartfelt responses."

Patrick Slattery, Professor and Regents Scholar, Texas A&M University

"This bold and wonderfully diverse collection of essays challenges us to re-examine and re-conceptualize embodiment. This book points to the fluidity of boundaries in very concrete and often provocative ways. Embodied difference is given an especially noteworthy and original treatment in this collection, making this book a must-read for those who take curriculum and pedagogy seriously, or indeed for any body."

Sandra Weber, Professor of Education, Concordia University, Montreal

Curriculum and the Cultural Body

A Book Series of Curriculum Studies

William F. Pinar
General Editor

Vol. 20

PETER LANG
New York • Washington, D.C./Baltimore • Bern
Frankfurt am Main • Berlin • Brussels • Vienna • Oxford

Curriculum and the Cultural Body

EDITED BY
Stephanie Springgay
and Debra Freedman

PETER LANG
New York • Washington, D.C./Baltimore • Bern
Frankfurt am Main • Berlin • Brussels • Vienna • Oxford

Library of Congress Cataloging-in-Publication Data
Curriculum and the cultural body / edited by
Stephanie Springgay, Debra Freedman.
p. cm. — (Complicated conversation: a book series of curriculum studies; v. 20)
Includes bibliographical references and index.
1. Body, Human—Social aspects. 2. Body image—Social aspects.
3. Body image in art. 4. Performance art. 5. Critical pedagogy.
6. Education—Curricula. I. Springgay, Stephanie. II. Freedman, Debra.
HM636.C87   306.4'8407—dc22   2006022449
ISBN 978-0-8204-8686-4
ISSN 1534-2816

Bibliographic information published by **Die Deutsche Bibliothek.**
Die Deutsche Bibliothek lists this publication in the "Deutsche
Nationalbibliografie"; detailed bibliographic data is available
on the Internet at http://dnb.ddb.de/.

Cover design by Sophie Boorsch Appel
Cover art by Janine Antoni

The paper in this book meets the guidelines for permanence and durability
of the Committee on Production Guidelines for Book Longevity
of the Council of Library Resources.

Printed in the United States of America

For Samuel and Maurya

Contents

List of Images xi

Acknowledgments xiii

Foreword xv
Madeleine Grumet

Introduction: On Touching and a Bodied Curriculum......................... xvii
Stephanie Springgay and Debra Freedman

Part I • Flesh Moves: Technologies and Virtual Bodies

Performing Embodiment: Pedagogical Intersections of Art,
Technology, and the Body.. 3
Yvonne Gaudelius and Charles Garoian

Experiencing Life Through the Body of Film: The Convergence of
Phenomenology and Cultural Curriculum Studies 21
John A. Weaver and Tara D. Britt

Not Without My Body: Embodied Learning With/In the
Online Learning Environment... 39
Debra Freedman = Iris Striedieck = Leonard Shurin

Body Interfaces in Curriculum 51
Karen Keifer-Boyd

Part II • Un/structure: Narratives of Bodies and Schooling

Silent Voices, Silent Bodies: Difference and Disadvantage in
Schooling Contexts.. 63
Dalene M. Swanson

Understandings and Communication Through Dress: Sartorial
Inquiry in a Secondary Art Class.. 79
Daniel T. Barney

Teaching Bodies Who Teach: Men's Bodies and the
Reconstruction of Male Teacher Identity in Ireland............................. 93
Donal O'Donoghue

Part III • Public Spaces: Mediating Embodied Difference Across the Curriculum

Life Goes On: Disability, Curriculum, and Popular Culture
Julie Garlen Maudlin 113

A Tail of Two Women: Exploring the Contours of Difference
in Popular Culture.. 131
Aisha S. Durham and Jillian M. Báez

Disrupting Mass Media as Curriculum: Opening to
Stories of Veiling.. 147
Diane Watt

Teaching Against Homophobia Without Teaching the Subject 163
Cris Mayo

Cesarean, Celebrity and Childbirth: Students Encounter
Modern Birth and the Question of Female Embodiment 175
Natalie Jolly

Part IV • Intersticial States: Performing Bodies

Intimacy in the Curriculum of Janine Antoni 191
Stephanie Springgay

Embodying Exile: Performing the "Curricular Body" 203
Barbara Bickel

Breathing Curiously: Queering the Curriculum Body 217
James Sanders

Notes 235
References 241
Contributors 263
Index 267

Images

Front Cover Image:

Janine Antoni, *Lick & Lather*, 1993. Seven soap and seven chocolate self-portrait, busts dimensions variable. Photographed by Lee Stalsworth at Hirschhorn Museum and Sculpture Garden. Courtesy of the artist and Luhring Augustine, New York.

Back Cover Image:

Janine Antoni, *Lick & Lather*, 1993. Two busts: one chocolate and one soap. Two pedestals 24 X 16 X 13 inches (60.96 X 40.64 X 33.02 cm). Photographed by John Bessler. Courtesy of the artist and Luhring Augustine, New York.

Performing Embodiment:

Stelarc, *Sitting/Swaying: Event for Rock Suspension*, Tamura Gallery, Tokyo, May 11, 1980, Photographer: Kenji Nozawa 3
Stelarc, *Handswriting: Evolution (extended arm)*, Maki Gallery, Tokyo, May 22, 1982, Photographer: Keisuke Oki 4
Stelarc, *Stomach Sculpture*, Fifth Australian Sculpture Triennale, National Gallery of Victoria, Melbourne, September 11—October 24, 1993, Photographer: Tony Figallo 4
Stelarc, *Exoskeleton Cyborg Frictions*, Dampfzentrale, Bern, November 25, 26, 27, 1999, Photographer: Dominik Landwehr 5
Guillermo Goméz-Peña and Roberto Sifuentes, *Mexterminator: Guillermo Goméz-Peña and Roberto Sifuentes*, 1998, Photographer: Clarissa Horowitz 6

Body Interfaces in Curriculum:

Mutual articulation in a simulated environment in a body interaction with EyeToy®. Courtesy of Hui-Chun Hsiao and Karen Keifer-Boyd 58

Understandings and Communication Through Dress:

Erik, *Wasted*. Courtesy of the artist and Daniel Barney 88
John, *Tied Down*. Courtesy of the artist and Daniel Barney 91

Intimacy in the Curriculum of Janine Antoni:

Janine Antoni, *2038*, 2000. C-print. 20 X 20 inches (50.8 X 50.8 cm)
Courtesy of the artist and Luhring Augustine, New York 191
Janine Antoni, *Mortar and Pestle*, 1999. C-print,
photographic assistance, David Allison, 48 X 48 inches
(121.9 X 121.9 cm). Courtesy of the artist and Luhring Augustine,
New York 197

Embodying Exile:

Barbara Bickel, *Living Inquiry,* 2006, video still I.
Courtesy of the artist 207
Barbara Bickel, *Living Inquiry,* 2006, video still II.
Courtesy of the artist 207
Barbara Bickel, *Living Inquiry,* 2006, video still III.
Courtesy of the artist 207
Barbara Bickel, *Living Inquiry,* 2006, video still IV.
Courtesy of the artist 212
Barbara Bickel, *Living Inquiry,* 2006, video still V.
Courtesy of the artist 212
Barbara Bickel, *Living Inquiry,* 2006, video still VI.
Courtesy of the artist 212

Acknowledgments

When Janet Jackson's costume "malfunctioned" at the Super Bowl XXXVIII the world came to a screeching halt. The exposure of a body part, and in particular a star studded breast, incited public protests and subsequently served as the stimulus for this book. Janet Jackson's "tit bit" was evidence that curriculum of the cultural body needed a critical investigation. This examination is part of a larger conversation about a bodied curriculum, a conversation that we have had with a number of individuals over the past few years. This book represents just some of these ideas.

Our thanks go to Elijah Mirochink, who invited us into this bodied conversation, brought the two of us together, and coined the phrase *Flesh Moves*, which we have used as our theme for Part 1. A special thank you to Bill Pinar, our series editor, for supporting creative work within curriculum studies. We'd also like to express our thanks to Madeleine Grumet for her introductory remarks and to Patrick Slattery and Sandra Weber for their insightful endorsements of the book.

To the authors, we cannot thank you enough for not only your written contributions but for adhering to our tight deadlines and for answering our frequent emails so promptly. We'd also like to thank our chapter reviewers: David Darts, Tina Thompson, Paul Duncum, Lisa Louzenhouzer, Sandra Weber, Dennis Carlson, Patrick Slattery, Will Letts, jan jagodinski, Stuart Poyntz, Dan Marshall and Marnina Gonick. Graduate students Dawn La Fargue and Sue Ritter deserve special mention for their assistance in helping us complete the tasks of putting the manuscript together.

Koushik and Paras you claim to not understand a word we write but our hope is that your "scotch night" conversations become fleshier.

A special thanks go to Stephanie and Deb. They deserve that gorgeous pair of shoes! Size seven.

Foreword

Madeleine Grumet

If we did not already know it, a visit to a kindergarten or first grade classroom quickly reminds us how much of education is about our bodies. In a recent visit to a classroom to observe a student work to integrate theater into the first grade curriculum unit on community, I was fascinated to see how constantly the classroom teacher and my student told the kids to sit down, move over, stay put, stop touching. My student was amazed at her own preoccupation with order. She had headed for this public school classroom bearing gifts of expressivity and creativity, and, as soon as she crossed into the room, had become a drill sergeant. We assumed that in addition to her desire to comply with the protocols she encountered, her own classroom memories of constraint, and discipline had been stimulated, and she had become the good little first grader herself.

I remember little from my early schooling experiences except strong images of constraint and humiliation. I remember a little pre-school place that an aunt we were visiting wanted to send me to: cots for nap time in a row, a chest of drawers with underpants for accidents. I put up a big fuss and didn't go. I remember waiting in lines outside the elementary school on freezing mornings before we were led into the building. By then I had learned not to make a big fuss, and I waited with the others, ears and fingers numb from the cold. I remember also, the sickening smell of the steam table in the basement cafeteria.

Disciplining and disappearing the body in schools are intrinsic to traditions of Western education and epistemology, and so it is no surprise that when we began to readmit body consciousness to educational discourse, in the very presence of toes or navels, gonads or drool, we stood mute and awed. THE BODY (whose, where, when?) as sensuous spectacle appeared in studies of gender, multiculturalism, ways of knowing, and identity, and we applauded the very fact of it. Nevertheless, as we celebrated its intervention, we often forgot that as we welcomed its sensuality, and materiality, we were replacing its absence with objectifications and stereotypes. The essays in this book, *Curriculum and the Cultural Body,* return our living, learning bodies to uncertainty and possibility, reminding us that there is no line to be drawn between subjectivity and what we know as we experience our bodies in the world and the world through our bodies.

Upon first encountering the text, I was surprised to see that its editors Stephanie Springgay and Debra Freedman had placed the section *Flesh Moves: Technologies and Virtual Bodies* first, before sections on schooling, difference, and performance, discourses about the body and education that are more familiar. But I soon discovered that the very defamiliarization achieved by these initial essays, is the project of this entire collection and the antidote to the awe and perhaps defensive hypostatization of our early responses to the sight of the body in the room.

It is ironic that the editors introduce this volume of essays by critiquing *Bodyworlds*, an exhibition that shows us what our bodies look like inside. What is "inside" has long fascinated curriculum theorists. We have sought it in the hidden curriculum, in the critique of hegemony and ideology, in the search for psychoanalytic understandings of desire and knowledge. Recent advances in neuroscience and imaging have advanced our convictions that we will understand human experience if we can grasp the working of synapses, and identify our genes. But the figure in *Bodyworlds* is the straw/plastinated man in the text, for in this collection of curriculum theory the distinctions between inside and outside are diminished as subjectivity, physical existence and history are all intertwined and synchronous in their transformations through our lives. And so, replacing our body-romance, these essays recognize the body as the medium for our knowing and work to understand how that recognition informs what we know and how we think about what we know. No longer fascinated with the Cartesian split, no longer invoking the body to critique idealism and rationalism, no longer confusing presence with revelation, *Curriculum and the Cultural Body* addresses the body as part of our act, as part of teaching, learning, knowing. Merleau-Ponty would be proud, and I can think of no higher accolade.

Introduction: On Touching and a Bodied Curriculum

Stephanie Springgay and Debra Freedman

The body has become a site of intense inquiry. We are enthralled by its ability to lose and gain weight, be surgically modified, pierced, tattooed, clothed, and put on display (Sweetman, 2000). This fascination with the body's intricate workings is personified by Gunter von Hagens's plastinated bodies.[1] His exhibition, *Bodyworlds*, has toured the globe since 1996 educating the public about the human body and its functions. These spectacles of anatomy present "real" human bodies that have undergone von Hagens's plastination process, which preserves individual organs and tissues.

Many of the plastinated "objects" are organs and tissues, for example, a healthy pink lung resting beside a blackened smoker's lung. In addition, whole bodies are arranged in poses that convey various actions from everyday life, such as playing soccer, tossing a basketball, riding a bicycle, and playing chess. Stripped of their skin the public presentation of the anatomical body produces the body as a kind of spectacle. What is preserved is no longer an individual body. Skin, facial features, eyes, and other identifiable markers have been destroyed or erased in the plastination process. The spectacle renders a collective homogenous identity; an erasure of difference. The body is at once fragile (i.e., a damaged and sick smoker's lung) and durable (plastination maintains the body; there is no decay). Education and freakshow (some of the bodies have glass eyes, bands of skin remain intact, makeup, added hair, or objects such as figure skates) collapse, while also further solidifying gender norms (Eddy, 2006).

The majority of the bodies are male and are arranged in poses that signify cognitive awareness, athletic prowess, and gender conventions. Male bodies play ball, they are labeled as "teacher," and they stand erect, looming large in the spectorial space. Women's bodies, fewer in number, engage in gendered activities such as dance, figure skating, ballet, or domestic activities like caring for children. Not one female stands upright with her feet firmly planted on the ground. A pregnant female and her fetus are presented with an additional disclaimer sign, reminding visitors that these individuals died of natural causes. While male bodies are splayed open in the name of education and science, the pregnant female body is grotesque, horrific, and in need of barriers. In addition, her body is presented in recline; a passive body lying in wait, while her male companions tower over her in athletic grandeur. Moira Gatens (1996) argues that the cultural imaginary of the female body as an envelope, vessel, or receptacle constructs woman as partial, incomplete, and lacking boundaries, which further serves to undermine women's status as subjects. Women lack integrity "precisely because they are not thought of as whole beings" (p. 41). The partiality of the female body is further reproduced in the cultural imaginary of the body politic, where the male body in its clean and proper state remains the privileged signifier of normativity.

Bodyworlds in its conscious attempt to educate the public about the human body constructs a visual spectacle of normativity. It reads the body through binaries: vibrant male bodies in opposition to sexualized and unclean female bodies; healthy bodies versus sick bodies; active bodies against docile bodies. Although the insides of the body are exposed, the leaky abject body is contained. Plastination replaces decay. The body presented is stable, static, and unified.

Moreover, it suggests that by becoming familiar with the "insides" of the body, viewers are able to know their body inside out and thereby to know themselves. Revealing inner life is a chance to see what you are made of. Identity is constructed through the compositions of outside (skin, hair, and other surface stigmatizations) and inside (organs, tissues, skeleton, and blood). As such *Bodyworlds* establishes identity as natural and biologically determined. At best it fails to recognize the imaginary body as a social product, which is culturally specific. Gatens (1996) defines the imaginary body as "those images, symbols, metaphors and representations which help construct various forms of subjectivity" (p. viii). Rather than a belief in the static, irrational, passive, and given body, the imaginary body reveals how bodies are constructed through psychic investments, symbolic renderings, lived experiences, and representational forms. As Elizabeth Grosz (1994) notes: "The body is an open-ended, pliable set of significations, capable of being rewritten, reconstituted, in quite other terms than those which mark it, and consequently capable of reinscribing the forms of sexed identity and psychical subjectivity at work today" (pp. 60–61). It is this ability of bodies to always extend the frameworks which attempt to contain them, to remain permeable and uncertain that serves as the impetus of this book.

Curriculum and the Cultural Body poses the question of how the body *as* meaning, rather than the container of meaning, disrupts normative assumptions and dualistic thought. While each chapter focuses on different understandings of the body with, in, and through curriculum, these questions inform our inquiries: How does cultural production contribute to building the conditions of bodied knowledge, relational practices of identification, and an understanding of a bodied curriculum? What is the role of the body in teaching and learning? What can be ascertained about how students understand, become aware of, and interpret body knowledge? What are the intersections between curriculum studies and the body as subject? And how might explicitly addressing body knowledge in education contribute to the philosophical sophistication of students' understanding of individual and collective agency?

Bodies have been accorded a place of central importance in recent scholarship as researchers attempt to construct the meanings of the lived body, the social body, and the imaginary body (e.g., Ahmed and Stacey, 2001; Grosz, 1994; Price and Shildrick, 1999; Turner, 1996; Weiss, 1999). Each discipline whether education, science, technology, sociology, sport, or visual culture has de-constructed and re-represented the body as subject. Subsequently, we believe that curriculum studies offers students and teachers a vital form of inquiry into bodies through a range of curricular practices.

However, curriculum scholarship often falls prey to an understanding of the body through binary opposites. More cogently, while the remnants of a Cartesian model have been replaced sporadically by a return to holistic or embodied curricular and pedagogical practices (e.g., Hocking, Haskell, and Linds, 2001), these interventions have not fully addressed the potential of the body in the construction of knowledge. Inside and outside of schools students encounter more or less implicit theories of bodies in which their bodies are marked as diseased, ugly, oppressed, and in desperate need of repair. For example, confronted with a healthy respiratory system in one display and a cancerous lesion in another, the public pedagogy (Giroux, 2005) of the *Bodyworlds* exhibit positions the bodies of the students/spectators within this paradigm where healthy is sought after, and the sick, freakish, and gendered is considered something to expel, heal, or suppress. The body in education has become a site of disempowerment and enervation.

Curriculum and the Cultural Body enters the discussion of body knowledge at these intersections and attends to the unspoken questions and practices in education that silence, conceal, and limit bodies. Each author explores the relationship between curriculum studies and the cultural body and, in particular, illuminates the complex intersections between knowledge, subjectivity, and experience. Embracing an understanding of curriculum as living, authors intersect spaces of pedagogical inquiry with curriculum theorizing. In doing so, this book argues that bringing bodies into the picture is crucial for education. This is not to say we are posing a model based on what the plastinated body offers, but rather as teachers and educational theorists we need to direct our attention to the realities of lived bodies in educational settings. While this collection is in conversation with the growing literature on the body, it takes as a central concern inter-embodiment, on ways of being-with others, where one touches and is touched by others.

On Touching and Inter-embodiment

Understanding the body *as* meaning, as opposed to a container in which we store or put meaning, problematizes the relations between inside and outside. In suggesting that bodies and minds are not in opposition and separate, or combined together to form a single autonomous entity, but somewhere *in-between* these two alternatives, we turn to the möbius strip (see Grosz, 1994). The möbius strip is a continuous surface of interconnected sides. Rather than a loop, that has an inside surface and an outside surface, in the möbius strip, through a kind of twisting or inversion, one side becomes the other. Inside and outside are no longer separate but intertwined, interconnected, and contiguous. The möbius has been used as a metaphor to help explain Maurice Merleau-Ponty's (1968) phenomenological understanding of the body as *Flesh*. Merleau-Ponty designated the term *Flesh* to support his idea that the body is neither material substance (biological) nor the container in which the mind is stored and hence separated from the world. Rather, *Flesh* is the intertwining of the material body and the world (experience) in mutual relation. *Flesh* denotes a body that is integrated with the mind, and enmeshed within experience. *Flesh* or the metaphor of the möbius is often conceptualized as in-between, where beings (bodies) constitute themselves not as objects, but as meaning, and as embodied existence. Embodiment captures a sense of the body's immersion in places, spaces, and environments in which it encounters the world. Likewise embodiment disrupts the notion that the inside (psyche) and outside (corporeal) are separate but rather flow one into the other and the surface or border becomes a place of interaction and transformation (Grosz, 1994).

Accordingly, curriculum scholar Ted T. Aoki (see Pinar and Irwin, 2005) reminds us that in traditional curricular spaces, fraught with standards, testing, and the corporatization of education, students become faceless, whereas in the embodied lived curriculum "teachers and students are face to face" (p. 212). Using the term "live(d) curriculum," Aoki folds the past, present, and ongoing experiences together in the situated image of the curricular landscape. Likewise, Bill Pinar (1975/ 2004), proposes an understanding of curriculum through "currere," which is defined as "to run the course, or the running of the course" (p. 35). Currere, argues Pinar (1975/ 2004), provides students and teachers with an embodied understanding of the *Currere* interrelations between knowledge, life experiences, and social reconstruction. Currere, like its counterpart self-reflexivity, "is an intensified engagement with daily life" (Pinar, 2004, p. 37), in which conceptions of self-knowledge are always understood in relation to others. Resonating with Megan Boler (1999), Pinar reminds us that self-understanding must be embedded with engaged pedagogical action, where the self and other become interconnected in the social reconstruction of knowledge, experience, and public life. In other words, curriculum understood as currere is an embodied awareness between inside and outside, and amongst bodies. Extending Aoki and Pinar's notions of curriculum as lived experience, this book proposes a *bodied curriculum* where the inter-embodiment between self and other performs curriculum as difference.

Inter-embodiment, an approach explored by feminist scholar Gail Weiss *Inter-embod-iement* (1999), emphasizes "that the experience of being embodied is never a private affair, but is always already mediated by our continual interactions with other human and non-human bodies" (p. 5). Inter-embodiment poses that the construction of the body and the production of body knowledge is not created within a single, autonomous subject (body), but rather that body knowledge and bodies are created in the intermingling and encounters between bodies. Curriculum theorist Madeleine Grumet (1988) shares this sentiment when she writes that:

> Trapped in the dualisms of individualism and idealism, we become convinced that whatever we see in our "mind's eye" is a private vision, split off from what others know and feel, split off from the synesthesia that integrates all our perceptions, split off from the body, the other, the world. (p. 129)

Rather, intersubjectivity, she argues is characterized as a sharing between self and others (Grumet, 1988). Such an understanding follows Merleau-Ponty's *Flesh* in arguing that bodies are touched; an experience which opens my body to other bodies. This intersubjective relationship between bodies can be characterized through the sense *touch*. Traditionally knowledge and perception have been associated with vision and looking, which is distant and objective, a perspective that posits the separation of mind and body (Foti, 2003; Vasseleu, 1998). "I see" commonly understood as "I know or I understand" reveals the use of sensory terminology to convey mental processes. The other senses marked by the body's effluence were historically separated from reason and knowledge. Engendering the body, the senses smell, taste, and touch became associated with women, characterized by proximity, birthing, and the home (Classen, 1993, 1998; Grumet, 1988). Understood as interior sensibilities, touch, taste, and smell establish boundaries between private and public, normal and abnormal, familiar and strange. In educational contexts, touch has remained colonized. The bodies of teachers and students are rendered "untouchable" (Grumet, 1988, p. 111) and set apart from each other. Grumet (1988) contends that the traditional seating patterns in classrooms fail to address inter-embodiment and bodied encounters.

> By arranging students in rows, all eyes facing front, directly confronting the back of a [student]'s head, meeting the gaze only of the teacher, the discipline of the contemporary classroom deploys the look as a strategy of domination. (Grumet, 1988, p. 111)

The impersonal "looking" further reinforces the rationalist boundary between mind and body, self and other. In contrast to just "being-seen" (my body sees the other body), inter-embodiment proposes that who we are and how we come to know is produced in the moment of an intertwining, inversion, and "touching" between bodies. To make sense of something, to know it, to create it, is to come into contact with it, to touch it, and thereby produce a body (Perpich, 2005). To touch, to feel, and to become embodied in the context of education, is a call for reciprocity (Grumet, 1988) and relationality (Springgay, 2005b).

As a contact sense, touch offers contiguous access to an object. Touch alters the ways in which we perceive objects, providing access to depth and surface, inside and outside. Touch as a way of knowing can be understood through two modalities. First, touch is the physical contact of skin on matter. The second modality is a sense of being in a proximinal relation with something. In visual culture this has often been addressed as synaesthesia. Synaesthesia refers to the blurring of boundaries between the senses so that in certain circumstances one might be able to say I can taste a painted image. A further understanding of proximity has been taken up by corporeal phenomenologists (e.g., Merleau-Ponty, 1968) and feminist scholars (e.g., Ahmed and Stacey, 2001; Grosz, 1994) who argue that knowledge is produced through bodied encounters, which can be interchangeable with the terms inter-embodiment or intercorporeality (Weiss, 1999). How we come to know ourselves and the world around us, our subjectivity, is performed, constructed, and created in relation with other beings. It is this relationality that is crucial. Rather than knowledge formed through the rational autonomous I, knowledge is the body's immersion, its intertwining, and interaction in the world and between others (Vasseleu, 1998). Our interest in touch and relationality resides in the notion that we are always "with" others. It is this intercorporeality or "being-with" (Nancy, 2000) that enables us to conceive of the body and a bodied curriculum outside of the normalizing discourses that have peeled back its skin and pumped it full of plastic.

As opposed to the relational, living, experiencing, and *Flesh*-y body von Hagens's spectacle presents to the public eye/I parts of the body typically hidden from view. Revealing the insides of the body, its organs and tissues, and thus, how the body "functions" he reinforces the notion that what we consider the body is simply its anatomical parts. The inside and the outside of the body are separate attributes. Furthermore, his plastinated bodies emphasize boundaries, containment, and the limits of the body, in direct contrast to the theories of inter-embodiment which pose bodies, body knowledges, and hence subjectivities as always already mediated by bodies in relation to one another. Through intercorporeality and touch the body's boundaries are fluid, interconnected, and permeable. The homogenized and normalized body in *Bodyworlds* fails to draw attention to the ambiguity, fluidity, and uncertainty of bodies, subjectivities, and knowing. In this sense, a bodied curriculum does not become another totalizing or homogenizing paradigm, but rather through inter-embodiment it questions, examines, and provokes the particularities of different bodies.

Intercorporeality *as* Difference

The concern for the particularities of difference within embodiment has been taken up by a number of scholars including feminist philosopher Moira Gatens (1996). Particularities are not limited to biological features, but rather, as Gatens contends, need to be understood from the perspective of the imaginary body. It is the imaginary body that forms and limits how we conceptualize the body in various ways. The imaginary body denotes "those ready-made images and symbols through which we make sense of social bodies and which determine, in part, their value, their status and what will be deemed their appropriate treatment" (Gatens, 1996, p. viii).

For example, in the *Bodyworlds* exhibit the female specimens' breasts and genital are displayed with the skin in tact. The areola, nipples, and labia have not been "dissected." While her male counterparts shoot hoops, the female body, in recline, pregnant, and with her genitals on display reinforces the sociocultural notion of the female body as sexualized, erotic, and offered up for consumption. In some instances the female specimens wear lipstick, further conforming to the cultural construction of the female body. In a similar vein, the lack of racial bodies, disabled bodies, and queer bodies in the exhibition, further reinforces a cultural imaginary of the excluded body. In contrast, it is not biology that gives meaning to the body, "but the ways in which the social system organizes and gives meaning to biology" (Grosz, 1994, p. 17) that continues to perpetuate systems of oppression and inequality.

The kind of curricular theorizing with, in, and through the cultural body, we are suggesting, would require a reconceptualization of the lived body intertwined with the imaginary body. The political practice imagined here is "one where difference could not be decided a priori but rather recognized in the unfolding of shared (or conflicting) aims and objectives of groups of bodies" (Gatens, 1996, p. 56). Difference is neither dichotomized nor neutralized. Embodied understanding takes place in and through "particular bodily existence" (p. 57). Moreover, Sara Ahmed and Jackie Stacey (2001) argue that if the separation of self and other "is undermined in the very intimacy or proximity of the encounter" (p. 6) then, "[i]f one is always with other bodies in a fleshy sociality, then how are we 'with' others differently? [And] how does this inter-embodiment involve the social differentiation between bodily others?" (p. 6). Such moves bring difference center-stage. Differences are not biological facts, but the "manner in which culture marks bodies and creates specific conditions in which they live and recreate themselves" (Gatens, 1996, p. 71). Difference is performed and produced in the very moment of a bodied encounter. What is crucial within education and curriculum studies is the ways that bodies become invested with differences. So, while many of the chapters in this book draw on phenomenology and lived experience, they also suggest that incorporeality "is subject to forms of social differentiation, although such differences cannot simply be found on the bodies of those who are marked" (Ahmed and Stacey, 2001, p. 6).

Rather than peeling back the layers of skin to reveal our "true" and "natural" insides and thereby become more familiar with who we are as bodies and individuals, this book thinks through the body as a *bodied curriculum*. A *bodied curriculum* attends to the relational, social, and ethical implications of being-with other bodies differently and to the different knowledges such bodily encounters produce. It is a practice of being oriented to others, to touch, to reflect, and to dwell with others relationally (van Manen, 1991). A bodied curriculum is an embodied activity where reflection is not simply an awareness of interiority (self-awareness) but a process that interconnects the interiority and exteriority of the body (intercorporeal). In her essay *Bodyreading*, Madeline Grumet (1988) suggests that "reading is an act that is oriented toward what the subject can do in the world" (p. 130). We liken this understanding of embodied reading to a bodied curriculum where

> curriculum, like language, is a moving form; conceived as an aspiration, the object and hope of our intentionality, it comes to form and slips, at the moment of its actualization, into the ground of our action. It becomes part of our situation. (p. 131)

It is this fluidity and openness to uncertainty that marks a bodied curriculum as disruptive and risky.

The disruption of normative assumptions of inside and out "Vanitas: Flesh Dress for an Anorectic Albino." The work is composed of 50 pounds (23 kilograms) of raw flank steak, the shorn edges sewn together to create a simple, elegant dress. The meat is fitted to a standard dressmakers form signifying a body turned inside out. Over time, the fresh meat shrivels and dries pulling taught and tearing from the underlying form. The meat darkens, the juices evaporate, and the marblings of fat thicken and harden (Baert, 2001). The body leaks and decay takes over. Renee Baert (2001) suggests: "This body is not a body contained and static. Rather, [t]his figure, as if with its inside out, imperils the very notions of boundaries and containment, and even desire. The object troubles borders of various kinds: it is a body and dress, inside and outside, animal and human, its contours in a state of flux, its acrid odours permeating the space around it" (p. 16). Through this irreducible corporeal existence "Vanitas" becomes a potent symbol of a bodied curriculum, a curriculum that is no longer based in universals, but one that emphasizes complexities, multiplicities, and difference. In contrast to von Hagens' contained curriculum, "Vanitas" invites "one another to risk living at the edge of our skin, where we find the greatest hope of revisioning ourselves" (Boler, 1999, p. 200).

Curriculum and the Cultural Body

The body of this book has been labored over through two pregnancies and births. What began as an idea while Stephanie's body swelled has become an actualized project in the final weeks of Deb's pregnancy (we're counting on her being late!). Between writing a prospectus, reviewing and editing chapters, and theorizing a bodied curriculum our own bodies have punctured this writing space. Our memories, sensations, understandings, and representations of (our) bodies have been mediated and complicated by our individual and collective experiences of pregnancy, birth, and becoming mothers. Our interest in "birthing" a bodied curriculum grows out of a desire to think about curriculum from a perspective that does not privilege mind and vision over the body and its other senses. Likewise, our concern for the absences of bodies in teaching and learning have propelled our search for bodied meaning in education. As curriculum scholars currently living and teaching in the United States, we are ever aware of the powers of standards and the oppressive capacity of normalizing discourses. A bodied curriculum not only resists the very notion of standards, hegemonic power positions, and categories of sameness, it dislodges and destabilizes "the center" from which binaries and dualistic logic are produced and maintained.

Curriculum and the Cultural Body is arranged in four thematic parts. These parts provoke and shape new understandings of curriculum and pedagogy through a bodied curriculum. In resisting the normative act to describe individual chapters, we embrace the interconnectivity of each text, and therefore focus on providing a context through thematic parts. However, we acknowledge that these are not exhaustive and that further possibilities of unraveling the body in and as curriculum exist.

Part I, *Flesh Moves: Technologies and Virtual Bodies,* explores the ways in which the body is endlessly subject to alteration through the techno-body (Balsamo, 1999). The techno-body exposes the breakdown of binaries between organism and machine, human and nonhuman while reflecting on the implications of alteration to corporality. Technology has often been viewed as a curricular tool—as something to be added to the body and/or curriculum, a position that situates technology as an appendage, a virus, or an intrusion. In contrast, the chapters in this section locate technology not as a "thing" or "tool" that is manipulated and controlled by a body, but as inter-embodiment.

Un/structure: Narratives of Bodies and Schooling is a thematic part that reflects on the ways that body knowledge is conceptualized in various teaching spaces and practices. Each chapter gives voice to the multiple ways that bodies are coded, organized, and produced in and through curriculum.

Part III, *Public Spaces: Mediating Embodied Difference across the Curriculum,* develops perspectives on the prevailing systems of meanings and values that inscribe the cultural body in schools and in larger social sites. The chapters consider the cultural body through what Henry Giroux (2005) calls a public pedagogy: "one in which the production, dissemination, and circulation of ideas emerge from the educational force of the larger culture" (np). Public pedagogy enables curriculum to be read and understood beyond traditional discourses of schooling.

Examining notions of performativity, embodied subjectivity, and relational knowledge, Part IV, *Intersticial States: Performing Bodies,* contests body-self boundaries. The performing body in these chapters, while located within discussions about performance art, is in fact something more complex. The performing body in this section examines the construction of embodied identity in both a discursive and material sense (Price and Shildrick, 1999) interrogating and disrupting patterns of existence in curricular spaces.

Ignoring the cultural body is virtually impossible in today's curricular spaces. As many of the chapters in this collection attest, the body is taken up through a host of possibilities such as: contemporary visual art, film, television, music and advertising, through technology, in schools, and the marketing of celebrity. Yet, despite this diversity of "appearances" society's fascination with the body is pervasive and at times intrusive, celebrating and reifying norms.

It has always amazed us how complete strangers fetishize the pregnant body, touching it, commenting on its size, and demanding intimate details such as trimester standing, sex, and amount of water retention. The pregnant body, like many other forms of bodily alteration, is understood as universal rather than particular, as if these standard codes of measurement (e.g., due dates and weight gain) mark all pregnancies as similar and thereby familiar. In contrast, pregnancy figured through inter-embodiment avows that a bodied curriculum conceived of as intercorporeal subjectivity emphasizes different ways that bodies make meaning.

Curriculum and the Cultural Body refuses to contain bodies or to impose frameworks that limit bodies; rather curriculum and the cultural body problematizes what it means to live as and with a bodied subject.

Part I

Flesh Moves: Technologies and Virtual Bodies

Performing Embodiment: Pedagogical Intersections of Art, Technology, and the Body

Yvonne Gaudelius and Charles Garoian

It's not a matter of being "kicked out of our bodies by machines." Our bodies are what they are. To be an intelligent agent is to be both embodied and embedded in its environment.

Stelarc (in Mulder and Post, 2000, pp. 30–31)

For the past four decades Australian performance artist Stelarc has pushed the materiality of his body to its limits to expose and explore its intersections with the mechanical and electronic apparatus of technological culture.

Stelarc, *Sitting/ Swaying*: Event for Rock Suspension, Tamura Gallery, Tokyo, May 11, 1980, Photographer: Kenji Nozawa

By suspending his body from large meat hooks and stretching his skin, in his early performances, Stelarc challenges our socially and historically constructed assumptions, the curriculum of the body's enclosure, the pedagogy of its circumscribed biotic perimeter, which separates its "meat" from the "machine" context of the world. Stelarc claims, "we can no longer see the skin as a convenient boundary between 'inner' and 'outer'" (Mulder and Post, 2000, p. 25). Stretching his skin, he distorts and ruptures his body's enclosure in order to cross the threshold that separates his body from the world. In doing so, he challenges the "skin" of Cartesianism, which separates our understandings of the body, language, and technology. Following these suspension pieces, Stelarc "started doing performances that didn't test the human body but extended it and augmented it with technical prostheses" (Mulder and Post, p. 26).

Stelarc, *Handswriting: Evolution* (extended arm), Maki Gallery, Tokyo, May 22, 1982. Photographer: Keisuke Oki

Stelarc, *Stomach Sculpture*, Fifth Australian Sculpture Triennale, National Gallery of Victoria, Melbourne, September 11—October 24, 1993. Photographer: Tony Figallo

By attaching an "Extended Arm" (1982), swallowing a "Stomach Sculpture" (1993), and inhabiting the robotic apparatus "Exoskeleton" (1998), which comprise his various prosthetic devices, he continues to question technological embodiment by ridiculing yet revering enfleshment, interconnectivity, and interactivity.

We watch Stelarc's cyborg body—his "prosthetic" extended arm moving, turning, and twisting through space in response to the signals that his body gives. Mimicking the "natural" arm, electrical impulses travel the nerves/wires, turn the cables/muscles and perform the body. Is his body obsolete, as he would claim? Do his mechanical prosthetic devices present us with a posthuman body, a body in which meat and machine are intertwined—a body that leaves behind the Cartesian separation of body and mind? What do Stelarc's metaphors of the prosthetic body suggest about embodiment? Given that his creative work represents an exploration and

Stelarc, *Exoskeleton Cyborg Frictions*, Dampfzentrale, Bern, November 25, 26, 27, 1999.
Photographer: Dominik Landwehr

critical examination of the posthuman body and its relationship to technology, what do his creative works suggest about embodied pedagogy and curriculum? What can we learn about embodied knowing from Stelarc's prosthetic body?

In yet another instance of art intersecting with technology and the body, La Pocha Nostra, the performance art collective consisting of Guillermo Gómez-Peña, Roberto Sifuentes, and Juan Ybarra, performs, mimics, and parodies the cultural tropes of ethnicity, racism and gender.

Guillermo Goméz-Peña and Roberto Sifuentes,

Mexterminator: Guillermo Goméz-Peña and Roberto Sifuentes, 1998.

Photographer: Clarissa Horowitz.

In their performance "Aztechnology," they construct and mimic differing Mexican and Hispanic stereotypes by dressing in clothing ranging from cowboy boots, sombreros, and bandoleros, to gang colors and knives while speaking "Spanglish," a hybrid of Spanish and English better known as "broken English," that performance artist and theorist Coco Fusco (1995) uses as a critical concept to interrogate the markers of "border" identities. Dead chickens hang from the ceiling, gang colors drape their bodies, as a neon halo flashes on and off, on and off, atop a large wooden cross, propped and ready for a crucifixion. Transfixiation, transubstatiation, transgression, transformation—whatever it takes to challenge the markers of Otherness.

In the background a strange mix of pop music and the tinny horns and guitar twang of a Mariachi band blast away. Religious, political, linguistic transgressions abound as these performance artists ironically perform a radical critique of the alterity of Mexican and Hispanic stereotypes by mirroring the gaze of Western European patriarchy. In doing so, their counter-mimicry disrupts the ways in which stereotypical representations function as disembodied technologies, linguistic management systems that disenfranchise and oppress people for their cultural difference. Contrary to the slick, "clean" and one-dimensional stereotypes of the nightly news, the spectacle of La Pocha Nostra's performances gives us "dirty" refractions (Haraway, 1997), occlusions and distortions that serve to disrupt the immutable "truths" of stereotypic representations. Their refractive performances challenge our understandings of curriculum and pedagogy in that they carry with them the power of the body, a power that enables a critical understanding of the images at hand.

La Pocha Nostra's parody of cultural stereotypes through performance art, their disruption of the categorization and classification of embodiment, coincides with cultural critic Susan Sontag's (1966) admonition against interpretation in art, which she claims "makes art manageable, conformable" (p. 8).

> Interpretations, based on the highly dubious theory that a work of art is composed of items of content, violates art. It makes art into an article of use, for arrangement into a mental scheme of categories...To avoid interpretation, art may become parody. Or it may become abstract. Or it may become ("merely") decorative. Or it may become non-art. (p. 10)

Manifesto-like, Sontag advocates a position of vigilance whereby the embodiment of technology is never assumed and any attempts at codifying that relationship are challenged. For Sontag, art is not teleological in that it does not serve as curricular illustration. We extend Sontag's argument by positioning art as a form of critical pedagogy that engages both the artist and the viewer in a process of critical citizenship. Art historians Amelia Jones and Andrew Stephenson (1999) argue that interpretation is a performative process "rather than an act with a final [illustrative] goal" (pp. 1–2), which parallels our notion of art as critical pedagogy.

Jones and Stephenson further claim, "interpretation is, we would argue a kind of performance of the object, while the performance of the body as an artistic practice is a mode of textual inscription. The body (as a corporeal enactment of the subject) is known and experienced only through its representational performances" (p. 8).

Accordingly, the performance artists whose work we discuss expose and critique the body's aesthetic relationship with technology and other cultural systems through performance art to raise fundamental questions and engage in a critical process of meaning making that constitutes an embodied form of curriculum and pedagogy. Hence the performance artworks of Stelarc and La Pocha Nostra lead us to the following questions, all of which have pedagogical and curricular implications. What is the nature of our interaction with technology? How have electronic and digital information technologies changed our understanding of embodiment and materiality? What do we mean by embodying technology? How is technology materialized in the body? Is technological performance disembodied? How do we perform embodiment? What difference does it make if our interaction with technology is disembodied? How do artworks perform embodiment and materiality? What role do visualization and the aesthetic play in embodiment and materiality? What is the difference between embodiment and materiality in everyday cultural work (e.g., teacher, mail carrier, chef), cultural work such as arts performances (e.g., music, dance, theatre, painting), and performance art where subjectivity and critical agency are played out through the body in a very conscious way in that these characteristics are made explicit and foregrounded? Given that performance art is the enactment of subjectivity how does it challenge prescriptive conceptions of curriculum and of pedagogy? We argue that within these questions lie critical understandings of the pedagogical and curricular relationships between the body, performance, and technology.

The "Embodied Body" in Pedagogy and Curriculum

While much of the artwork of the 1980s and 1990s investigated issues of identity and its relationship to the body, the emergence of virtual, digital, and cybernetic discourses and practices have led to a shift away from the *embodiment vs. the body* (handwritten)

essentialized modernist body and toward a posthuman, contingent understanding of technological embodiment as theorized by literary critic Katherine Hayles (1999a). Locating the body as a locus of investigation, while important, had the effect of inadvertently enforcing a mind/body split, as "the body" was investigated in a manner that was separate from the mind. Within such a bifurcated yet closed system, the body is paradoxically rendered as standing alone yet complete in its duality, a sign of what is written on the body through a number of visual, textual, and cultural discourses. "The body" suggests an interchangeable, emblematic body, a universal body of the enlightenment. In contrast, embodiment carries with it an understanding of the cultural location and the specificity of the posthuman body. It suggests a self-reflexive skepticism of our bodies, an unwillingness to believe in its naturalized constructions. Embodiment is not about identity per se, a topic of earlier performative representations, but about subjectivity. As such, embodiment is not an immutable signifier of identity, but is a signifier of multiplicity existing within a complex web of cultural understandings and significations (Garoian and Gaudelius, 2001).

In addition, we refuse to dematerialize embodiment; hence our discussion of embodiment and materiality assumes a dialectical relationship between body and technology. Whereas Cartesian dualism locates body and technology as distinct objects in the world as seen from outside of themselves, a dialectical relationship is in and of itself an embodied one in that its dichotomizing boundaries are porous (Leder, 1990) and permeable (Hayles, 1999a). Contrary to "one-dimensionality," described by cultural critic Herbert Marcuse, the contradictions of dialectical thought are two-dimensional in that a "critical tension" defines their ontology (p. 111). Thus for Marcuse, the framework of Cartesian dualism resides in a "total empiricism" (p. 24), which suggests that as concepts and objects in the world the boundaries and characteristics of "body and technology" can be laid bare and exist in a condition that Heidegger (1962) refers to as "present-to-hand" (pp. 54–55). Heidegger outlines the differences between "present-to-hand" and "ready-to-hand" (p. 68) as follows. Present-to-hand is the tool that is broken, different, or new. It is the foregrounded object laid bare for critical examination and creative re-presentation. In marked contrast to this, ready-to-hand is the tool that becomes part of our being, a familiar object that is known, assumed, and taken for granted by us through our routine use of it.

Using Heidegger's concept of present-to-hand as compared to ready-to-hand, science philosopher Robert Crease (1993) argues, "a tool is conspicuous when our attempts to use it meet interference. We need to call someone, but the right means is not at hand; we experience an 'un-ready-to-

present-to-hand vs. ready-to-hand (handwritten)

hand,' we experience something as 'un-useable;' the telephone on our desk that does not work obtrudes on us as something we need to have work" (pp. 62–63). The "obstinate and independent" workings of interference that Crease points to in his example of the telephone are performative qualities that present the possibility of exposing cultural difference. As such, interference is not a negative outcome but a position of possibility from which we can understand the contradictions and complexities of the refracted images of technological systems that Haraway (1997) suggests. Interference disrupts and transforms the dualism that distinguishes the body from technological, pedagogical, curricular systems into a dialectical play or performance where their assumed differences beg the question of each other in the form of "argumentative analogy." Crease (1993) suggests that this play between the two represents "a tool whereby a structured set of relations present in one area [the body] is introduced into another [technology]" (p. 76).

The significance of dialectical thought notwithstanding, its potential for curricular and pedagogical connectivity is limited. Although the dialectical relationship between the body and technology renders their boundaries porous, even within this relationship "body" and "technology" remain separate entities. Hence the focus of the dialectic becomes the point of tension where the body (human) and technology (machine) intersect, which suggests a difference that is maintained by the skin. As we discussed earlier in this article, it is this point of tension that Stelarc exposed by the puncturing, stretching, and suspending of his body from his skin. Such a truncated discourse essentializes the assumptions of the body and technology at the expense of any divergent, disparate, and contingent circumstances among and within which they are situated. In doing so, a "biunivocal" intersection is created between the body and technology similar to a tree and its taproot (root-tree system) that delimits the "understanding of multiplicity," claim cultural critics Gilles Deleuze and Félix Guattari (1987, p. 5). Instead of the root-tree, they offer the metaphor of a rhizome, a reticulated system of roots with unlimited nodes of interconnectivity. Arguing against dialectical processes whose efforts to thwart dichotomy are limited to bilateral exchange, Deleuze and Guattari (1987) claim that the problem with "these linguistic models is not that they are too abstract but, on the contrary, they are not abstract enough" and instead they propose that we consider a rhizomatic structure that "ceaselessly establishes connections between semiotic chains, organizations of power, and circumstances relative to the arts, sciences, and social struggles" (p. 7).

In spite of their differences, the root-tree dialectic and the multiplicity of the rhizome as pedagogical and curricular metaphors can be considered in mutually dependent ways. While dialectical thought is limited in its interconnectivity, it nonetheless provides an essential means to disrupt Cartesian dualism and to materialize a link between the body and technology in such a way that they are embodied within each other. Thus a dialectical intertwining of body and technology systems challenges "us and them" and "machine and meat" dichotomizations, which enables an open discourse to ensue between the two. In doing so, this dialectical exchange represents the "first step" in rupturing Cartesian dualism and enabling a multicentric critical pedagogy to occur on the scale espoused by Deleuze and Guattari.

The Materiality of the Body

Judith Butler (1993) argues that the activity of the body during the process of social construction gives the false impression of a "willful subject." This impression notwithstanding, Butler claims, "construction is not an activity, but an act, one which happens once and whose effects are firmly fixed [as regulatory cultural norms]. Thus, constructivism is reduced to determinism and implies the evacuation or displacement of human agency" (p. 9). To counter willful construction, the body being inscribed or performed upon, Butler posits "citationality" as the body performing its own subjectivity. In doing so, citationality refers to the body's agency, the disclosure of its social and historical context in which the citation exists. Contrary to construction where reiteration reproduces the oppression of the body, the performance of citationality represents for Butler, Lacan, Deleuze, Irigaray, and Haraway a reiterative process that counters cultural norms and stereotypes through parodic distortions.

Such distortions for psychologist Jacques Lacan come in the form of anamorphosis, a parody of the gaze of ocular technology, which is enabled by geometrical perspective. Anamorphosis, claims Lacan, is a method of representation "that makes anything appear at will in a particular stretching…[it] complements what geometral researches into perspective allow to escape from vision…[the stretched, oblique image of anamorphosis serves as] a trap for the gaze" (pp. 87–89). If we were to apply the distortion of mimesis enabled through anamorphosis to a critical end we would move toward a notion of parodic mimesis. For example, feminist critic Susan Kozel (1996) points to Luce Irigaray's notion of the critical function of parody. "Through mimesis, she [Irigaray] offers what seems to be an indirect and often parodic rendition of that which has been left out of the text that she examines" (p. 118). Similarly, Linda Hutcheon (1985) conceptualizes parodic distortion as différence. Invoking the theoretical writings of critical theorist Gilles Deleuze about the subject (1986), Hutcheon argues that "parody is repetition, but repetition that includes difference; it is imitation with critical distance, whose irony can cut both ways" (p. 37). Thus for Deleuze and Hutcheon, difference is exposed when a subject is read and interpreted both in and out of context, which suggests a transcontextual inversion of its socially and historically constructed assumptions.

Similarly, cultural critic Donna Haraway (1997) claims that the transcontextual convergences of the body (organic), the textual (language), and the technical (cybernetics) "are more important than their residual oppositions...[as such] bodies have become cyborgs—cybernetic organisms—compounds of hybrid techo-organic embodiment and textuality" (p. 212). What is significant about her argument is the fundamental importance that she ascribes to context, "not as surrounding information," but as a co-structuring of the inner "technics and biologics" of the body's immune system with ecosystems outside the body (p. 214). Haraway points to Terry Winograd's (1992) concept of "breakdown" to characterize the co-structuring of communications pathologies, the distortions brought about by stress in the body's immune system as well as those of electronic management systems. Winograd claims, "breakdowns play a central role in human understanding. A breakdown is not a negative situation to be avoided, but a situation of non-obviousness, in which some aspect of the network of tools that we are engaged in using is brought forth to visibility (becomes 'present-to-hand')" (p. 164). Similar to Haraway's cyborgian trope, Winograd's concept of breakdown provides yet another example of parodic mimesis insofar as it exposes difference—the discreet, hidden heterogeneity imbedded in electronic management systems as compared with their universal representations and applications.

Thus, according to the aforementioned theorists, parodic mimesis renders the invisible visible. Its critical pedagogy reveals the discrete, hidden agendas, norms, and stereotypes of social construction, and in doing so, it critiques and disrupts the gaze of patriarchal culture. Parodic mimesis exposes difference—multiple readings, interpretations, and representations of social norms. The critical perspectives of performance artists like Stelarc and La Pocha Nostra represent ways of parodying, distorting, breaking down, and disrupting the electronic gaze of cyberculture. They create ideas and images that are "situated," a cultural positioning referred to by Haraway "where partiality and not universality is the condition of being heard to make rational knowledge claims" (1997, p. 195).

[handwritten: Relationship to Curriculum → phenomenology?]

Given that the social construction of pedagogy and curriculum dematerializes the body and delimits its creative and political agency, Butler (1993) proposes that the body be theorized as "matter" so that the cultural norms that constitute its identity can be exposed, examined, and critiqued. In doing so, she locates identity as embodied; the materiality of the body and the materiality of knowledge, language, and identity are intertwined.

Stelarc's prosthetic devices and La Pocha Nostra's distorted stereotypes as embodied performances correspond with philosopher Maurice Merleau-Ponty's (1968) conception of materiality as the intertwining of the body and the world, a condition of "enfleshment" wherein the body's knowledge of phenomena is perceived only as flesh rather than the illusions transmitted by our senses. What we see, hear, feel, taste, and smell represents information—knowledge about the world that can only be understood in the material composition of the body. Accordingly, the books we read, the music we hear, the people we touch, and the technologies that we use are not external to, but intertwined with the body. *[handwritten: "enfleshment" → all experience is embodied]*

Yet when Merleau-Ponty (1968) makes this argument he writes not of the materiality of the body, of the meat of the body. Instead, "flesh" represents our embodied engagement with the world. As such, he argues that "the flesh we are speaking of is not matter. It is the coiling over of the visible upon the seeing body, of the tangible upon the touching body" (p. 146). He goes on to write "we must not think [of] the flesh starting from substances, from body and spirit—for then it would be the union of contradictories—but we must think it, as we said, as an element, as the concrete emblem of a general manner of being" (p. 147). Merleau-Ponty is characterizing what it means "to be in the world," hence his discussion of flesh can be misread as an empiricist being-in the world through the flesh of the body, or the body ready-to-hand, to use Heidegger's term. For Merleau-Ponty, the flesh of the body is folded over and into the flesh of the world and the flesh of history. We can never step back and view this flesh, for Merleau-Ponty dismisses the notion of the objective humanist viewer, what Haraway (1997) has called the "modest witness." For this reason, Merleau-Ponty shifts from notions of the viewer and viewed, subject and object, body and mind to "the visible and the invisible."

Historian Martin Jay (1994) has argued that Merleau-Ponty's "new emphasis on the 'flesh of the world' rather than the lived, perceiving body meant that the notion of vision itself began to assume a post-humanist inflection, comparable to that of Heidegger's, which made it less obviously a term referring to what is normally thought of as human beings looking at the world" (p. 316). Jay goes on to write, "what consciousness misses in Being is the invisible inextricably intertwined with the visible in a chiasmic exchange that never achieves dialectical sublation. Being is in the interplay of the visible and invisible, which no humanist subject can ever truly see" (p. 320). Within such a framework the objectivist stance of Enlightenment humanism is impossible to maintain.

Despite all that Merleau-Ponty has to offer, his work has been criticized by a number of feminist theorists (Butler, 1993; Grosz, 1994; Irigaray, 1992; Olkowski, 2000; Sullivan, 1997; Young, 1990). Much of this critique focuses on Merleau-Ponty's positioning of "experience" as the point of view from which knowledge is constructed. Olkowski (2000) writes that "the acceptance of experience as unproblematic criterion for the assessment of knowledge overlooks the fact that experience is already determined by the cultural and theoretical milieu and so is not ideologically free." Philosopher Shannon Sullivan (1997) points to Merleau-Ponty's concept of the "anonymous body" as especially problematic in that it erases markers of difference.

Nevertheless, Hayles (1999a) intentionally intertwines the materiality of text and technology with that of the body which enables markers of difference through text, an extension of Merleau-Ponty's claim that knowledge is enfleshed. Given that differentiated bodies are socially and historically codified, their materiality is similar to that of literary texts. If what we read is only known in our body, then the texts of our identities are enfleshed with our bodies. Moreover, considering that our bodies are socially and historically constructed suggests a technological materiality. Our bodies are as much machines as machines are flesh given that our knowledge and experience of them is known exclusively in the body. Hayles (1999a) argues, "because they have bodies, books and humans have something to lose if they are regarded solely as informational patterns, namely the resistant materiality that has traditionally marked the durable inscription of books no less than it has marked our experiences of living as embodied creatures (p. 29).

In keeping with Hayles's intertwining of the materiality of technology and the body, art educator Carol Gigliotti (1999) claims that embodiment lies "at the heart of all ethical and aesthetic investigations" (p. 55). Her call for an embodied ethics and aesthetics corresponds with the aim of artists like Stelarc and those of La Pocha Nostra whose performances serve to expose, examine, and critique dualistic, rationalistic and deterministic assumptions of electronic management systems, which dematerialize the body and render it powerless, if not obsolete. Gigliotti (1999) states:

> [it] is not that we must transcend this envelope of skin in order to act morally, but that the body allows us to be of and in the world at the same time. We may act,

[handwritten margin notes: "Argument against humanist", "Feminist response to Mer.-Pont."]

think, grasp, be individuals and yet part of the whole. We collaborate with the world, and at the same time we are the world. (p. 55)

Gigliotti's notion of the aesthetic dimension enables interconnectivity through "absorption," a process of "bidirectional incorporation" that constitutes a "one-body relation," to use philosopher Drew Leder's terms (1990, pp. 164–165). It is within the realm of the aesthetic that the intersection of the body and technology can be imagined and performed because, as Marcuse (1977) claims: "The world formed by art is recognized as a reality which is suppressed and distorted in the given reality" (p. 6). The given reality that is being addressed by the performance artists and theorists discussed in this chapter is the oppressive world of information management systems that dematerializes the body and in doing so renders it politically impotent within cyberculture. The critique of these systems by these artists and theorists has implications for an embodied pedagogy and curriculum that promotes critical citizenship and the attainment of creative and political agency.

Technology, Agency, and Politics

Historian and philosopher Ivan Illich, in a brief yet provocative 1982 speech that he delivered in Tokyo, Japan, at the Asahi Symposium "Science and Man: The Computer-managed Society," claimed that electronic information technologies are capable of programming environments where "people in them become indolent, impotent, narcissistic and apolitical. The political process breaks down, because people cease to be able to govern themselves; they demand to be managed" (p. 1). Illich's critique of programmed environments echoes the cultural critiques of Herbert Marcuse, who wrote about the "one-dimensional" thinker, and Terry Winograd's "rationalist tradition." For Marcuse (1972), "one-dimensional thought is systematically promoted by the makers of politics and their purveyors of mass information. Their universe of discourse is populated by self-validating hypotheses which, incessantly and monopolistically repeated, become hypnotic definitions or dictations" (pp. 25–26). Similarly, Winograd (1992) refers to such management as the embodiment of "systematic logical rules that can be used to draw conclusions" (p. 154). Peoples' loss of creative agency and their acquiescence to management, which Illich, Marcuse, and Winograd refer to and which is often achieved through pedagogy and curriculum, represents a condition wherein peoples' life experiences and learning are disembodied and isolated from the world.

To illustrate his point about the environmental degradation of electronic programming, Illich invoked a metaphor of ecology—a trope previously applied to interconnected biological systems, which in recent years has served to represent interdependent social, political, and economic issues and concerns. For example, he advocated an approach to dealing with the issue of electronic management critically through "political ecology," a process by which a "politically organized general public analyzes and influences technical decisions" (p. 1). To support his claim for political resistance against the perils of electronic management, Illich (1983) drew upon his knowledge of historical systems, which were deployed to manage and exploit the environment. In doing so, he distinguished between two kinds of public environments: "the commons within which peoples' subsistence activities are imbedded, and resources that serve for the economic production of those commodities on which modern survival depends" (p. 2).

The purpose of the embodied environment of the commons then is transformed through electronic management systems into a disembodied resource whose sole purpose is its own social, political, and economic survival. Under these egregious conditions the human body is rendered obsolete, suggests performance artist Stelarc. Disembodied information and experience are at the core of electronic management systems given that the body and identity are tele-constructed, tele-archived, and tele-ported globally, all of which reconfirm the dichotomous relationship between the body and the world posited by Descartes. According to Illich (1983), this transformation of the commons into a resource for capital happens through "enclosure," a process that

> inaugurates a new ecological order...through which the environment became primarily a resource at the service of "enterprises" which, by organizing wage-labor, transformed nature into the goods and services on which the satisfaction of basic needs by consumers depends. This transformation is in the blind spot of political economy. (p. 3)

It is precisely this blind spot in the information economy, pedagogy, and curriculum of cyberspace, its oppressive and enterprising disembodied policies and procedures that artists like Stelarc and La Pocha Nostra expose, explore, and disrupt with their interventionist tactics of performance art. Their objective is to re-claim the body and to reconstitute its agency as a critical citizen in contemporary culture.

The colonization of the commons of cyberspace by corporate advertising and sales, and by xenophobic hate groups, sexual predators, and sleaze merchants is confirmation of Illich's harbinger of management systems transforming the commons of cyberspace into a resource for capital. To illustrate the corporate takeover of the commons by technology, Illich cites the impact of the introduction of the first loudspeaker on an island on which he landed in 1926.

> Up to that day, all men and women had spoken with more or less equally powerful voices. Henceforth this would change the commons. Henceforth the access to the microphone would determine whose voice shall be magnified. Silence now ceased to be in the commons; it became a resource for which loudspeakers compete. Language itself was transformed thereby from a local commons into a national resource for communication…Unless you have access to a loudspeaker, you now are silenced. (p. 4)

Analogous to Illich's example, various extremist groups purveying their ideologies and vying for the public's attention now pervade the commons of cyberspace. Their "access to the loudspeaker" of the Internet silences democratic discourse in the commons and transforms its open public space into places from which to market its resources to the public through spectacularized propaganda and advertising. In an essay written with performance artist Guillermo Gómez Peña, performance theorist Lisa Wolford (2000) makes ironic reference to this corporate enterprise in cyberspace as "sili-colonization."

Corresponding with Illich's notions of disembodiment, the indolence and impotence of the body in electronically managed environments, historian and philosopher Michel Foucault (1977) argues that such impelled discipline or subjection produces "docile bodies." He claims, "discipline increases the forces of the body (in economic terms of utility) and diminishes these same forces (in political terms of obedience)" (p. 138).

Both Illich and Foucault agree that disembodiment results from programmed (Illich) or disciplined (Foucault) environments. For example, while Illich defines the curriculum of "enclosure" as a circumscribed space whose sole purpose is to function as a resource for capital, Foucault defines "enclosure" as a space determined or specified by a disciplinary force: "a place heterogeneous to all others and closed in upon itself" (p. 141). Accordingly, both scholars point to an existential condition in which the body's facility and mobility are managed and distributed by a disciplinary regime. In cyberculture such disembodied experience is manifested through electronic delivery systems that dematerialize the corporeality of the body in order to re-materialize it as digital code ready for electronic distribution. The interventionist objectives of performance artists are the obverse: to dematerialize or deconstruct the oppressive discourse and practice of cyberculture in order to re-materialize the body and its agency.

To resist the subjection of programmed and disciplined environments, both Illich and Foucault call for political vigilance and action. Positioning the body politically requires challenging and disrupting the Cartesian duality of body/mind and Enlightenment taxonomic systems, which a programmed, disciplined environment like commercial cyberspace depends upon for its construction. Disembodiment assumes the materiality of the body and the materiality of knowledge, language, identity, and technology as isolated and separate phenomena. As long as programmed environments like cyberspace assume that information, knowledge, and identity are separate from the body, both are vulnerable to being dematerialized through social inscription and construction.

According to Butler (1993), institutionalized power in the Foucauldian sense is performed on the materiality of the body. It is the material and subjective conditions of institutions that impose upon and displace the body's attitudes and behaviors, its choices and desires. A "reformulation" of the body's materiality requires an "understanding of performativity not as the act by which a subject brings into being what she/he names, but, rather, as the reiterative power of discourse to produce the phenomenon that it regulates and constrains" (Butler, 1993, p. 2). In other words, the pedagogies of culture and power are not inscribed as curriculum on the body as if it was an empty slate, a common earlier view of pedagogy, curriculum, and learning. On the contrary, the body's biological predisposition is always already implicated in the cultural assumptions that construct it insofar as the body cannot be understood without understanding the cultural conditions with which it is intertwined.

Likewise, the historical and social conditions of culture cannot be understood separate from the contingent circumstances of the body. As such, the materiality of the culture and the body are intertwined as suggested by Merleau-Ponty (1968), however, with the understanding that this intertwining does not occur separate from the cultural conditions of difference within which the body and culture exist. This intertwining represents a metonymic relationship between the body and culture in that they are contiguous with one another rather than dialectically opposed. Moreover, this contiguity of the body and culture enables the possibility of Deleuze and Guattari's (1987) rhizomatic understanding of subjectivity. Similar in its operation to the dialectical structures rejected by Deleuze and Guattari, the enabling facility of metaphor is limited by its subject/object relationship, which cultural critic Edward Shanken (2000) characterizes as an "active-passive" condition of agency (pp. 73–74) that is similar to the critical position "against metaphor" proposed by Kristine Stiles and which echoes

Sontag's position "against interpretation." Shanken (2000) writes, "Stiles has theorized that the conventional metaphorical function of art was appended by an interactive metonymical function that emerged when the human body became the primary medium and content of visual art" (p. 74). Within this theoretical framework, Stiles has positioned performance art as enabling, "a subject-subject relationship between artist and spectator" and hence holding "the possibility for a more connected relationship" (p. 74).

Such an intertwining of metonymy and rhizomatic is what performance artists like Stelarc and La Pocha Nostra create, and what an embodied pedagogy and curriculum of resistance requires. By exposing, examining, and critiquing the normative discourses and practices of electronic management systems, they disrupt our naturalized understandings of technology's relationship with our bodies. They challenge our limiting assumptions about technological intervention, a paranoia whose pathology traces back to the dematerialization of the body by Cartesian and Enlightenment philosophy. Contrary to such social and historical categorizations of the body, which foster a fear of the disembodied other, the performances of these artists enable viewers' political and creative agency— their ability to re-claim, re-construct, and re-present the body and technology as imbedded within each other.

The body materialized in technology represents for these artists and theorists an interconnective relationship that ruptures binary logic, passes through the dialectical, and opens to the multiple possibilities of the rhizome for interaction and interconnectivity. Rather than standing outside of regimes of power, these artists and theorists create disruptive spaces within these ideologies to enable critical agency and subjectivity. As such, their performances represent radical forms of democracy and pedagogy, the practice of critical citizenship within the constricting circumstances of prescribed management systems such as schools and curricula. Unlike the silenced, mute, and complacent spectator who has succumbed and assimilated to the disciplinary laws and practices of management systems, the critical citizenship of performance art involves artists, theorists, teachers, and students who speak and act out about disembodied subjectivity in contemporary culture through civil disobedience.

Experiencing Life Through the Body of Film: The Convergence of Phenomenology and Cultural Curriculum Studies

John A. Weaver and Tara D. Britt

> In a search for rules and principles governing cinematic expression, most of the descriptions and reflections of classical and contemporary film theory have not fully addressed the cinema as life experiencing life, as experience expressing experience.
>
> (Sobchack, 1992, p. 5)

We want to introduce the work of Vivian Sobchack as it may apply to the reading of popular contemporary films. Particularly we want to focus on her ideas concerning the bodily experience of films, filmmakers, and spectators and how the film body acts as an extension of the human body. Then we want to offer our own phenomenological reading of a popular, contemporary film, *Minority Report*. We focus on this film since within the history of film criticism and theory the tendency is to ignore these types of film and focus more on *avant garde*, international, or select Charlie Chaplin or Alfred Hitchcock films. The one exception to this practice is Robert Warshow (1946/2001), who sought out the "immediate experience" of popular films to demonstrate how films touched the minds and bodies of viewers. After our readings of *Minority Report* we turn to the influence of montage and the digital image in constituting identities and how the digital image is changing the relationship between the body and cinema. Films still serve as extensions of the body but through an excursion into the work of Mark Hansen (2002, 2004a/b) we will see that the body's function becomes more pronounced in relation to the digital image. We then end with a section that contextualizes the body, technology, and film within cultural curriculum studies.

The Embodiment of Film

Traditionally in film theory, from Hugo Munsterberg (1916/1970) and Siegfried Kracauer (1947) to Gilles Deleuze (1986, 1989), the focus has been on the aesthetic dimensions of film or a psychoanalytical reading of film's content. The same thing can be found in film readings in curriculum studies. In most writings dealing with films the focus is on the political dimensions of films (see Giroux, 2002) or pedagogical content readings (see Gough, 1993). What is often left out of these readings is the experience of films or how bodies interact with film and film's technology. It is Sobchack's work that can help reconnect cultural curriculum studies and phenomenology. Film, of course, is never a complete embodied experience—that would require a complete sensory interconnection between the body and film. As films are created now, they are "an act of seeing that makes itself seen, an act of hearing that makes itself heard, an act of physical and reflective movement that makes itself reflexively felt and understood" (Sobchack, 1992, pp. 3–4). Because of this sensory and cognitive connection between films and the body, "cinema thus transposes, without completely transforming, those modes of being alive and consciously embodied in the world that count for each of us as direct experience" (Sobchack, 1992, p. 4). Films open us up to the world; they are just another important way in which we see and live in the world. For Sobchack this seeing and living in the world through the mediation of film possesses a double nature. Film presents the world to and with spectators but it also creates the world for and with spectators. Film is more than a technology, more than a mechanical device to present an image of/to the world. It is an experience that "opens up and exposes the inhabited space of direct experience as a condition of singular embodiment and makes it accessible and visible to more than the single consciousness who lives it" (Sobchack, 1992, p. 9).

This double nature of film to mediate and create the world does not relieve the viewer of any creative or interpretive responsibilities. As Sobchack notes, the viewer's role in this phenomenological relationship with film has a double nature. "The viewer...shares cinematic space with the film but must also negotiate it, contribute to and perform the constitution of its experiential significance. Watching a film is both a direct and mediated experience of direct experience as mediation" (1992, p. 10). When we read a film we always inhabit two worlds, it is the world of our body's relationships and experiences with the world beyond film, and the world of relationships that the film captures and reveals to spectators. What film reveals and what those outside relationships with the other are, depends on the spectator, both their individual experiences with the world and with the common but varied experience of watching a film. Given this double nature of film, we can never leave the world of direct experience but we must always include in this list of possible direct experiences with the world the mediated experience of watching films. *Mediation & Direct Experience*

As a result of the doubled nature of films and direct experiences, films are neither transparent, nor completely morphed with our bodies, nor are they alien appendages, or some kind of violations of the pure experience of our bodies. Instead, films are extensions of our bodies, extensions of our experiences, or experiences and bodies of our extensions. In the words of Sobchack (1992), film is a "cinematic apparatus as an intentional technology. This way of considering technology animates human artifacts that extend and alter human existence with human function and significance" (p. 165). Film becomes a means for individuals to extend their bodies into the world—a means to see and touch the world beyond the physiological limits of our bodies. Just as our bodies extend our consciousness, film is "an enabling technology, for it enables intending consciousness itself" (Sobchack, 1992, p. 167). This ability to enable sensory experiences like other dimensions of Sobchack's phenomenology of film is doubled. Not only does film technology enable individuals to experience the world and extend themselves into the world, film as an extension describes "cinematic ontology: the emergence of the motion picture as a unique form of communicative existence" (Sobchack, 1992, p. 168). Suggesting that film has an ontology implies that Sobchack is not viewing film as an object—a thing that spectators and filmmakers manipulate or use. By suggesting that film has a being, Sobchack is suggesting that film, like humans, has its own embodiment that gives it a life-of-its-own. This life-of-its-own manifests itself through the camera for the filmmaker, and the projector for the spectator, and therefore is limited to an embodied vision as seen through a lens. No matter what the embodied limitations are of either film or individual, acknowledging the ontology of film suggests that the relationship between the individual, film, and technology is never monologic but a dialogic experience that requires an interaction between bodies in order to construct or negotiate meaning. *(Film & Ontology)*

To understand the extended body or posthuman body of the individual spectator and the cinematic body and their relationships, Sobchack relies on the work of Don Ihde. Both embodied individuals and embodied films represent a materiality that enables perception of and within the world. Films enable individuals to see the world beyond its immediate sensory capabilities and individuals enable the film to share its cinematic vision. This materiality is temporal and serves as a conduit for perceiving different parts of the world represented in different times. Film enables individuals to transcend its own immediate temporal limitation—living in the now—while it brings the past and even future possible worlds to the individual. Film also brings together other individuals. The film through the camera brings the director and actors to the spectators and through the projector brings the spectator to the filmmaker and the worlds that the projector enables. At the same time, individuals bring their own temporal space as their own experiences and perceptions shape what they see and feel while viewing the film. What is established in this relationship is a phenomenological instrumentalism, or as Ihde notes, a "human-machine relation"; "an experience through a machine" (Sobchack, 1992, p. 180). Traditionally, curriculum theorists and critical theorists have defined instrumentalism as something that stunts the development of the individual. In film and from Ihde's perspective, it is any mechanical device. Furthermore, instrumentalism is the only way we can experience the world. For instance, the camera is how "the filmmaker's body can see the world and also reach out and touch it just as the projector enables the filmmaker to touch the spectator and for the spectator to see, reach and touch the world" (Sobchack, 1992, p. 183).

Sobchack and Ihde believe that the relationship between human and machine, as they co-exist in the world, is limited to sight and hearing. This, we think, ignores the ability of films to touch us through the sensory experience of feeling. Warshow (2001) believed films offered spectators "the actual, immediate experience of seeing and responding to the movies" (p. xi). The idea that people respond to movies implies they feel it in some way. This can range from a visceral response, rejecting or accepting the film on many levels, or a more emotional response that can encompass hair standing on one's skin when watching a horror film or a feeling of elation as a film inspires. The immediate experience of feeling a film further extends the ability of spectators to experience the world.

In recent writings, Sobchack begins to recognize that there is a feeling to movies that exists beyond seeing and hearing. Sobchack recognizes that in film criticism the body is often ignored. "Thus, if we read across the field, there is very little sustained work in English to be found on the carnal sensuality of the film experience and what—and how—it constitutes meaning" (Sobchack, 2004, p. 56). From this limitation in film criticism,

Sobchack attempts to give a body to our vision and hearing. "Our vision is already "fleshed out," Sobchack (2004) admits.

> Even at the movies our vision and hearing are informed and given meaning by other modes of sensory access to the world: our capacity not only to see and to hear but also to touch, to smell, to taste, and always to proprioceptively feel our weight, dimension, gravity, and movement in the world. In sum, the film experience is meaningful not to the side of our bodies but because of our bodies. (p. 60)

Laura Marks (2002) calls films that connect to our sensory perception "haptic cinema." This body of film that Marks refers to "appeals to a viewer who perceives with all the senses. It involves thinking with your skin, or giving as much significance to the physical presence of an other as to the mental operations of symbolization" (p. 18). We could not agree more and hope that we can demonstrate how our bodies and the bodies of film influence how we experience the world, physically and symbolically. This we argue is only enhanced and magnified more with the advent of the digital image.

One final note is important to highlight in regards to the embodied connections between humans and machines to experience the world through film. The human-machine relationship is transparent. That is, morphing of spectators and films to create immediate experiences of the world is never complete to the point where one cannot notice where the spectator ends and the machine begins. This is what Sobchack (1992) refers to as an "echo focus." The echo focus represents the reality that "the mechanism [film, camera, projector, sound system] is never wholly incorporated into the spectator's lived-body" (p. 178). There may come a time when the technology becomes so advanced that we are unable to sense where our sight, hearing, and feeling begin and where the images of the film end. The lines between human senses and film images are no doubt blurring and collapsing with the development of digital images but spectators are able to distinguish still between the two. What the "echo focus" offers is yet another opportunity for spectators to interrogate film and other dimensions of reality at a technological level.

Reading Popular Contemporary Films Phenomenologically: *Minority Report*

We have selected *Minority Report* to read phenomenologically for two reasons. First, as we noted earlier most film theorists ignore popular, contemporary films in their analysis. This is a long tradition that has its roots in the early criticism of film found in such critics as Rudolf Arnheim (1957) and Edwin Panofsky (1995), who were educated in art criticism and merely transplanted their tastes and predilections about culture into the realm of cinema thereby ignoring the artistic potential of any popular film. Second, we look at this film to demonstrate that any genre of film can be read phenomenologically.

From Sobchack's phenomenology of film, we are going to read *Minority Report* with three issues in mind. First, because of Sobchack's emphasis on films as an extension of the body into the world we will explore how this film extends our bodies into the world—the world of film and the world in which we live. Second, Sobchack suggests there is an ontology or a being of films; therefore we want to interrogate *Minority Report* in order to determine how a film expresses its body in the world. Third, we contend that film not only extends our bodies through sight and hearing but also enhances our ability to feel. As a result, we ask how one might come to feel this film or how any film might bring about certain feelings in a spectator?

Minority Report

The film *Minority Report* is based on the novel of the same name, written by Philip K. Dick. This science-fiction thriller centers around the character of John Anderton, police chief in Washington, D.C., in the year 2054. This officer of the law is responsible for the pre-crime division of the police force, a relatively new system devised to catch murderers before they have the chance to commit the crime. Unfortunately, John is haunted by the disappearance of his own child and the plot centers around his struggles of dealing with this sad occurrence. Through the manipulation of a myriad of technologically advanced paraphernalia, John ultimately ends up fighting for his own freedom against the very system that he represents. The film's message is one of warning against the abolition of our civil liberties and it works to extend the body of the spectator into the future through its shockingly realistic depiction of ways in which the government could possibly control the lives of its citizens.

The film opens with a montage of scenes running backward. The clarity of the events is limited: the spectator sees them as if viewing them from underwater. However, it is clear that the situation involves a man killing a woman who is in bed with another man. The scene switches to that of John Anderton. He is arriving to work at the police station, where his colleague, Chad, tells him that there is a new case that has just been reported by the "pre-cogs." The "pre-cogs," as the spectator finds out later in the story, are the children of drug addicts who, because of their severe mental birth defects, have been taken way from their parents. Researching how to help these children, a scientist discovered their acute abilities to see into the future, thus the acquired name "pre-cognitive." The pre-cogs, working in groups of three, are housed at the police station in a pool of solution called "the temple," calibrated to keep them calm and alive as footage from their brains is recorded as predictions of the future. When the three pre-cogs perceive a future murder, a machine produces unique wooden balls with the names of the victims and criminals engraved on them. In this first scene, John is shown "scrubbing," or reviewing through advanced physical manipulations, the file footage. This video is saved and projected onto plasma and with the touch of a gloved hand John can rewind, fast-forward, zoom in or out, extract, or freeze various frames. This scene is an excellent example of how montage, a topic we will return to in the next section, affects the spectator. The film's audience sees a character within the film producing a form of montage in order to understand reality. For example, John Anderton slices and dices the file to investigate where and how the murder will take place, just as a filmmaker does with film and as a spectator does with the perception of reality. Through this overt example of montage, the body of the spectator is exposed to methods of visually organizing experience, thus causing the spectator to mentally (and possibly physically) interact with the film in a way that may go undetected. The spectator's body is extended into the lived world at this juncture involving considerations of how s/he internalizes events in a film and uses them in the future to help process her/his perception of reality outside of the film experience. The spectator's body and the body of the film work on one another: the film works to influence the spectator while the spectator works the film to understand self and how self perceives reality.

Eventually, John and his team of police pursue and apprehend the suspect of the murder investigation, at which time the suspect is "haloed": a headband that seems to control the criminal's body and mind is placed at the temples and around the back of the neck. The scene quickly changes to focus on a commercial that is eliciting votes for the approval of pre-crime during the next electoral opportunity. This commercial is not being viewed on television; rather it is being projected in a public place while at the same time other projected images (possibly commercials as well) can be seen. The familiar format of commercials is used in conjunction with a new method of dissemination—a physical montage of media. The commercial ironically declares, "vote yes" to keep us "safe and free." The public in the film appears to be impervious to its effects but the spectator might be caught off guard at the profound intrusion of such advertising. This extension of the spectator's body into the assaults of the media of the future could be cause for alarm. As we were watching the film, we were at first astounded by the blatant intrusion of the media into the minds of the passers-by in the scene, and then it occurred to us that just such non-critical perspective of the media exists now. This depiction of a future society as it is presented in the film is a mere reflection of what currently exists in our lived experience of society. As spectators, we felt this scene opened up our minds, or extended our bodies, into the future so that an exploration of what might be to come may be reflected upon critically. Such a critical reflection is necessary to deal with the multiple and various forms of media that are and will be projected at us in this increasingly technological world that we inhabit. The spectator could learn from the technique of montage: by cutting out unwanted frames of experience, the spectator can exert control over her/his formation of identity. This "radical reflection on ourselves as viewing subjects who are aware of our own immediate and mediate access to the world and others" (Sobchack, 1992, p. 54) is necessary for a cognizant and informed realization of experience as it becomes our perception of reality. We suggest that we, as spectators, take time to "experience" our experiences, that we should be reflective, that we should consciously ingest what is presented to us, paying attention specifically to the body of film. "The screen is a space in which viewers can identify with an image that is not of them—the screen is not a mirror—but that confirms their existence and reflects back on them" (Marks, 2002, p. 25). The give and take between the spectator and the film should flow between the two bodies, like the brushing of the wind on a pool of water, each body performing in its reflection on the other.

The next case is announced via files produced by the pre-cogs, and as John is watching, he realizes that he is the murderer in the scene. He quickly hides that frame of the montage so that Chad cannot see it and sends his co-worker out for a break. As John is reviewing the file again, seeing himself shoot a man that he has never met, Wally, the pre-cog technician also views the footage. Wally gives John a two-minute head start before sounding the alarm and the action begins. John is on the run because of a murder he has not yet committed nor has any intention of committing. Regardless of his attempts to flee in order to solve this mystery and prove his innocence, the police know where he is through various technological mechanisms. When he is on foot and on the subway, they detect his location with scanning machines set up across the city that detect who people are through retinal recognition. And at this point he is not even safe from commercialism: as he passes the various projected commercials the retinal scan allows the commercials to call out his name. ("John Anderton, you need to get away" one commercial for a vacation coos.) When he is in his car on the futuristic highway where the cars seem to run by some magnetic force, the police are able to lockdown his car. John goes to great lengths to evade the police, including an eye transplant so that at one point when he is hiding in a run-down apartment complex he can escape the robotic "spiders" that come to seek out warm bodies with eyes to scan: his eyes do not read as those of John Anderton, and so he is left alone. These examples of extreme surveillance dominate the tone of the film and affect the body of the spectator as it extends into the future. As we watched the film we were struck with such thoughts as, "what if the government could really do this; what if there was a never-ending flow of commercials directed at us by name; what if the only way to prove your innocence was to flee?" During these scenes we found that our hearts were rushing to pump faster and faster, that we were holding our breath or, alternately, breathing heavily, and that our muscles were taut as our minds filled with all the questions that fear propels forth. The body of the film, through the technique of montage and through the nature of the story, evoked fear from within the body of the spectator and it was a fear extended toward the future. This phenomenological style of spectatorship that causes the body to respond physically, mentally, and emotionally provokes the viewer to think. "Spectatorship defined this way is less a matter of aligning oneself with an all-powerful gaze or perish, and more a matter of trying on various viewing positions, not untraumatically but not entirely destructively" (Marks, 2002, p. 76). Being a spectator requires the viewer to open her/his mind, to be active and to mediate the experience of media.

Montage and Film as Identity Formation: The Digital Challenge to Come

> Montage is the principle governing the organization of film elements, both visual and audio, or the combination of these elements, by juxtaposing them, connecting them, and/or controlling their duration.
>
> (Aumont, Bergala, Marie, and Vernet, 1992, p. 45)

Through this organization, the spectator catches glimpses into the world created by film: this world is an illusion but at the same time is a representation of reality. The technique of montage tricks the eyes of the spectator in order to produce certain effects that encourage her/him to believe that what s/he sees is a product of one, seamless camera view, despite the sometimes unnatural nature of the scene construction. The normal spectator is typically so engrossed in the narrative or plot of the film that to break from that hypnotic state of watching in order to analyze editing in its entirety is rare.

According to Aumont et al. (1992) "the first function of editing or montage...is actually its narrative function" (p. 47). Montage provides a method through which physical movement, whether that is of actors, scenery, or sound, creates a story. Through the cutting and sequencing of scenes, the film is molded into a visual representation of the written script, producing a unique version of the narrative. (How many versions of one script could be created if various combinations of directors, producers, editors, actors, and crew were used?) This montage-produced narrative is the spectator's access to an illusory world within which exists a very real immediacy. For example, films which, through the technique of montage, incorporate "digital images are more exciting, lively, and realistic...[The spectator's] desire for immediacy is apparent in the increasing popularity of the digital compositing of film and in Hollywood's interest in replacing stunt men and eventually even actors with computer animations" (Bolter & Grusin, 1999, p. 23). This editing that produces immediacy mimics the speed and rhythm of the experience of the lived world. Spectators absorb this speed and rhythm of the edited film just as they absorb the speed and rhythm of lived experience. Montage as "the creation of a sense or meaning not proper to the images themselves but derived exclusively from their juxtaposition" (Bazin, 1967, p. 25) allows for interpretation by the spectator.

Beyond the idea of montage in general and more specific for our argument here is the notion discussed by Aumont et al. (1992) of the "productive montage" (p. 48). If montage is said to be the layout of shots in selective conjunction with one another, then productive montage is that layout with a motive: the motive to make something stand out in importance and to evoke response from the spectator. As Aumont et al. (1992) point out, "Jean Mitry defines 'productive' montage (or the 'montage-effect') as the result of an association, whether arbitrary or not, of two images that, when related to one another, cause the viewer to perceive an idea, emotion, or sentiment in his or her consciousness that is not present in the individual images" (p. 48). Film used to manifest feeling? Why not? If such is the goal of art, and film is a form of art, then film most certainly can be used in the same manner. "Productive montage" is a conduit for meaning-making. Opening up opportunities for the filmmaker to communicate with the audience and for the audience to respond, it is the portal through which the spectator is able to observe, experience, and absorb film as a representation of reality.

Montage "has as its task to influence or 'shape' the spectator" (Aumont, et al. 1992, p. 65). As part of the constitution of the film, montage challenges the spectator to do more than merely watch the film: montage invites the spectator to participate in the world of film and to be enveloped into its body. Sobchack (1992) proposes that "[t]he primary function of cinematic technology…is to enable acts of introceptive perception and their expression" (p. 205). We interpret this to mean that the spectator must digest and analyze what it is that they encounter in film and then must recognize the ways in which the messages themselves were received. Participating in such a practice requires that the spectator allow the experience of film to flow over her/him like a wave. First, comes the visual stimulation of the film, which can be represented by the small rise of the water at the beginning of the wave. Second, arrives the understanding of the narrative, which can be understood as the increasing push of the water as the crest arrives. Following is the awareness of the convergence of the visual and the meaning of the message, which correlates to the moment that the wave reaches its peak. Finally, internalization occurs. It is an internalization of the film experience as a whole, which is comparable to the force of the wave as it crashes down. "This fluid, centered and decentering intentional encounter with a sensible and significant world implicates a bodily being in and of it and indicates a consciousness able to sense and make sense through movement and sight and reflection upon movement and sight" (Sobchack, 1992, p. 218). Through this sensing and reflection, "shaping" such as is mentioned by Aumont, et al. takes place.

We argue that this "shaping" is one manner through which the spectator forms their identity. The spectator's senses are engaged, s/he attends to the physical and emotional effects that the senses produce, and this process and its product becomes a part of who s/he is. How does this happen and in what ways is this process similar to that of montage in film? Through an exploration of the ideas of mediation, these questions may be addressed.

If, as Aumont et al. argues, montage "becomes the single and central principle controlling all production of meaning" (1992, p. 65), then a parallel can be drawn between the function of montage and the function of the spectator as editor. First, it is necessary to determine exactly what is meant by the idea of spectator as editor. To best accomplish this, let us turn to a discussion of the act of remediation as is presented by Bolter and Grusin.

Several definitions of remediation are presented by Bolter and Grusin (1999), including the ideas that remediation takes such forms as restoration, improvement, and representation (pp. 53–62). "Any act of mediation is dependent on another, indeed many other, acts of mediation and is therefore remediation" (p. 56). This idea echoes other various cyclic relationships, such as iteration and reiteration and the digital phenomena of zeros and ones: to have one, there must exist the other, and from that relationship emerge infinite possibilities. In montage, the film editor selects from a collection of recordings, scenes and shots. This act in itself is a form of mediation. Once those selections are melded together to create the film, the presentation of those once separate elements as one embodies a type of remediation. A similar event takes place as the spectators watch a film. They are presented with the final version of the montage, during which, as they watch, they consciously or subconsciously pick out images, combinations of images, or entire scenes that come together to create their perception or recollection of the film. In this way, they become the editors of their mind's version of the film, just as the film editor creates the montage that makes up the film as a whole.

Because "the image is evaluated not according to what it adds to reality but what it reveals of it" (Bazin, 1967, p. 28) montage and spectator both must demonstrate the ability of discernment. Such discernment is needed to maintain a healthy perspective on the message of film so that the focus does not turn into simple mimicry. For montage, the discernment is a narrowing down of multiple views, angles, and shots to the perfect one that expresses the message of the film (or the version of reality that the film intimates) in the best way. For the spectator, the discernment is a recognizing of the film editor's selections and how those shed light onto some perspective of reality that may be novel. This act of recognition shapes the spectator's identity in that s/he is responding to stimuli on various conscious and subconscious levels. According to Douglas Kellner (1995), "[t]heorists of identity from Hegel through G. H. Mead have often characterized personal identity in terms of mutual recognition, as if one's identity depended on recognition from others combined with self-validation of this recognition" (p. 231). We would argue that this self-validation occurs through the conscious and subconscious spectator as editor through the viewing of film. The spectator takes in a film, finds connections between situations and characters within the film, experiences emotional and physical responses to the film, and thus feels a form of self-validation. Identity is in this instance mediated through film, and despite the "multiplicity of possible viewers" (Bolter and Grusin, 1999, p. 81) every spectator in some way can find validation through film, even if it is only to say that s/he does not prescribe to the version of reality presented by the film.

Being both the subject and the object, the spectator has the capacity to determine which aspects, if any, from film will be allowed to add to or subtract from her/his identity. Although it is obviously apparent to the spectator that film is a mediated representation of reality, the spectator finds herself/himself in a situation where s/he must actively participate in making meaning. The "instrument-mediated perception is never experienced as exactly as identical to direct perception, that is, perception experienced introceptively through the lived-body as ['her/his own']" (Sobchack, 1992, p. 178). The "pressure and resistance" which result from this situation extend themselves in two ways and are what Sobchack calls "echo-focus" (p. 178). In the first extension, there is a meeting of the spectator's physical limitations of viewing as is defined by the film screen in the theater and the actual limitations of the projection of the film itself: the spectator's visual parameters echo that of the projector's projection parameters. In the second extension, Sobchack (1992) juxtaposes the person and the machine in that "the spectator's bodily space/projected visual space...echoes the different situations of the spectator's body and the film's body and creates in the spectator resistance to the projected perception, an inability to absorb it totally" (p. 179). We propose that the spectator's inability to totally absorb the experience of film is a reflection of the spectator's parallel inability to totally absorb the experience of real life. This inability in real life is what constitutes one's individual perception of reality and how that differs from other's perceptions. However, something is absorbed and we contend that those absorptions lend to the acceptance of the represented reality in film and that identity is, as a result, affected. Sobchack (1992) reminds us that "instrument-mediated perception...is a genuine perception of the world as it exists in an embodiment relation with technology. Instrument-mediated perception is an extension and transformation of direct perception but is enigmatic in that extension and transformation" (p. 186). As film mediates the world, so too must the spectator as editor mediate the experience of film and in doing so remediates her/his identity.

The necessity of films to mediate worlds, and the spectator to act as editor, are only more enhanced and crucial with the rise of the digital image. Sobchack ends her treatise on the phenomenology of film with a warning of a pending crisis for lived-body experiences and film.

> The intelligibility and meaning of the film experience originates in the embodied experience of perception and its expression...If we are to understand how we understand the film experience, why it has significance for us, and why we care about it, we must remember that experience is located in the lived-body. Indeed, at this historical moment...the lived-body is in crisis. (Sobchack, 1992, p. 300).

The culprit creating this crisis, according to Sobchack, is the digital image. It is creating a "crisis of the real" and a "crisis of the flesh" (Sobchack, 1992, p. 300). In her latest work Sobchack (2004) continues her belief in a crisis of the flesh. She writes: "we can see all around us that the lived body is in crisis. Its struggle to assert its gravity, its differential existence, status, and situation, its vulnerability and mortality, its vital and social investment in a concrete lifeworld inhabited by others, is now marked in hysterical and hyperbolic responses to the disembodying effects of electronic representation" (p. 161). Our contention is this crisis, if it is even a crisis, of the digital image is not of the lived-body. If anything is in crisis, it is the film body. We want to end this section by showing how with the advent of digital images, the lived-body experience is more pertinent for film studies than ever before, and therefore, is not in crisis—just transformed. We want to demonstrate our point through the important theoretical work of Mark Hansen on the digital image, and then suggest how the film body is perhaps the subject in crisis. For now we want to stress that even if we could argue that the film body is in crisis, it is not a crisis of identity or existence. Instead it is a crisis that will open up numerous opportunities to read films not just phenomenologically but in many theoretical ways.

Theorizing the Digital

It is our contention that the digital image is changing phenomenological readings of films. As media theorist Mark Hansen (2004a) notes, "the digital image explodes the frame … it need no longer be so bounded. Regardless of its current surface appearance, digital data is at heart polymorphous: lacking any inherent form or enframing" (p. 35). This explosion of the frame, Hansen believes, has profound implications for our aesthetic sensibilities. Most media critics and theorists often use film as the embodiment of the digital image. For Hansen, this tendency enframes the potential of the digital image, reduces its power to a technical explanation, and ignores the necessary role of humans to create meaning. Hansen (2004a) proclaims that "as long as it [the digital image] is tied to the image-frame of the cinema, this polymorphous potential will remain entirely untapped" (p.35). The untapped potential of the digital image is found in its expansion outside of any frame, and more importantly, how the digital image is able to latch onto the human body as a supplement and demand more creatively and physically from any human individual who comes in contact with the digital image. What Hansen is trying to do in tapping into the full potential of the digital image is not to grant more power to a technological device than is necessary or possible. On the contrary, Hansen creates a theoretical space to bring the body back into the technological realm of the digital image and directly challenge those scholars such as Friedrich Kittler who argue that the posthuman age no longer needs human beings. For Hansen, the posthuman age marks the return of the human morphed with the technological.

To understand how Hansen's understanding of technology is different from most Western philosophical traditions, it is important to return to his first book, *Embodying Technesis: Technology Beyond Writing*. Technesis for Hansen (2000) is "the putting-into-discourse of technology" and "forms a common…reductive strategy that allows for a progressive assimilation of technology to thought" (p. 4). This reduction of technology to discourse limits the potential of technology to transform our thinking and bodies and erases what Hansen refers to as the "robust materiality of technology." This robust materiality comes before and cannot be fully comprehended by thought. The sensorimotor skills of the body are the most adept way to capture the full meaning, potential, and reality of technology as it connects and relates to the body. By limiting current theorization to technesis, contemporary theory acts in a similar manner as Hansen believes film does. Just as film limits the untapped potential of the digital image to the cinematic frame, technesis also enframes technology within the parameters of discourse. Hansen is by no means suggesting that contemporary theories are fatally flawed in their reduction of technology to the discursive. However, he is suggesting that when technology is approached poststucturally, deconstructively, or psychoanalytically the following are erased: the affective and material dimensions of technology as supplement; the untapped potential of the digital image as a frameless existence; and the active role of the human body.

If the digital image is marked by a frameless existence, and if technology is a supplement to the body, then what is the role of the body in the realm of digital images? For Hansen, this question can be understood if we simultaneously reclaim the meaning of the affective and envision the body's role in the digital image as having a primary framing function. The framing function, center of indetermination, permits individuals to feel the power of technological images, tame the untapped potential of the digital image and create (frame) meaning of each individual image and its morphed offspring, thereby extending the power of the individual to feel the world beyond their natural means. This last point is what Hansen (2004a) refers to as "affectivity: the capacity of the body to experience itself as 'more than itself' and thus to deploy its sensorimotor power to create the unpredictable, the experimental, the new" (p. 7). It is this ability to extend one's sensorimotor experiences that mark the posthuman condition, not some dystopic science fiction proclamation that technology no longer has any uses for the human.

If Hansen wishes to reclaim the affective and reconstitute each individual as a center of indetermination in order to interact and live in the world, then each individual has the ability and responsibility to act as a framing function in and of the world. This means that each individual enters into a frameless digital world, where information flows freely, meaning is never a given but must be constructed. For Hansen, the only way individuals can do this is through our sensorimotor skills. As digital images act as canvasses that give color, shape, texture, and potential to the world, it is the individual who feels, smells, sees, and hears the world that gives meaning to what is. Technology only enhances our proprioceptive abilities.

If individuals are the center of indetermination and the digital explodes the frame, then the relationship between individual bodies and cinematic bodies changes. First, the cinematic body is no longer stable. Films still animate our bodies and serve as a medium to live in the world but this living and mediation is much more fragmented. With the increase of DVDs and different versions of films, how a film mediates the world for individuals is more tenuous. If I purchase a new DVD of a film and included in that DVD are multiple versions of the film or never before seen cuts of the film previously edited out of the screen version, how an individual interprets a film will depend on which version one finds most appealing or which version touches their affective sensibilities more. Second, the transparency or "echo focus" of films is becoming less and less obvious. With the advent of digital imagery and creative editing skills, the ability to tell where an actor ends and a digital image begins is challenged. This requires film, cultural studies scholars, and educators to rethink the interpretive requirements of the spectator as the demands of the film increase.

Technologically Embodied Cultural Curriculum Studies

> We live in a still-Enlightened culture that, despite its current post-Enlightenment fascination with and fetishization of "the body," regards the body as an alienated object quite separate from—if housing—the subjective consciousness that would discipline it into visible shape or visibly shape it into a discipline.
>
> (Sobchack, 2004, p. 185)

Analysis will have to become performance, a creative experimentation with the possibilities for our future technogenesis…What this means, however, is that cultural studies must become embodied experimentation.

(Hansen, 2004b, p. 17)

We wish to conclude this chapter with two suggestions and observations. First, if we find the epigraphs to this section even somewhat intriguing, those of us in curriculum theory or other fields of study within education have to begin to rethink the importance of technology in experiencing our embodied world. The tendency within education is to think of technology as a tool—an instrument for better instruction—or it is the tendency of critical scholars to suspiciously dismiss technology as an infringement on our identities. With the rise of the digital image and interactive technologies, technology is not an infringement but a supplement or an extension of our bodies. Even perhaps more risky, we can posit that technology has become the beginning of our experiences in the world or, as Hansen (2004b) suggests, "our future technogenesis" (p. 17). To view technology as a tool is then to view the body as tools. This might serve neoclassical economists and free market ideologues well but will it serve educational scholars? To dismiss technology as an infringement is to dismiss the issue of embodied identities. We suggest curriculum scholars begin to experiment with the many possible ways that our bodies are supplemented with and through technology to understand how students and teachers interact with each other and the world.

Our second and final comment relates to the unruliness of the digital image and the primary framing function of the embodied individual. If Hansen is correct in asserting the individual as the primary framing function, then the importance of the body is supreme. But not just any body, the individualized wired body is important in the process of meaning making in the digital age. As Marks (2002) states, "[b]ecause movies engage with our embodied memories, each of us experience a movie in an absolutely singular way" (p. 122). Meaning is made in the material connections between our bodies, the body of the film, and the bodies, animals, vegetables, and minerals recorded by the film. The digital image only magnifies this engagement and relationship. If the technological frame of the film no longer contains the meaning of films, then the power of the individual to create meaning and interaction with the film is essential. For educators this means we have to nurture the interpretative faculties of our students so they can fine-tune their framing functions. To do this it is important that we begin to create what we call a digital aesthetics. It is the realm of merging technology with aesthetics, with our bodies firmly connected to both, that we will begin

- Curriculum and the Cultural Body

to create interpretive frameworks to understand our worlds phenomenologically or otherwise.

Not Without My Body: Embodied Learning With/In the Online Learning Environment

Debra Freedman = Iris Striedieck = Leonard Shurin*

The purpose of this chapter is to explore the ways that embodied learning e/merged within an online, graduate-level education course. Specifically, we look at the ways students made sense of select course readings and experiences, and connected themselves within a learning community through detailed narratives of their body memories (Irwin, 2000). These embodied learning moments seemed to propel students forward, connecting mind and body in ways that contributed to a fuller, richer, and more textured theoretical understanding of course topics.

One perspective that informs our thinking is Janet Emig's (2001); in particular, how she classifies embodied learning as "the learning that can take place only through transactions with literal others in authentic communities of inquiry" (p. 272). However, in Emig's view, "authentic communities of inquiry" exist only within the context of a traditional classroom. She expresses her concern with the use of online learning environments:

> We must make the case for what embodied learning represents and achieves over cyber learning. Otherwise, our grounded, subtle, and complex knowledge will not, I believe, prevail—politically and economically—against the seductive simplicities of technological models that confuse the acquisition of information with the comprehension and creation of concepts. (p. 273)

As teacher educators (Deb and Iris) who instruct online classes, of concern for us is Emig's (2001) belief in the "simplicities of technological models that confuse the acquisition of information with the comprehension and creation of concepts" (p. 273). Her implication that online learning is simplistic and devoid of comprehension and the creation of concepts makes assumptions about the ways students learn and access information. As well, her assumptions portray students as passive, disembodied consumers of technology.

We believe, however, that an online classroom, designed to be interactive, group-work intensive, and insistent on thoughtful student participation, can be a medium that has the possibility of facilitating full engagement between mind and body. That is, online course experiences can open up spaces for embodied learning, and can, using Emig's words, become "site[s] where students are required to acknowledge human complexity, situational ambiguity, vexed, even unanswerable questions about self and society" (p. 279). In addition, we believe it would be remiss to think that while people convey ideas and engage in discussion in the online environment that their bodies simply cease to exist.

Course Context and Methodological Choices

We gathered data—asynchronous threaded discussions and email exchanges—from a 15-week online master's-level course that focused on school supervision and teacher leadership. The course structure provided for a variety of learning activities: shared and personal readings, book clubs, and individual and small group projects. Our goal was to develop an environment rooted within democratic pedagogy, one that fostered trust, inclusion, freedom, self-determination, human development, reflection through deliberation and scrutiny, and consideration of multiple understandings of ideas and experiences (Lummis, 1996).

The online environment challenged us as curriculum developers to think of approaches that moved away from individual accountability toward strategies that fostered a community of practice whereby individual and group responsibilities prevailed, for instructors and learners alike. As such, we created learning activities that built on connections developed among students, with a preference for group needs over individual needs (Beyer, 1998). Our research questions explored the ways in which students (7 female, 3 male) entered into online learning experiences. How did the online learning environment facilitate open participation? How did the online learning environment make possible complex understandings of student lives? How did the online learning environment enable learning experiences that allowed for those involved to become collaborative, skilled, and engaged participants (Beyer, 1998)?

Once we began analyzing the data we began to notice how students mediated the online environment and fostered dialogic communities through their bodies. Initially, we saw this insertion of the body as a way to connect visually with others in cyberspace. One student emailed a short vacation video, many posted photographs that smiled back at you when you received an email or looked at a personal webpage. On one occasion, a student detailed the ways his body was tossed about during a car accident noting: "I'm battered, bruised, bloody, and sutured, a little disoriented, but otherwise OK, with no broken bones." Yet, as we explored the data further, we began to notice the increasingly complex ways students coupled bodied experiences, specifically body memories (Ahmed and Stacey, 2001; Butler-Sanders and Oliver, 2001; Springgay, 2003), with their learning experiences.

While we collected a great deal of data for this project, in this chapter we highlight one student, Leonard, a white male, age 53, as an illustrative example of embodiment. Specifically, Leonard's embodied online narratives provoked other students to become aware of their interactions, their embodied pedagogical encounters with/in their traditional classroom contexts, and fostered democratic, dialogic encounters that acknowledged human complexity and situational ambiguity.

Body Memories and Stillness

Research concerning online learning practices often takes no notice of the body (Lander, 2005). Most often, research concerning online learning environments focuses on the differences between what is called "face to face" learning or traditional learning in classroom environments and web learning (Wingard, 2004); or equivalency in time-on-task between "face to face" learning environments and the online learning environments (Bender, Wood, and Vredevoogd, 2004; Watkins and Schlosser, 2003); or learners' and instructors' experiences of online courses (Conrad, 2002). However, we wonder "[a]re we really able to eliminate physicality so easily, or does [the online environment] give us pathways that are wide enough for us to leave parts of our physical selves to help reach each other?" (Argyle and Shields, 1996, p. 63).

Rita Irwin's (2000) work is helpful to our understanding of the ways in which embodiment takes place within the online learning environment. And while Irwin's work does not connect specifically with online learning environments, her theorizing concerning body memories helps us to better understand the ways students connect with each other with/in the online learning environment. She explains that "[s]ometimes going back to our childhood memories of our bodies puts us in touch with our selves" (p. 83).

Recounting memories of afternoons wandering through the grain fields with her dog or walking silently down a country gravel road, Irwin remembers the silence that allowed her to feel and learn through her embodied experiences—whether the feel of a wheat shaft against her leg, or hearing sounds of crickets, or seeing the changes after a heavy rain. She writes, "Dreaming great thoughts, imagining new ideas, creating incredible stories, these were days in which I knew my soul through my body" (p. 83).

We understand body memories to exist within a complex dialectic (Hayles, 2003), one in which body memory and stillness work in relational and reciprocal ways to facilitate learning with/in the online learning environment. Irwin explains that learning from body memories comes out of the stillness, out of the silence of the journey; that is, in moments of silence one is able to face one's self and re-discover and re-connect.

> It is in stillness that we allow ourselves to face ourselves. It is in stillness that it becomes possible to appreciate the sounds we have taken-for-granted in new ways. It is in stillness that we can envision new ways of being in relationship with others. It is in stillness that we can begin to understand that in any pedagogical moment, it is an openness to complexity that allows us to enter into the experiences of our students. At that moment we are experiencing the beginnings of an embodied pedagogy. (p. 84)

That is, body memories and stillness complement, supplement, and define one another (Hayles, 2003). As well, the connection between body memories and stillness has the ability to facilitate communication, allowing for new understandings, and allowing for the realization of others' embodied knowledges (Burkitt, 1999).

We understand this complex dialectic of body memory and stillness as a challenge to what Megan Boler (2002) refers to as "drive-by difference." Boler explains:

> In virtual interaction, there is a high likelihood of what I call "drive-by-difference." For example, computer-mediated expressions of experience related to oppression are unlikely to engage the reader in the kind of "bearing witness" necessary to transformative dialogue. It is very difficult to demand attentive listening and deep grasp of another's experience within the context of fast-paced, multitasking, impermanent traces of digital interaction. Computer mediated communication encourages, at best, the superficiality of drive-by difference. (p. 338)

As instructors, curriculum developers, and researchers with/in the online environment, we have come to understand the ways in which body memory and stillness can challenge fast-paced multitasking, drive-by-difference, and impermanence with/in the online learning environment. Moreover, we have come to recognize that online learning environments that facilitate and welcome the insertion of body memories open up spaces that allow for an understanding of the complexity of students' lives and allow for those involved in the conversations to enter into complex learning relationships.

Self-imposed Wait Time

At different times throughout the day, throughout a given week, students would log on to the class site, read the assigned readings, post responses to discussion prompts, and respond to each other's postings. Students were rarely online at the same time. Moreover, logging on to read postings and logging on to respond to postings were often two separate events. We understand the time between reading and posting as a self-imposed wait time—a time to think, a time for contemplation, a time to connect theory to practice, a time to get lost in the stillness. This self-imposed wait time is much different than the often uncomfortable five to seven seconds of silence that teachers in traditional classrooms allocate between their question and a student's answer. This self-imposed wait time, these moments of stillness, allowed students to respond in their own time, to consider postings carefully, to enter into complex relationships, and to react in thoughtful ways that moved thinking and conversation forward.

For Leonard, the self-imposed wait time, the stillness, allowed him to connect theoretical learnings with body memories of childhood. During one activity in which a group of students led a discussion on issues of power and privilege in relation to the role of the school in the community and broader culture, Leonard posted the following:

> Although I am a white male, I have felt the sting of prejudice, and I didn't like it, and I don't want anybody to feel that hurt for any reason. What was the prejudice I felt? It was poverty. I grew up very poor. When I was growing up I knew what it was like to go to bed hungry and to go without a coat or jacket. I grew up in the fifties, and times were much different then to what they are now. Now if a poor person needs a winter coat, there are agencies like Salvation Army or Goodwill. Thank God for them today, and there are food banks now, so that is an improvement.

> I remember waiting in line with my disabled father in the fifties for the surplus food the federal government handed out. It was not uncommon to wait in line for three hours in the freezing cold for some surplus beans, flour, and beef (never any fresh vegetables or fruit). We would go to the

back of grocery stores and root through the vegetables and fruit that was thrown away to find something edible. No, I am not making this up...it happened. That was the culture of poverty. I have yet to attend a high school reunion (the 35th one is this year) because of the cruelty from classmates who tormented me and others like me. Yes, it was a culture of poverty, and I think in many communities the teachers and the supervisors must face this problem as well as all the other educational problems we face, because a child who is hungry can't learn.

As a teacher or supervisor, to understand how poverty affects a child in the classroom, do not eat anything for 2 or 3 days. You can have water, but no food. On the 4th day, you get one slice of bread with ketchup on it for the whole day. Try it, you won't die, I tried it many times because that was all there was to eat on many occasions when I was a child. Try functioning on that, and you will know what many children in the culture of poverty in our country feel (20% of U.S. children, according to government statistics, live in poverty).

I stopped for gas in the west end of town today. I noticed three ragged boys, probably around 8–10 years old, hanging around the entrance. They were waiting for a car to drive away. Underneath the car was a half-empty soda pop (that's what we call a soft drink in western Pennsylvania).They picked up the soda pop and shared drinking it. They apparently had checked over the garbage can, too, by the entrance to the store, and were waiting in anticipation for one of the store employees to drag a large garbage can out to the storage area behind the store. I observed an employee doing that, and as soon as he went back in the store, they were searching through that garbage can for food.

I resolved at that moment...that if I ever became a supervisor at a school, no student in my care would go hungry, no matter what. When we talk about the school and community and culture, to me that is what we are facing—children who do not have enough to eat in my community. I don't know if I'm addressing the issue here as well as I should, but I think you can see that it is a major cultural issue, and it is only getting worse.

By the way, I thought I would point out to you one of the by-products of going hungry as a child. As an adult, I never, ever, diet. I eat anything I want, and I never worry about fats or carbs or anything like that. Always, in the back of your mind, is that little voice telling you that you may go hungry again someday.

Here, Leonard expresses a knowledge, a learning, an awareness through his body memories. His descriptions of going hungry, of lacking proper clothing during the winter months, of waiting in line for government surplus food, of fearing that someday he might be hungry again, these are poignant moments that make his body tangible and place his body in relation to others within the learning environment (Burkitt, 1999).

Mairs (1990) explains, "It is precisely this willingness to give voice to what our culture tells us to shroud in silence that creates freedom, bringing the body into the plain light of shared human experience" (p. 92). A peer replied to Leonard's posting:

Leonard, thank you for sharing your story. For the past three years, I have been concerned about the students in my class. The majority of who live in poverty and foster care. We try so hard to make sure they have opportunities to do things in the classroom that we know they do not do at home. At Christmas my first year, we made cookies. Two of my students told me they never made cookies at home, even at the holidays…Since then I have included crafts and gift and cookie making so that each of my students can make and take home cookies or gifts for family members the entire week before break. They love it. This year we had one student who was homeless when he came to us. His mom has issues, but dearly loves her son. She works now, but barely makes ends meet. He wears the same two pairs of jeans and four t-shirts all the time. I wasn't sure if I was overstepping boundaries, but I was determined to help this little boy. My best friend has a son the same age/height and Alex is growing so fast that he can only wear his clothes for a short time and then she donates them to Goodwill. I told her about my student and Alex gave him a bunch of his new clothes that he had not worn yet. My mom told her boss, and she went shopping for my student too. It was so cool. I told my student that my friend wanted to know if I had any students who would appreciate Alex's clothes since he could not wear them before he out grew them. I told him I thought of him first and another student that I wanted to help too. This boy took a few things and said he wasn't going to take all the clothes in case someone else needed them in the class. Then he asked to make thank you cards! Since then, he and I have a little different rapport. None of the other kids in the class know what I did, but it really made him feel good about himself for a day. I wonder if he thinks I did this because I felt sorry for him. I just think this boy has a really awesome character. How many 11-year-olds do you know that ASK to make thank you cards? Your story made me think I did the right thing. I also will make a point to be even more observant in the future to my students' personal needs.

In this particular encounter, Leonard's act of remembering in the present touched this student and caused her to face herself, to reflect on action and prompted an emotional, pedagogically situated response, as evidenced in the final sentence of her posting, "Your story made me think I did the right thing. I also will make a point to be even more observant in the future to my students' personal needs." Leonard, responded, connecting with this students' experience and offering alternative means for action:

When I worked at the Vo-tech, we took over a small room and made it a donation center for unused or unwanted clothing. We did it very secretly. I never even knew who all was involved, because we wanted to protect the children who benefited from the clothes. I knew two of the teachers who were involved, and I would ask them to help a child, and like magic that child had clothes, a coat, shoes, whatever was needed.

No one ever talked about this clothing room…it was like being in the French underground in World War II. We also had suitcases and overnight bags because there were children who, when they went on an overnight school activity, brought their change of clothes in a garbage bag! I thought you would appreciate what a few determined teachers can do. I also noticed that, just like the little boy in your class, these children were very appreciative.

As someone who was in their shoes at one time, I can tell you that as good it will make you feel, helping these children, believe me, you are making an incredible difference in some child's life, because now he or she knows someone really does care, and there is mercy and goodness in the world. You can't show mercy and goodness as an adult if you never knew it as a child. We talk about community in our class, and that type of work is real community action.

The same student responded again to Leonard's body memory:

Thank you Leonard, you have put things in a perspective once again that I had not thought of before. You have also given me an idea for next year. Our school population will be changing from a more affluent to a less affluent one, especially the migrant population. I know a few angels in our county office and our school that might be willing to assist in the coatroom idea. Thank you for sharing your story. I agree, experiencing mercy and humanity as a child really does affect you as an adult.

The above narrative could be read from varied perspectives: a focus on issues of personal or collective charity; an analysis of systematic changes in curriculum and school structure. In our class context, what we noted, was that the self-imposed wait time, the stillness, allowed students to enter into complex emotional relationships with one another and allowed students' thoughts to become part of an embodied social activity (Burkitt, 1999) focused on learning, challenging, and thinking. As example, Leonard's body memories caused students to question broader social and curricular issues. Another student responded to Leonard's posting:

I was struck by the concept of prejudice of poverty. Isn't this a huge, and largely overlooked, issue in our schools and our culture today? When was the last time you saw a poor child in your school who was popular? Had friends? Held her head high? From very early on these children are seen as "different" and are most often ostracized. What do our schools offer these children, other than a tormented existence until they reach 16 and can escape the daily degradation from their fellow students?

Full of questions that evidence connection and attentive listening, the above response to Leonard's body memory reveals new understandings about schooling, society, and about the complex realities that educators encounter and embody on a daily basis. In particular, the stillness of the online environment enabled this student to interconnect her own embodied narratives of schooling and learning with Leonard's body memories to unravel, to question, and to wonder about the ways in which school culture maintains in/exclusion, as well as the ways school culture maintains broader membership in the larger culture outside of school. This type of embodied learning did not happen the first time Leonard shared his body memories within a traditional learning environment. He recounted an experience while attending a Governor's school for teachers:

We were in a seminar and we were requested to bring up a memory, good or bad, from childhood. Almost all the teachers had a good memory to share. All I said was, "I remember being poor and hungry." Everyone stopped talking and just stared at me. It was as if I had said I had leprosy when I was a child.

The physically present body articulating memories of hardship made people feel uncomfortable which in turn made Leonard feel insecure. His body memory perceived in a traditional learning environment as unpleasant, something that fellow attendees were not prepared to hear about or acknowledge. Perhaps the other teachers in the room felt manipulated by the disclosure. Perhaps the other teachers felt that Leonard had disclosed too much information about his childhood. Perhaps the other teachers did not want to complicate the simple, superficial relationship they had with Leonard. Perhaps the more traditional learning environment did not allow the distance, the time to think through Leonard's disclosure, or the access to stillness that the online learning environment provided. The self-imposed wait time, the stillness of the online learning environment, seemed to facilitate connection with Leonard's body memory. In contrast to the traditional learning environment, students in the online environment embraced Leonard's virtual body and entered into a learning, challenging, thinking relationship.

Embodied Learning With/In the Online Learning Environment

The learning represented in the above responses contrasts many scholars' concerns with online learning environments (Boler, 2002; Emig, 2001). Boler (2002), for example, voices apprehension about learning in the online environment—"how can we measure dialogue in its transformative sense as engaged in computer mediated communication" (p. 338)?—and wonders how transformation and risk taking can take place in the "absence of face-to-face communication" (p. 338). Yet, we believe that encounters in the online learning environment can be understood as virtual face-to-face encounters. In the online learning environment a posting can be seen or read as a person's face, a reflection of a person's re-presented embodied identity. In Leonard's case, his memories of his body, his postings, were read as virtual embodied representations that revealed a seeing, feeling, touching, breathing, smelling, longing, thinking, experiencing, and (at one time) starving body. In a sense, in the stillness of the online learning environment, Leonard's present understandings of his body memories became a theoretical construct for knowing and learning.

Our goal for this course was to develop an online learning environment reflective of democratic pedagogical practices: a learning environment built on trust, inclusiveness, freedom, self-determination, human development, reflection through deliberation and scrutiny, and consideration of multiple understandings of ideas and experiences (Lummis, 1996). We wanted students to experience a genuine participation that opened them up to new understandings and possibilities and that moved them toward pedagogical awareness. As a result, moments of stillness allowed for a pedagogical thoughtfulness, mindful of the ways thought and soul become embodied with/in a moment (Pinar and Irwin, 2005) as well as a pedagogical attentiveness perceptive of the ways that stillness causes us to face ourselves. Irwin (2000) explains, "By facing ourselves through stillness and permitting the loss that precedes transformation, we are better able to be fully awake pedagogues who embody our own convictions and who, in turn, can awaken students to face themselves" (p. 85). Leonard's body memories, presented within the stillness of this online learning environment, facilitated these moments of deeper understanding and affected students in ways that moved them to realize new ways of understanding and being in relationship with others (Burkitt, 1999).

* An equal sign (=) appears between the names of authors to acknowledge the collaborative and shared responsibility amongst the contributors (see Mullen, 2003 for a further discussion on this practice).

Self-imposed wait time allows for the students to avoid the awkward 5-7 seconds in a face-to-face setting.

Body Interfaces in Curriculum

Karen Keifer-Boyd

Living in a technologically engineered and information-rich environment brings with it associated shifts in habits, postures, enactments, perceptions—in short, changes in the experiences that constitute the dynamic lifeworld we inhabit as embodied creatures.

(Hayles, 2002, p. 299)

L earners understand the world through their body's perception, contemplation, and communication with others. This body knowledge is not isolated from the technologies that mediate and interact with the body. In this chapter, I discuss what bodied interactions through simulation and virtual articulation mean for a curriculum of the body. I examine the relationship between virtual reality and a bodied curriculum that introduces students to mutual articulation. I argue that the construction of the body, in and through virtual space, is a mutual articulation of knowledge formation arising from the body's interactions with virtual objects in a simulated environment. It is mutual articulation that alters notions of corporeality. The implications of such alterations impact student understandings of body knowledge.

The term "mutual articulation" refers to a movement of assembling, not to the content of what is assembled. Mutual articulation emphasizes uncertainty about the origin of actions. Rachel Prentice (2005) defines mutual articulation as "an interface that becomes increasingly differentiated as it interacts with more elements of the world" (p. 841). Prentice's theory of mutual articulation emphasizes the mutual construction of the body within digital technology. Prentice (2005) contends that:

The computer requires experiential knowledge of difference to be articulated as mathematical values…The [body] model's deformability does not, cannot, exist apart from the thing it interacts with…Deformability is a quality of model bodies defined exclusively at their interface with other bodies. Values of tissue-feel used in deformable models are products of the mutual articulation of bodies. (pp. 854–855)

She regards simulations as mutual articulations where "acquiring knowledge, whether through the senses or through the mediation of instruments, becomes a process of articulating differences in the world" (Prentice, 2005, p. 841). Simulations involve action and sensation that are a form of body knowledge. Simulations convey the body as an interface and articulate the physical connection between body and machine in graphical, haptical, and mathematical terms so that the body and machine intertwine "visually and semiotically, with knowledges culled from engineering and computer science, and physically, with sensors, wires and processors" (Prentice, 2005, p. 847). Likewise, simulations use mathematical constructions to articulate embodied actions. This focus on embodiment as mutually articulated in a movement or process of interaction, with no clear source of origin, is the starting point of my investigation of embodiment in virtual environments.

Embodied/Body Knowledge

Actor-network theory (ANT) is a process philosophy, which offers a way to understand embodiment and body knowledge. It is not based in cause and effect notions of how the body knows, but instead focuses on body knowledge as mediated or mutually articulated in interactions between networks of actors. Such networks include technology interfaces with simulated environments.

Actor-network theory has affiliations with process philosophy. John Dewey (1859–1952) is probably the best-known process philosopher to educators. "Process philosophy holds that the ultimate entities in the universe are not enduring things or substances but processes" (Dusek, 2006, p. 208). ANT perceives technology integration through processes of interaction in networks with life-forms and systems, including environmental and social systems. Embodiment as a process of interaction has significant implications for curriculum. For example, in curriculum the content for study and how the content is organized from an ANT standpoint suggests that "the production of the network is central and is prior to or at least not built up from its atomistic individuals" (Dusek, 2006, p. 209).

The term actors refers to human and non-human mediators in an action or event. Actants can be humans or technologies recruited by organic or inorganic "actors" in a network. The network of "entangled interactions" is "characterized by the way it gathers together into new shapes" (Latour, 2005, p. 65). Furthermore, ANT is "a movement, a displacement, a transformation, a translation, an enrollment" (Latour, 2005, p. 64).

There are distinctly different ways to conceptualize body knowledge including: developmental cognitive psychology theories concerning sensorimotor, visual-spatial, and lexical-semantic body knowledge. Slaughter and Heron (2004) summarize the focus of these conceptualizations of body knowledge:

> Sensorimotor body knowledge is responsible for on-line control and movement of one's own body and may also contribute to the perception of others' moving bodies; visuo-spatial body knowledge specifies detailed structural descriptions of the spatial attributes of the human body; and lexical-semantic body knowledge contains language-based knowledge about the human body. (p. vii)

The problem with these ways of looking at body knowledge is that the body is viewed as a discrete entity and measured against a perceived cultural norm. This norm, which history has shown is political and ideological, is often manifested in everyday language about the body.

Understanding embodiment through ANT is important for defining a bodied curriculum. Embodiment is not the body's materiality, but movement. This movement, I argue, can be understood from the perspective of mutual articulation.

Embodiment as mutual articulation draws on Jean Baudrillard's (1983/ 2005) cultural theory of reality, particularly his investigations of simulation, and Donna Haraway's (1991, 2003) cyborg theory, which blur boundaries between organic and inorganic, between the human body and its natural, cultural, and technological environments. Haraway (1991) and Latour (2004, 2005) emphasize, "the hybrid or intermediate beings, as in Haraway's use of human-machine combinations, such that intentionality is not attributed to humans alone" (Dusek, 2006, p. 209). This view of body knowledge focuses on the interaction between bodies as the site of meaning making. Body knowledge involves the ever-changing combinations of the body in dynamic, entangled interactions with other things. Therefore, embodiment is not durable, solid, and inert. How then can something in flux be considered knowledge of any sort, let alone body knowledge?

I turn to ANT as a way to support my argument that embodiment is a fluid mutually articulated process between things—human and human, or human and non-human. This view of embodiment changes the way that curriculum is constructed.

Embodied experiences are particular lived-experiences such as "experiences from the inside, from the feelings, emotions, and sensations that constitute the vibrant living textures of our lives" (Hayles, 2002, p. 297). Embodiment, from ANT position, includes digital and physical selves and environments in a dynamic interplay of networks (Latour, 2005; Law and

Hassard, 1999). Today, students who learn to become art educators; perform surgery; create architectural spaces; or understand that political, economic, and social systems have opportunities to enact and react to cultural body knowledge in simulated worlds through bodily interaction. Embodied engagement with virtual simulation environments tends to enhance understanding and memory in processes that require body knowledge (Prentice, 2005).

Virtual Simulation Environments

Virtual simulation environments are communicative membranes between knowledge and bodied interaction in a virtual environment. They change what we know and how we know it. Simulation experiences are situated in cyberspace. Ron Burnett (2004), a new media theorist, cautions that:

> one has to be careful because simulation seems to suggest a sense of loss, or a loss of control over what one defines as real to one-self. Clearly, the feelings associated with simulation are powerful. But they are limited by the interfaces and by the fact that they are always mediators among experience, fantasy, and simulation. (p. 194)

Burnett directs our attention to how embodied feelings in a simulated experience are attached to mediators or interface technology devices. His view is similar to ANT, which revisions existence as enacted attachments, as interactive networked processes. The term *mediator,* in this context, refers to being embodied in a large network of attachments that make actions occur and subjectivity felt. Simulations mediate experiences in which there is a "mutual articulation of bodies in and through the machine" (Prentice, 2005, p. 1).

Architect and new media artist Petra Gemeinböck (2004) explores the negotiation of real and virtual, "confusing actual and virtual, present and past" (p. 17). She describes that:

> [T]he virtual projection seems to gain more active, "material" power over the real object, for it is able to redefine, amplify, and even genuinely recreate the real. In the force play between two or more real spaces, an inverted, negative space emerges, in which the real and the virtual can shift places—negotiated secretly in-between. (Gemeinböck, 2004, p. 20)

Gemeinböck's art is an example of ANT in praxis. For example, in her work "Veil of Illusion," two bodies at remote sites interface together with a computer projection in a virtual encounter and thereby transform all of the actors, both human and machine, recruited in this network.

Thus, new media is not about new tools but about new forms of mediation, that is, new ways that a medium enables interaction from one place to another. For example, fiction writer Margaret Atwood, tired of book tours, invented a way to autograph books remotely. According to GadgetGrocer.com (2006), "The author writes a message using a stylus pen on a computer tablet. On the receiving end, in another part of the world, a robotic arm fitted with a regular pen signs the book. The author and fan can also chat via webcam" (p.1). This example suggests society's acceptance of the virtual body prosthesis as communicative of the sensation of being-in-the-presence of the writer celebrity and her physical act of writing. Atwood's robotic arm collapses space to mediate an experience of an in-the-presence encounter of two people.

Hayles and Gessler (2004) argue that subjectivity, which is in a constant struggle between inscriptive and embodied practices, does not reside solely in either the computer or the body. They write:

> Whereas first-generation theorists of virtual reality tended to regard simulated worlds as separate from real life, current trends in miniaturization, implants, wearable computers, and embedded sensors have shifted the emphasis to "mixed realities" mingling computationally intensive simulations with input from the real world. (Hayles and Gessler, 2004, p. 482)

Moreover, Prentice's (2005) concept of feedback looping to explore types of actions between humans and technologies that connect physical and virtual spaces supports the premise of embodiment as mutual articulation.

Feedback Looping

Prentice (2005), in her research of surgical simulations, discusses three types of looping: virtual-feedback loop, mechanical-feedback loop, and embodied cognitive-feedback loop. In these loops humans become aware that their actions impact something. The virtual-feedback loop provides haptic and visual feedback. There is a sense of integration, of being recruited by the *actant* into a simulated network. The mechanical-feedback loop provides body knowledge to the machine. In this type of looping the computer recognizes human responses, sometimes as subtle as anxiety or other emotions conveyed in brainwave fluctuations, eye movement, heartbeat, or skin moisture levels. The embodied cognitive-feedback loop is concerned with how a body learns from tactile and kinesthetic actions such as how much speed, pressure, or tautness is needed in a surgical operation.

In a simulation experience, motion created from virtual, mechanical, or cognitive loops articulates meaning. In learning to perform surgery in a simulated environment, Prentice (2005) describes how body knowledge is constructed from body interaction with other bodies:

> When I clamped the instrument onto a virtual ovary, for example, I felt a distinct snap as the instrument locked onto it and resistance when I pulled the virtual tissues. In reality, all I pulled was the physical interface handle; on the screen, the instrument tip retracted, pulling the ovary with it. (p. 855)

Spatial and tactile knowledge feels and looks "real" when the physical body interacts in a simulated environment. Prentice further emphasizes body knowledge as especially acute through touch. She argues that "the dual nature of hands—they are sensors and actuators—connects actor to object much more directly than vision, smell, or hearing. Hands simultaneously perceive an object and act directly on it" (Prentice, 2005, p. 860). The body both feels and acts, and it is this mutual articulation in simulated worlds in which powerful learning experiences emerge.

Through touch, one understands in a brief moment a multitude of information. The three feedback loops suggest that deep understanding can occur when one's hands or body interacts with virtual matter. The looping that occurs in mutual articulation in a simulated experience is understood as simultaneously a real and unreal "in-between" space.

A Curriculum of Mutual Articulation

To explore a curriculum of mutual articulation I invite pre-service art education students to question their relationship to digital technologies. I introduce, for example, the EyeToy® product, which enables students to use their body to play in a virtual space. In doing so, these future educators consider EyeToy® and other body/technology interfaces as embodied experiences and imagine mingling physical and virtual subjectivity to reveal and to reinvent the cultural body.

I begin my undergraduate visual culture and educational technologies course with a discussion of the students' experiences and understandings of technology. I ask students to respond to the following questions: Why do you use technology? How would you like to use it? What are your fears about technology? Who uses digital technologies? How do artists and art educators use digital technologies? How does electronic/digital media change our experiences, and therefore, our perceptions and expressions?

Students respond with conflicting views about electronic/digital media. They believe that: digital media negates intimate, in-person, and private communications; new media connects people who are physically distant; digital media can provide diverse multisensory experiences; shopping, entertainment, education, and friendships are homogenized when all these experiences are reduced to one's digits moving on a keyboard or fingers manipulating a hard surface.

As a counter response I use the Hayles (2006) definition of interface as a "device to allow communication between two embodied entities, e.g., a computer and a person or one computer and another" (np). This, I posit, is the network created when the students' fingers touch and move on the keyboard. These actants each have their own networks that mesh in that moment of touch and human motion. There is a mutual articulation as the body responds to the machine, and the machine responds to their physical touch on a keyboard, or with other technologies through virtual touch (e.g., one taps the air, virtually hitting the start button that is a projection of light made of digital code). This dynamic process creates meaning, and thus, understanding is formed through touch and motion.

Following class discussion, I encourage students to use their whole body to do things in a virtual space. Especially popular in the past three semesters are the special effects in EyeToy® in which students appear to dematerialize or leave traces of color as the students move in front of a miniature camera. The EyeToy USB camera, attached to a *SONY Play Station 2®*, snaps a photograph of one or more players and places their image in a virtual space selected by the players. Press start and the character projected in a computer monitor, television screen, or on a wall with an LCD projector moves according to the players' movement in front of the camera. EyeToy®'s camera captures body movements in real-time to make it appear like one is gesticulating in a fantasy place.[2]

I am not implying that embodiment is merely about moving our bodies, but instead that body knowledge comes from the actions of our body in interaction with something else. Embodied knowledge involves an action and reaction; a motion or touch and felt response. The origin of who or what recruited the actor into the network is uncertain because the attachments to any action is vast. For example, a pin in one's finger may seem like the cause of the prick, but questions can spin out to consider attached networks of activity, such as asking, why is the pin in the finger?

The impact for curriculum is that corporeality is understood as mutually articulated. Subjects/subjectivity construct and are constructed by the technologies they experience. Technologies that are interfaced with the body, such as EyeToy® and iBrush® reconstitute subjectivity as a network. iBrush® is a brush that contains a video camera. When the brush is stroked over an object it records and then paints the movements, such as blinking eyes, on a touch projection screen (Ryokai et al., 2005). To record a body movement and then construct a dynamic image that contains that action with other actions might seem at first to dismember or disembody subjectivity. Rather, it is understood as a process of mutual articulation. In using technological interfaces such as iBrush® or EyeToy® from an actor-network perspective is an example of a virtual-mechanical-cognitive feedback loop where subjects/subjectivity is reconstituted by looping.

Mutual articulation in a simulated environment in a body interaction with EyeToy®.

Courtesy of Hui-Chun Hsiao and Karen Keifer-Boyd.

Subjectivity

To further explore subjectivity as mutually articulated in simulated experiences, I guide students to generate internal simulations from the textures of lived and imagined experiences. This exercise explores the different needs of different bodies and the reliance our bodies have on technologies. I ask students to draw from personal and cultural body knowledge through sensory memory. Sensory memory considers and values lived experience as mutually articulated.

Students generate ideas of how to incorporate body knowledge from interaction in virtual spaces. From their body interface play with EyeToy® they explore subjectivity and examine how subjectivity is formed in relationships. They consider why and how they are recruited as participants in technological networks, and whether the mediated communication process forms a type of community. One student related to the class that before her own students use EyeToy® they "would discuss what the terms 'identity,' 'relationship,' and 'community' mean" (January 17, 2006). Another student stated, "I think that by expecting my students to be active participants…using tools like EyeToy® [would] encourage exploration of self-identity" (September 14, 2005). The pre-service educators describe that they experience a heightened sense of awareness in enacting and interacting with the body in relation to human and non-human bodies/networks. The performative aspects of body movement in virtual spaces with EyeToy® type technology increases self-awareness of "the body in relation to other bodies and the ways in which knowing and being are informed through generative understandings of touch, fantasy, and performance" (Springgay, 2003, p. 1). Few educators are involved in developing body-mediated experiences in virtual educational environments, and thus a bodied interaction curriculum that introduces educators to mutual articulation in virtual simulations is paramount in preparing future art educators.

Guy Debord (2006), in discussing the goals of a 1968–1972 activist art group known as the *Situationalists,* also recognized the radical curriculum of body knowledge as a space of interaction. He states, "We must develop a systematic intervention based on the complex factors of two components in perpetual interaction: the material environment of life and the behaviors which it gives rise to and which radically transform it" (n.p.). Technology-body interfaces offer this interaction. Moreover, participation in construction of the interface, that is, the mediated hybrid third space of interaction, can lead to an awareness and transformation of cultural body knowledge. Hybridization, which Latour refers to as the *third space,* is "the process of moving beyond subject/object relationships" (Burnett, 2004, p. 176). It is a "hybridized third space of interaction" (Burnett, 2004, p. 182). Hybrid connections of material and virtual bodies recontextualize the body in the performing feedback looping spaces of interactions. Virtual traces of virtual travel in imaginative play are new forms of mediated communication significant to curricular development and study.

Today, "hybrid processes are about new levels of materiality that are the product of a series of interactions and transformations that may not have been built into the original technology, nor have anything to do with its initial purpose" (Burnett, 2004, p. 172). Materiality for Hayles refers to "what performances the work enacts" (2004, p. 71). Thus, meaning comes from the signifying strategies of enactment, which is a movement or an action. When there is uncertainty or conflict between epistemic and motivational representations, humans tend to seek coherence (Castelfranchi, 2004). This desire for coherency is perhaps why intentions enacted in the virtual space are believable to the enacting body.

Moreover, "technologies are born out of needs, amplify and extend those needs, and then help in the redefinition of what it means to be human" (p. 174). Yet, what it means to be human should be grounded in a consideration of mutual articulation and the notion that virtual space is embodied. In considering body interfaces, curriculum should explore and critique mutual articulation in simulated worlds and hybridized spaces of material and virtual interactions.

Un/structure: Narratives of Bodies and Schooling

Silent Voices, Silent Bodies: Difference and Disadvantage in Schooling Contexts

Dalene M. Swanson

Within the sunken recesses of an imposing indigenous landscape, there is a place that breaks through the integument of a magenta-soiled Body-Earth. It is an eclectic montage of corrugated iron and hardboard, splitting the brush strokes of nature to expose its grit and bone…it is the skull of my country,[3] its lived and unlived moments, bearing the teeth marks of a protracted history of *oppression*, a peopled past-place of pain and *struggle*.

It is from this place, this informal settlement, that the children come…and they walk many a mile to a community missionary school. Perhaps, they come in the hopes that through their education, they might rise above the material and historical conditions of socially engineered "poverty," beyond the land-locked, community-locked, bodily situated localities of established "disadvantage" frozen in time. Or perhaps, ironically, they come because this school represents for them a "protected place," where all children "are equal in poverty," a place in which they may assert the wealth of their humanity, divorced, momentarily and contradictorily, from the outside conditions of a world which "others" them and holds their bodies to prescribed spaces of "deficit" and "disadvantage."

I open here with an excerpt from my doctoral dissertation that sets the scene on an informal settlement community within a context of socioeconomic poverty, in the Cape Province of South Africa. My recent research in Curriculum Studies and Mathematics Education explores sociopolitical and cultural perspectives, and embodiments in a range of diverse curricular and pedagogic contexts. This excerpt relates to one community context of fieldwork experiences in socioeconomically, culturally and historically diverse schools in post-apartheid South Africa.

The narrative sets the stage for a performative discourse that contributes to understanding more broadly the intersections of race, class, gender, poverty, and other constructions of social difference and the ways in which these interrelated positions produce meanings through the body as lived experience (Merleau-Ponty, 1962; van Manen, 2003).

I explore the multiple articulations of the body as it finds place within the paradoxes, dilemmas and ambiguities produced through discursive and embodied productions and ideological performances within localized contexts, in particular contexts of poverty. My research looks at how global discourses are reconfigured or recontextualized (Bernstein, 2000) within situated locations in ways that are often oppressive. This global-to-local recontextualizing may serve to enact a symbolic—and often physical—violence on bodies. Nevertheless, the chapter provokes questions around how the recontextualizing of discourses opens up a range of spaces of possibility or constraint in and through bodies in performance, and what positions of resistance toward transformation become possible, if at all, with(in) such contradictions.

Furthermore, I address how bodies act as visible markers of sites of struggle and relations of power, and raise questions about how silence may be voiced through bodied constructions relating to social difference. In so doing, I bring into debate critical sociocultural and political perspectives in mathematics education discourse and practice, addressing the comportments of bodies in accordance with how school mathematics, in these instances, is variously constituted and (re)produced in contexts that are delimiting or enabling. This research makes visible some of the hegemonic practices in mathematics education as social texts of "difference" and "deficit," and it aims to contest some of the curricular, pedagogical, and pathological practices in mathematics classrooms and communities of practice that construct and enact learned, lived, and embodied "disadvantage." In this chapter, I engage with these concerns and debates through narrative excerpts culled from my doctoral dissertation. Restor(y)ing the excerpted narratives in the context of this chapter also facilitates a further "coming to know" through an interpretive discursive dance and a layered writing on the body.

Interpreting the body as constituting and constitutive of relations of power, assists in hypostatizing the many relationships, contradictions, and ambiguities produced through constructions of the body in situated contexts, and the contextual dilemmas produced through marked bodies in performance. In this sense, it opens up a space for reflexive narratizing[4] in addressing the relationship between social difference and constructed disadvantage. Furthermore, it highlights how this relationship becomes "pedagogized and pathologized"[5] through a multiplicity of complex, discursive, and somatic performances in the production of power and identity.

The embodied implications of pedagogized and constructed disadvantage leads to a notion of "corporeal situatedness": how the body might mark out the place of agency and contestation where the body becomes the very site of struggle for competing discourses and ideological positions in context. In exemplifying this corporeal situatedness, I return to my research vignette. I am back in the missionary school in the informal settlement in the Cape Province of South Africa. I am hoping to be a participant observer in the classroom, but the shape of that experience has not been as I expected.

And so it came to be that I found myself in the midst of "the multitudes," a class of fifty grade 7 children from this shanty community. Their teacher had already abandoned them for more than three weeks, but they came to school nonetheless. And I can only assert that they were compelled to come, not by the promise of pedagogic and, consequently, economic empowerment as promised through globalizing progressivist modes of ideological engagement, as the paucity of subject-based knowledge mitigated against this, but—as I see it from my researcher's vantage point—by a sense of commonality, community, and a "place of belonging."

"Would you like me to teach you some mathematics?" I offered. "Ja, asseblief, mevrou! Ons sal baie daarvan hou! Ja, asseblief mevrou!" ("Yes please ma'am, we would like that very much!"). They began to dance in their desks with excitement at the prospect of learning something...something new perhaps? Learning something from me? I was moved and heartened and I began to bless and break the bread of my mathematical knowledge, my own empowerment, and divide it with affection and compassion and I broke of this body to give of the light and joy of this subject I loved so much...offering it in tasty morsels...this was surely more than mere fishes and loaves!!

And after a short while, the children began to answer my questions and even to ask questions and participate in the discussion, giving meaning through their bodies, giving back unsparingly of their enthusiasm. I was greatly heartened as I saw this as tremendous "advancement" in such a short time. For children that I had witnessed as having been exposed to nothing but transmission, rote-learning, and proceduralism, this was surely an "opening of minds," an "awakening of spirits," a "pedagogic achievement," a "progressivist success!"

I was elated, ecstatic! I was performing a miracle. I was proving that the miracle was possible; that my miracle could set a spark in the dry veld of despair and disillusionment and would Light the Dark and heal my whole country with a Sanctifying Fire. And just when we were about to consecrate the communion of Mathematical Thought, there was a Divine Visitation. The door swung open and a child entered. He handed me a crumpled white bag and was gone as suddenly as he had come.

A cloud passed over the sun and, through the broken panes of the classroom window, the streaks of golden sunlight dulled and disappeared. The atmosphere cooled; the mood of the children changed. And then there seemed to be a movement, indiscernible at first, and then ever Increasing, a spiraling force drawing the atmosphere inwards, like a vortex, deep, downwards into what I was holding...a crumpled plastic bag! The children began to move around in their desks in agitation. They were no longer focusing on the mathematics we had been doing, just the bag in my hands. The moment of Mathematical Mastery, of Conceptual Glory was shattered!

"It is the white people, ma'am, that give us our school lunch. It comes from the children in the privileged schools, ma'am. It is for us, ma'am." Their hands began to touch on the sides of the open bag, to touch my hands, to look inside the bag. Was there enough food today, perhaps? No never enough! I looked into the bag and saw a few sandwiches and fruit. White children's discarded lunches that had been collected for the day and brought to the school under the guise of "assistance" from the surrounding community. I realized that I had the impossible task of having to decide who eats and who goes hungry that day. Everything had seemed to change, or had it? I had offered to teach these children mathematics; now I was expected, to preside as judge and jury over their bodies. I was no "liberator" or Great Redeemer, but an accomplice coerced into the discourse and practice of Oppression!

The rules of the discourse of mathematics had shifted to a new discourse whose dominant and uncontested rules won the day. I realized that I could not perform the miracle of "fishes and loaves." Just as I was not able to perform it pedagogically, so I could not physically break up the sandwiches and divide the fruit equitably among 50 children so that they all may be satiated. Who would have to starve? White chalk dust from my fingers billowed in a fine mist as the movement of small black hands over mine disturbed it. For a moment it clouded the view of the contents of the bag and I thought I saw through the mist, the skull of my country looking back at me and in it was my own skull. I had tried to provide a skin over that skull, to give it substance and embodiment through my own mathematical empowerment in a context where pedagogic possibilities are reduced to the rules of "poverty." My body had become the site of cataclysms between colliding ideologies, and all of ours together in a vortex of situational immediacy, of corporeal situatedness. The struggle between the ideology of Africanisation—and the celebration of indigenous knowledge, people and power, and that of neoliberalism—that limited empowering possibilities and maintained existing hierarchies and hegemonies, enacted itself through the situational dilemma and contradiction, and performed the ideological contestation through our marked bodies. What did I think I was going to do? What Messiah did I think I was? Was I going to "uplift" this community, provide their children with the pedagogic promise of something "better" than fishes and loaves? What "good" did the patronizing offer of food for "disadvantaged learners" do for this community's educational, political and socio-economic empower-ment? In what way did my actions or those of the other do-gooders address the structural and material conditions of the lives of the children and people of this informal settlement?

From this research narrative, I move back into the textual place of this presence, shifting weight as my stance changes from writing research to writing the writing of that research, a process of writing an un-writing on the body. And so I ask: Whose voices, whose bodies are silenced in this process and how is this achieved? What does an embodiment of curriculum and pedagogy of social justice look like in such a context? What does the pursuit of democracy feel like inside of the contradictions? Where do we place the ambiguity, the deferred, the immediacy, the moment of engagement along the journeyed route of "restorative egalitarianism," and the decolonizing project? Through reflexive body writing, a dialogue is set up that raises questions about intentionality and purpose, about social action in dilemmatic contexts, of hidden ideologies that compete for hegemony, sited in/through the body and made visible through contradiction and disjuncture. Actions have color, and intention colors action. The sociohistorical cannot be divorced from the moment of intention, as social domain discourses vie for supremacy and control, articulated through the social, ideological, and biological subjectivities of the body. The ethical, moral, critical, practical, and spiritual intersect and validate their multiple and often divergent purposes in social actions. These mark our bodies, as they mark our souls.

Colonization takes on many modes of dress, and Western mathematics curricula across the world take on the layered forms of colonization in the classroom.[6] Placing school mathematics in social and historical context, informed by the historical and ideological developments of the discipline of mathematics, masterfully made "neutral" and "objective," school mathematics enjoys a position of eminence in "the social division of labour of discourses in schools" (Bernstein, 2000, p. 6). Hiding its cloak of ideological materiality, school mathematics comes to us as a masculine white body, colonizing the places and persons of its influence, most often deceitfully in the name of social and economic community advancement or democracy through its techno-centric and industrial utilitarianism (Swanson, 2004). In teaching school mathematics in diverse socioeconomic and cultural contexts over many years, I have grappled with the multivalence and incommensurate ideological positions underpinning understandings of mathematical empowerment—for whom, where, why, how, by what means? Does empowerment imply access to the regulating principles of mathematical discourse (Dowling, 1998); to enable individuals through access to economic and intellectual means within the prevailing global, social, and economic relations; or does it imply the critical capacity for its collective resistance? I embrace an understanding of school mathematics embodied colonizations as it acts divisively upon persons, evoking a form of intellectual apartheid, thereby affording access and opportunity for some, while denying it to others along the lines of constructions of "ability" and other social difference discourses.

Living a pedagogy of hope in mathematics education, has, for me, come to mean engaging in multiple forms of resistance on several fronts within school mathematics discourse and practice. These multiple resistances hold school mathematics to account by demanding that questions of democracy be asked of its practices. It is an orientation that informs my philosophy of teaching and learning. Hope and possibility lie at the intersection of different embodied engagements with mathematics education in ways that reconstitute mathematics in the classroom. While noticing what the visual anthropology and geography of the mathematics classroom might be, and how this shapes discursive and somatic performances within it, a further commitment to reconstituting mathematics as both science and art affirms embodied pedagogies of teaching and learning. A different configuration of somatic performances is enacted. Mathematics can be taught through dance movement, drama, visual art, music, and literature. The preserve of mathematics as describer-of-all-reality needs review, just as the time has come for the "Queen of the Sciences" to be dethroned. Further, narrative approaches to teaching mathematics that resist Piagetian-inspired hierarchies—hierarchies that lay open a door to skills-based approaches and proceduralism—need to be embraced. Just as the body articulates narratives of everyday life and human creativity, so too the cultural body of school mathematics needs narratives of everydayness and imaginative contexts of engagement.

Mathematical narrativity integrates the arts and sciences, liberating the body of these dualisms. Such engagement in integrative pedagogies provides an alternative to the cognitizing of social difference and the "pedagogizing of disadvantage" (Swanson, 2004) by re-conceiving the living body in non-objectifying, non-dichotomous, socially responsive and holistic ways that integrate mind, body, and soul in understanding how meaning and possibility are produced.

Embodied approaches contest the dualistic way in which the body is conventionally conceived, that often relate to the dichotomizing of the arts and sciences in pedagogic contexts. These Cartesian dualisms inform gendered and socially constructed conceptions of the mind and learning processes that mark bodies in multicultural or situated contexts. Not only does this integrative, embodied perspective offer opportunities to renegotiate the body and disrupt its conventional role in pathologizing disadvantage, but it opens a space for collapsing destructive binaries and oppositions, and blurs the boundaries of science and art through a holistic conception of body, mind, and spirit. It proposes an anti-oppressive perspective on teaching and learning through approaches that legitimize bodily knowledge, and place the heart at the forefront of pedagogical purpose.

Rendering embodied ways of knowing and "coming to be" as crucial to learning and living, engaging a pedagogy of heart, and privileging the emotive and spiritual over cognitive or intellectual considerations, offers hopefulness to a philosophy of teaching and learning, but it also informs an ethics of being in research. Our ontological and epistemological convictions draw currency from a sense of moral presence, of "how we are in the world," the statement we make upon the earth through the complex interplay of our bodies, minds, and spirits. Our moral commitments, set against the ideological terrain of our actions and the possibilities they endorse or prevent, are often instantiated in dilemma, ambiguity, and paradox. Our being in the world in particular ideological ways often signifies the effacement of that moral commitment, or acts as an undoing of pedagogical purpose. The variegated nature of purpose and possibility confuses attempts to find coherence in understanding social action toward egalitarianism and democracy, but roots/routes meanings back toward presence, relationships with Others, and ways of being and becoming, rather than knowing. Writing reflexive research serves as a place of performative engagement in grappling with the ethical dilemmas, contradictions, and paradoxes that decide the integrity of pedagogical and academic commitments. And so I move back into the textual domain of an excerpted research narrative to exemplify the performative nature of pedagogy and research practice, where our bodies perform an ideological dance of seeking ethical resolution, social justice, and ways of becoming.

"All these new methods and this progressive education thing," the principal of the missionary school in the informal settlement continues—after a long pause, "...and these kids still don't know their times tables! So what is the good of all of it?" At first he assumes the posture of someone in debate, but then he jumps up and starts to stride across his office, gesticulating as he talks. I sit on the other side of his desk as he performs for me, explicating his argument against progressivism in an extemporaneous and agitated dance. "When I grew up, we did it by rote, and at least I can work out my budget and do multiplication without having to reach for a calculator. But these kids today, if you ask them: what is two times seven, they don't know." He goes on: "But we have to embrace this progressive education thing."

My mind is trying to reconcile this outburst against progressive education with the very traditionalist and procedural practices[7] I have evidenced in the classroom. And I am trying to provide it with political place and voice. But where is this voice coming from and why? And how does this measure up to the practices I have observed within the classroom? And where and how come is he making the assumption that I am an unquestioning advocate of progressive education? Is it something that I said or something that I appear to be or appear to stand for? And so, I begin to see where the thread of the argument is going, and in it, I think I see the source.

I realize that this statement has more to do with his positioning of me as "a white South African mathematics teacher, or even more so, a white Canadian researcher," and his own relational positioning in this context, and in the take-up of these positions, (that is, how they shift and are reconfigured and established in a local context within a broader context of constructed "disadvantage," and of the other social domain discourses which inform it), than it is about the pedagogics or politics of educational progressivism itself. The motivating principles lie in the multiple voices, authorial and distal, that overlay and undergird the present context; and contextual agency is rooted in the routedness of the argument, in the network of dialogues that construct and assist in the maintenance of the discourse of "disadvantage" itself. I infer from this that the meaning lies, not in any "truth" of the statement itself, but behind this "truth," in the interstitial spaces of silence within a broader structure, that either obscure meaning, or generate other meanings, meanings seldom straightforwardly articulated.

And despite this, for a moment, I want to ask what I think are crucial questions, which, for me, highlight the contradictions of the statements I have just heard from the principal of this elementary school. I want to ask him, why it is, that, from my perspective, I have not really evidenced any real attempt to engage in any progressive education practices within these classrooms, why I have seen so much rote learning when any pedagogic learning took place at all? Or why I have seen, from my perspective, so much apparent indifference? Why so many of the teachers are so seldom in the classroom when the current National Minister of Education has made urgent and repeated appeals to teachers across the country to take their jobs seriously for the country's sake, for the sake of our youth and the future generation of South Africa now in creation? Where does the proverbial 'buck stop,' who is responsible, who cares, why not, and how can we make a difference? I want to ask him why he closes the school early so frequently, causing very small children to have to walk home alone, often unescorted back to their homes in the informal settlement where they are not attended to or protected because their parents or caretakers are at work? Where does his responsibility to the community end or where does it start? Why does he use class time to have meetings with his staff, and why so frequently is learning interrupted for apparently, from my perspective, inconsequential issues? Why does he legitimize teachers' missing classes by engaging in these practices himself? Why can't meetings take place after school?

I think of how the school day ends at 2:00 pm sharp, 1:00 pm on Fridays, and how the gates are bolted and chained by 2:05 every day, 1:05 on Fridays, after which an unnatural silence pervades the school grounds. I think of how the school day ends early on days when the staff attend workshops run by the provincial department of education and I see them all climbing into the school's mini-van, apparently eager to attend, waving and smiling at me as they drive off together: "Wonderful workshops!" they tell me, "with innovative ideas on how to teach mathematics and some good progressive techniques!"

Again, as I have felt many times before, a strangeness and awkwardness overcomes me, and I begin to feel a sense of alienation and hopelessness!

And yet, a part of me wants to speak out. I want to tell him what I think. I want to tell him that I think it is not right. That this is "just not good enough!" Is this what we were all liberated for? Wasn't it to try and make a difference, to turn it around, to "fight the good fight!" Not to give in to oppression; not to submit to the authority of poverty and consequently the authority of privilege that establishes the poverty; not to succumb to the worst form of oppression, in Freirian terms, when the oppressed begin to oppress themselves.

I want to ask him why? Why he is not seeing it, why he is so bound by this model of oppression, this discourse of poverty and situated experience that he cannot step outside of it, even for a moment, to see what it is like. Is it that poverty is so rooted in 'situatedness,' that it is so delimiting, so strangulating, that we cannot create even a momentary spark of insight? Does it require a stepping aside, a looking awry, a new platform, another place, a firm patch of new ground, to find it, to visualize it, to imagine? Does envisioning require the separation or abstraction from local context and its firm-rootedness to be able to provide perspective, generate new interpretations and conceptualizations, provide them with the flesh of real hope, of tangible possibility?

And then the blinding moment of anger passes and I am back within this situated reality. I look out of the window. I see two girls scuffing their shoes in the red dirt, the dry dust rises in a small wisp of smoke. Then one girl suddenly grabs the other girl from the back by her hair and pulls her down into a kneeling position. There is anguish on the victim's face, but she doesn't resist. And it appears to me that this, or more, has happened to her many times before and she is no longer indignant, resistant, affronted, was she ever otherwise given the space to be such, I wonder? Her hopeless resignation angers me.

I jump up and move to the window looking down onto the scene in the courtyard, the crisscrossing Euclidean grid of the window frame between us, the bully turns her eyes toward me and looks through the pane/pain, looks through her own pain, even with a blank undaunted stare. Staring into my face contorted with a horrible mixture of anger, disappointment, and pity. The Principal sees my reaction and he too jumps up to have a look at what I am looking at. He swears under his breath in Afrikaans, "darrie blêrrie boggers van graad sewe kinders…uit die blêrrie klasskamer alweer."[8] His composure is broken, the posturing has disappeared, we are back to the immediacy and brutal "reality" of the moment and partially recovering his previous tone, he relays to me in English: "Their teacher isn't here again today," as if I might not have known this self-evident piece of information. "Excuse me a minute," he says brusquely, and walks hastily out of the office, across the courtyard, up the steep steps and stops in the open doorway of the offending classroom.

From my visual perspective, the classroom behind the principal's dominant form is dark, unseeable, and formless, like an auditorium when the lights have gone down—ready for the performance, a performance on a "stage-in-the-round." The two girls have already disappeared back into the same room, caught out, scampering, like a pair of frightened rabbits back into their dark burrow. I can see the principal shouting and gesticulating threateningly. He is silhouetted against the dark doorway, delineated by the door, and through the windowpane I can hear nothing of what he says—there is only silence and it is loud in my ears. It is as if I am watching an old-fashioned silent movie, being played out before me, a performance in silence on the theme of silence, visible, audible silence.

I stand silently in the room, waiting and watching, waiting for the principal to return. The clock on his desk ticks quietly, time passes.

I am trying to comprehend the scene. I think back on what precipitated the current chain of events, to make sense of it. I think of the two rabbit girls scurrying away when the Voice of Authority entered the scene. I am a schoolgirl again, waiting in the principal's office. I am remembering the fear of bullies, bullies that took all forms, classmates and teachers. I am remembering the smell and taste of fear, the fractured, brutal, images of authority and its violent sting. I feel the same sick feelings coming back, deafening fragments of memories. I feel like a bewildered animal caught in the headlights of this strange blinding reenactment of repeated repressive realities.

At that moment, and it was not an epiphany, but a slow blurred form taking root, re-rooting in my mind. It was a slow re-realization of what I had done by wanting to "peak out" and to tell this principal that I thought it was "just not good enough". It was a re-cognition of my own voice of violence, of what brutality I had done in feeding into the discourse on "disadvantage." I re-realized that my thoughts, framed within the discursive roots of my socialization, my education and knowledge, my own perceived empowerment as an adult, and my own experience of teaching—had established that "disadvantage" as "plain to see".

I began to re-realize that in my initial thought-words of anger, I had been taking on the colonizing voice which produces the deficit, and that creates, validates, and establishes "the problem" from outside, from a place out there that can speak unmonitored by its own surveillance. I had been doing the same thing as that which I had surveyed in the courtyard. I was producing and reproducing the very conditions that produced the bully/bullying in the first place, ensuring its reproduction through my own voyeuristic perspective and reproductive deficit language, albeit a silent language of thoughts.

I too had become a bully. I was complicit with a system or discourse and a well-entrenched paradigm of thinking that constructs "the problem," establishes the "truth" on "deficit," and lays blame.

I realize that my vantage point was at fault. That, in some of the contexts in which I had practiced my profession as a secondary school mathematics teacher, the practices I was criticizing now would not have been possible, that teaching time was sacred, important, urgent and that time was of the essence, a resource of which there was never enough. From this vantage point, I notice the inversion and the contradictions.

In a suburban schooling context, material resources are relatively plentiful, paper, equipment, classroom space, computers, libraries, photocopy machines, photocopy assistants, new technology, availability of resource materials, curriculum materials, pedagogic assistance, all within a community of Pedagogic Knowledge Experts, but time was a precious and limited resource, urgent, sought after, coveted. Here it was the opposite—confined space, discomfort, lack of privacy, lack of expertise, lack of pedagogic support, noise, dust, the smell of dust, too many bodies, huddled bodies, wriggling, no space to think, no space to prepare, but all the time in the world in a sort of time-warp...in a mental, psychological, sociological, human landscape of foreverness.

These are the power principles that inform not only the political gaze from the perspective of the self, but also control the distributions of the spatial/temporal dichotomy and that define the political economy of context by assisting in the production of the poverty/privilege hierarchy, and which define the roles of subjects in context.

These are the principles of the politics of context that either delimit or allow spaces of possibility in accordance with the social division of labor of discourses (Bernstein, 2000) in the social domain in which the discourses of context are invested, discourses which depend/suspend entirely on the stringently policed rules of relations of power. This is how the principles of "progress" operate across the temporal and spatial, in the race toward "future advancement." And defined by its own rules, it ensures very few "winners," and many "losers!"

I hear the deficit voices again, bullying voices, some voices of educationalists, specialists, and well-known people in authority in South African Education, people in the "new arena" of post-liberation education. "The problem lies with our teachers...they are underqualified, demotivated, lacking experience and expertise...and there is not enough of them...our failures in mathematics can be directly attributed to the teachers...they are our problem."

I realize that in my own way, I was feeding into this, re-creating this monster, re-establishing this deficit discourse. I realize that in creating the teachers, principal, and their pedagogic practices in this "disadvantaged community" as lacking, as the "real problem," it was an escape, a way of not facing up to not understanding, not seeing the source of power and how it threads its way into the repressive web.

Yes, I had become the bully. And the bully in the courtyard was as much, if not more, my victim of constructed "disadvantage" and the pedagogy of pain and poverty that it produces, as she was a bully in herself. The principal was a victim of it too, and I had not even begun to imagine the strangulating and delimiting conditions that this discourse served to produce and in which he was constrained to operate. This was the "pedagogizing of difference" indeed, and a discourse in which I had participated. This was how the construction of disadvantage begot pedagogic and contextually produced disadvantage.

The principal came back into the room, looking a little harassed. A "sideshow" had interrupted "Our Performance" and had seemed to detract from "the conversation." But, in fact, it was a critical fragment of the whole, a necessary contribution to understanding the resolution of the narrative, and in which our initial "polite" conversation preceding "the sideshow" had been the essential exposition. I, myself, had moved through several modes of looking, premised by various experiential podiums of perspective. Consequently, when I had been angry and critical my vantage point had been the more privileged context of some of my teaching experience. When I had overcome my anger and realized my role in the co-constructed authorship of power I had returned to my early youth and to remembering, remembering what it was like to be bullied and to feel the hand of violence and the voice of humiliation. And it was only then that I could begin to understand—feel with a deeper listening.

It had required a range of senses as it had required a shift in perspective. I had moved from a "looking on" and the voyeuristic power instantiated in perspectives of "seeing," to a "listening to," where the eyes are quieted by the sights and sounds within darkened silence, and the sense of hearing is peaked, tuning into silence.

This had been my route. Instead of trying to find the "root of the problem" and trying to "root out the problem," like a cancer from living tissue, instead I was moving toward searching for "the source." The source of the problem lay silently behind the construction of "the problem" itself and threaded its way, like a tributary, to my very doorstep. I too was complicit, a collaborator of deficit discourse, a root of "the problem's" routedness. Now I became responsible as well, through acknowledging that responsibility.

The I-you dichotomy had been broken by the emergence of a new bond of responsibility, a humbling togetherness! I needed to listen collaboratively to that "source" in collectively finding a way together of "re-sourcing" toward non-impoverishment, other possibilities, and mutual healing.

Experiential, situated, sensory, and somaesthetic awareness provide meaning and possibility within sociocultural contexts of teaching and learning, and being in research. Through reflexive narrative that calls upon the social, spiritual, embodied, and emotional domains of experience, misconceptions and prejudices can be analyzed, felt, and innately understood within the terms of a particular set of embodied performances. The body makes visible incommensurate discourses that collide and confound meanings in situated contexts, producing a quagmire of ethical and contextual dilemmas through marked bodies in performance. Constructions of disadvantage are pedagogized through ways in which communities, students, and teachers' bodies are temporally and spatially conceived of in context. Consequently, validating the relationships between culture and embodied ways of knowing, and the silences within and between bodies in corporeal situatedness, provide opportunities for viscerally understanding the multiplicity of complex, discursive, and somatic performances in the production of power, pedagogy, and identity.

To recapitulate on some of the theoretical approaches and ideas addressed in this chapter, these present opportunities for deconstructing the body as object and its Cartesian-imposed distinction from the cognitive and affective domain of perception. Michael Peters (2004) explains Merleau-Ponty's notion of "body-subject" in these terms: "The body is not an 'object' in the objective sense through its spatial properties and its location; neither is the body limited to cause and effect descriptions. Rather, the body is the subject of action: it is essentially a practical, pre-conscious subject in the lived world that possesses both 'intentionality' and 'knowledge'" (p. 20).

The body as the subject of intentioned and knowledgeable action further offers an opportunity to embrace understandings of the political and cultural body in its many manifestations of relations of power and enactments of discursive and ideological disjunctions. The relationality of the individual body with the collective, and the blending of corporeal boundaries or their visibility as sites of irresolvable difference, sanctions interpretations of a political body that is constitutive of experience—resistant, compliant, unstable, agentive, relational, un-unified, and subjective.

Subjectivity is multiple, fragmented, situated. It modulates its form as it is mediated in and across contexts. Certain priorities and positions are fore-fronted in the take up and recruitment of particular subjectivities, as others are back-grounded (Ensor, 1996), in particular evoking contexts (Bernstein, 2000) through a set of discursive and somatic performances that interplay with the webbed textu(r)ality of the place of such performances. For Cindy Patton (1995), "understanding the place of various strategies, tactics, and the actants they produce and which deploy them requires us to say more about the 'context' or 'stage' of performance/performativity" (p. 192). The body is the textural, intersubjective agent of performance. For Charles Garoian (1999), "performativity" in cultural production "represents the performance of subjectivity" (p. 8). The performing body creates the knowing dialect of interaction—it performs itself as articulation of knowing and unknowing, and the corpus of meaning making. As such, the body may be understood in terms of the multiple, complex, and interrelated ways in which it informs the production of subjectivity in particular curricular, pedagogic, and sociopolitical contexts and how this concomitantly shapes and mediates our consciousnesses and the forms of knowledge produced and legitimated.

And so, I re-invoke these earlier questions in our journey toward more insightful and visceral understandings: Whose voices, whose bodies are silenced in this process and how is this achieved? What does an embodiment of a curriculum and pedagogy of social justice look like in such a context? What does the pursuit of democracy feel like inside of the contradictions? Where do we place the ambiguity, the deferred, the immediacy, the moment of engagement along the journeyed route of "restorative egalitarianism" and the decolonizing project? But these questions evoke further ones as they commit, simultaneously, to personal and collective resolution, over seeking a unified "solution" to the "problem" of contradiction. Perhaps, most of all, we need to ask ourselves of what we become through our greater embodied consciousnesses, our new collective humanity. How is our ethical, moral, social body placed in the context of this new knowing, new becoming, new arriving? How do we situate ourselves within the ambiguities, dilemmas and paradoxes we proliferate yet avoid, residing instead with contented corporeal presence within the uncertainty, challenging—while also embracing—the ironic embodiments of our own and our collective contradictions?

It is about moving out and coming together simultaneously, it's about digging down and pushing up, like a plant searching for anchorage and light at the same time, it is about at once finding place and searching for a new course and it is about rootedness in routedness and finding routes toward roots. It is also none or any of these, but all of these at once—not in a moment of time, or even in a temporal continuum—but ever present, past, and future blended together in a bodily soulscape, and ever-interconnecting in a storied journeying, journeying towards sourcing, and re-sourcing with earth and air and sun.

Understandings and Communication Through Dress: Sartorial Inquiry in a Secondary Art Class

We as teachers like to think it's only words and actions that we are embodied—how can our bodies teach, but we are embodied beings—how can our bodies NOT be a part of the teaching act?

Daniel T. Barney

> When a teacher enters a classroom for the first time, it is not necessarily her or his ideas that first attract students' attention. It is the body and how it is adorned and clothed—how it looks, sounds, moves and smells. Whether or not we realize it, the image we project precedes us, introduces us, and inserts us into the communication we have with students.
>
> (Mitchell and Weber, 1999)

Clothing in schools explicitly deals with codes of conduct, namely dress codes for students, staff, teachers, and administrators. These codes are used to communicate a hierarchy of power that sets one apart from others, for example, the student from the teacher, the teacher from the administrator, and the lunch worker from the custodian. But, perhaps there is more to clothing than its seemingly banal materiality. What can be learned from curriculum as inquiry through dress? In this chapter I discuss clothing and art as communicatory processes. Traditionally, clothing and art are viewed as objects to be studied. My analysis positions clothing as art, as a process, a way of understanding self and the body. As such, I propose a sartorial artistic inquiry that calls attention to a thinking through the body as communication. Sartorial is used as a non-gendered term denoting: relating to tailoring, clothes, or style of dress. Several secondary students' work, as well as my own, will be presented to illustrate this potential.

> body art as well- tatooing, piercing, hairstyles

Clothing as Communication

While clothing serves to protect the body or to cover it in modesty, John Carl Flugel (1971) argues that it is improbable that modesty and protection are the primary motives for clothing the body. Instead, clothing is a ubiquitous signifier that appears in magazines, billboards, radio, television, and also in everyday discussion, like, "Where did you get those shoes? They are to die for." In addition, television shows about fashion, with titles such as *How Do I Look, Fashion Police, The Look for Less*, and *What Not to Wear,* embody the practice of the make-over, where those who have fashioned themselves incorrectly can be saved. Similarly, clothing and how one dresses is monitored and displayed in schools. Teachers, staff, and administrators prescribe and/or succumb to dress norms. Students are labeled and self label themselves using thrift shop chic, Skater wear, BMX wear, Jock wear, Lolita wear, Cyber wear, Goth wear, Straight Edge wear, Emo wear, and the like. These are all active means of communicating one's identity (Cunningham and Lab, 1991; Hebdige, 1979). Irit Rogoff (2000) agrees, stating that clothing is a common means of marking the body in the "signification of identity" (p. 144). Dress can also be an uninvited display of one's place in a socioeconomic order (Roach-Higgins, Eicher, and Johnson, 1995) or other hierarchical structures such as gender, age, or politics (Damhorst, Miller-Spillman, and Michelman, 2005). Therefore, clothes are more than objects of technology used solely to protect oneself from nature or to satisfy a cultural or universal sense of modesty; they are also a form of non-verbal communication.

Malcolm Barnard (2002) reviews two models of communication in relation to clothing and fashion: (a) the process model and (b) the semiotic model. The process model of communication is described "as a process in which someone says something to someone else in one or other medium or channel with some or other effect" (p. 30). Within the context of clothing, a garment wearer or the clothing designer sends an intended message that is transmitted to another person via the garment. For example, the rubber boots that I am wearing communicate that I am expecting rain, or the yellow shirt I am wearing communicates that I am happy. As Barnard points out, this school of thought is problematic. The intentions of the sender are central to this view, as expressed in the statement, "I am wearing yellow to send the message that I am happy." Also, the transmission process in this view is significant, for if the intended message reaches the receiver in an altered form the communication is seen as unsuccessful. For example: "He is wearing yellow because he is eccentric, or tacky," rather than the intended

How do teachers
We as teachers read dress—process
(parents, etc.) or semiotic?

Understandings and Communication Through Dress • 81

message of happiness. Finally, in this view of communication, the receiver, or spectator, must be affected by the communication in the intended way. "I see that he is wearing yellow because he wants me to know that he is happy." Hence, the "sending and receiving of messages" (Barnard, 2002, p. 32) in the process model are problematic because we "read" messages in complex ways. An individual selects clothing for various reasons depending on complex variables from his or her socioeconomic standing to her or his cultural understandings regarding gender, politics, ethics, and other social constructs.

The second model of communication—semiotics—deals with the negotiation of these complex interactions to produce meanings. In this model, the ambiguity of clothing is not seen as a failure to communicate, but is expected. The wearer and the viewer negotiate meaning making through their unique cultural experiences. If, for example, I am informed that yellow is the "new black," I must negotiate what I should do with this information. Do my finances allow me to purchase a new yellow wardrobe, if I do not own any of the "new black?" Do I want to appear "cool" and start wearing yellow before everyone else? Will others have heard that yellow is the new black? Is this a phenomenon that is local, regional, national, or global? Will I be obligated to wear yellow or face social consequences like being ostracized? Will I protest the statement until the fad subsides or will I be obliged to submit to marketing or cultural norms to buy yellow attire? What intensity and value of yellow? For which age or gender is this yellow the new black? What styles, cut, fit, and accessories are connected with this idea? Can I wear this in all settings, casual and formal, rural and urban? Individuals must negotiate numerous texts—clothing and other cultural phenomena—to form understandings regarding clothing. According to Susan Kaiser (1997) these negotiations are sometimes made consciously and at other times they are made subconsciously: "Some people are more attune[d] to, and conscious of, their own appearances along with other situational cues" (p. 201).

In *The Fashion System*, the structuralist Roland Barthes (1983) examines fashion using linguistic analysis. Describing fashion as a vestimentary code, Barthes demonstrates that fashion is a communicative text. To Barthes:

> Fashion is stripped of content, but not of meaning. A kind of machine for maintaining meaning without ever fixing it, it is forever a disappointed meaning, but it is nevertheless a meaning: without content, it then becomes the spectacle human beings grant themselves of their power to make the insignificant signify; [f]ashion then appears as an exemplary form of the general act of signification, thus rejoining the very being of literature which is to offer to read not the meaning of things but their signification. (p. 288)

How about post-colonially? or is semiotic model doing this? (Can dress communication or wardrobe read this way (structurally) or is it positioned to be read post structurally as well?)

Therefore, fashion's stability of form with an unstable content creates signification, a process of an endless seeking of an elusive meaning.

Anne Brydon and Sandra Niessen (1998) see the meaning of clothing residing "in practices which frame the object, and not in the object itself" (p. xiii). Using Erving Goffman's (1959) analogy of life as a dramatic performance, also known as dramaturgy, Brydon and Niessen purport that, "[t]he wearer of clothing must know the [contextual] meaning of apparel items and be skilled in performing the nuances which shape their interpretation" (p. xiii). According to Brydon and Niessen, "[t]he actor must 'get it right' to situate himself [sic] comfortably in his [sic] time and place" (p. xiii). This view implies a call for a vestimentary literacy, which entails (1) the ability to read, or understand the socially constructed meanings, and (2) write, or communicate those meanings through clothing.

Troubled by the neglect of appearance in the study of communication, Kaiser (1997) states, "it is important to recognize that appearance is a form of communication in its own right, and it is not the only type of communication that is frequently overlooked or taken for granted" (p. 229). She asserts that nonverbal communication includes gestures, tactile sensations, smell, taste, and sounds other than verbal language. However, examples provided later in this chapter will illustrate how even these are relevant to a sartorial artistic inquiry. Kaiser identifies four types of nonverbal codes applicable to clothing. These are: (a) artifactual codes, cultural artifacts like clothing and art are both things and signs—such as cultural codes and aesthetic rules—that carry meaning and "express identity or intent" (p. 229); (b) body code communication, including body form, surface, and motion, convey messages, which are enhanced when joined with clothing. For example, how a military salute or other hand gesture is understood depends on contextual information beyond the observed person's attire; (c) media codes are understood as "appearance imagery through mass media," such as, movies, billboards, advertisements, magazines, and the Internet that "influence our interpretations…in everyday communication" (p. 234). These act as a type of formatting of stereotypes that facilitate a shared understanding. And perhaps less applicable to this chapter; (d) spatiotemporal codes, which deal with one's "use of space and time in terms of social interaction" (p. 234).

For example, according to Martha Davis and Shirley Weitz (1981) and Nancy Henley (1977) male bodies tend to take up more space than women, sitting with their legs apart rather than crossed. Alison Lurie (1981) claims that "clothing and dress, including hair styles, bodily attachments, and decorations, are languages that have a vocabulary and a grammar like other

[handwritten: what kind of vocab & grammar > is culture influ. this? How?]

spoken and written languages" (p. 4). Margaret Maynard (2004) questions Lurie's arguments stating, "clothes are the precise markers of status, region, sexuality, class, ethnicity and gender" (p. 3). Maynard examines clothing as a language that is fragmented and complex. She "considers dress at a more symbolic level of indication, as a manifestation of the variable, sometimes contradictory social tactics of individuals and groups as they seek advantage and register their momentary place in the world" (p. 3). She reports that individuals of varying socioeconomic status or cultures "make informed and strategic decisions about what they wear" (p. 4). To Maynard, "clothes don't just inform, people use them tactically to define, to present, to communicate, to deceive, to play with and so on. They are central to identity but not in a deterministic way" (p. 5).

[handwritten: Do you believe Maynard or Lurie? Why?]

Art as Language

As an art teacher, I have been trained to think of art as a visual language. During a critique of my artwork my professors might have asked me, "what are you trying to say by painting this red line there?" or "I am reading this area here (professor points to a portion of my artwork) as unfinished, or overworked, or a passage of calmness." I find myself, as a classroom teacher, asking my students the same types of questions. I approach an image with the intention of reading it, to make a connection with it, to reflect, to understand something in a new way, to confirm something I have experienced, to question, and to converse. Artists and art educators often use the phrase, "As an artist you should engage in a dialogue with your art."

Many educational scholars, but particularly within art education, argue the parallels of language and visual art. John Goldonowicz (1985) suggests that art is a language like English, French, or Spanish and can be learned and understood (p. 17). He states the following: [handwritten: Does the lang. inform the culture of the lang of the art?]

> [Art] is a form of communication that one can learn to read and speak through study and practice. Reading art means understanding a visual statement. Speaking art means creating a visual statement. When art seems strange or meaningless, it is only that this language is yet to be understood. (p. 17)

Renee Sandell (2006) calls for educators to teach art "as a qualitative language" (p. 33). Mary Burns and Danny Martinez (2002) transfer the semantics and syntax of language to a visual literacy framework. They state, "[v]isual literacy uses the same competencies as phonetic literacy—decoding and comprehension—to decipher, comprehend, and interpret images, and critically evaluate the messages such images attempt to convey" (p. 34). Roy

When we teach visual literacy → from What theoretical per. do we teach it from → and how does this inform stud. What eng ō ?

84 • Curriculum and the Cultural Body

Harris (2005) explains how ambiguities, "where x might correlate with more than one y...can be applied to both pictorial and verbal communication" (p.182). Kristin Congdon (2005) implies a need for knowing a cultural or contextual language of art and artists when she states, we "often miss the key message of an artist because we don't understand the language" (p. 144). However, Mary Ann Stankiewicz (2004) warns against limiting the framing of art as a language as has been done in the past. She proposes that art "as a visual language is as limited in its potential functions as the language of a primary school reading series" (p. 90). She implies that making art should "communicate understanding of the individual's life-world, social and cultural landscape" (p. 90). Paul Duncum (2004) attempts to encourage art educators toward multimodal, multiliteracy, and multisensory sites of engagement in the following:

> The consequence for art education of sign systems working together in the dominant cultural forms of our day is the need to rethink our traditional, exclusive focus on things visual. Having decided to study the visual culture of contemporary life, it is necessary to acknowledge that no matter how important the visual characteristics of contemporary cultural sites are, in various ways and in varying degrees, they all involve other sign systems and appeal to multiple perceptual systems. The study of contemporary visual culture thus poses a major challenge to the basis on which we have long advocated and justified visual arts education, namely the exclusively visual nature of visual imagery. (p. 253)

In 1970 Edmund Feldman defined contemporary art as (a) a needed object, commodity, property, an investment; and (b) an interest in innovation, originality, and stylistic succession. However, he also noted that educators should be "interested in the connections between art forms and everyday living" (p. 21). Feldman's suggestion to art educators is congruent with the following statement by Duncum (2004):

> Since art is everywhere around us—in the design of the large-scale and the small-scale environment—teachers should try to enlarge their pupils' concept of art so that they can help bring about its integration—naturally and officially—with the rest of our common existence. They must learn to perceive form and meaning not only in pictures but also in every aspect of personal and social life. (pp. 21–22)

Dress fulfills these calls for alternative sites, including everyday life, and cultural landscapes. It also addresses the other sign systems and multisensory, or "multiple perceptual systems," as directed by Duncum (2004).

John Shotter (2004) presents a unique thesis of communication than those previously presented, but one congruent to Springgay's (2005 a/b) view of thinking through bodies. Both scholars discuss understandings in terms of intercorporeality. These notions influence my conceptualization of sartorial inquiry and communication. Shotter states that communication involves our living bodily experiences. He suggests that individuals are participants in "an indivisible living whole" (p. 452), and posits a re-thinking of everyday life "by taking corporeal forms of reciprocally responsive expression as central" (p. 444) to communication and understanding. Springgay (2005a/b) challenges us to "consider the possibilities of interactions between bodies—knowledge as intercorporeality" (p. 37). Calling for a reading of texts—which would include clothing, art, and bodies—as "real presences" (p. 454), Shotter states in the following:

> Not feeling set over against thought and action, nor action set over against thought and feeling, but thoughtful action as felt, and responsive feeling as thought, and all as aspects of a living whole with specific internal relations with each other that are at once both inter-animating and in tension with each other. It is to the spontaneous expressive responsiveness of our body's living activities that we now must turn, and especially, to the strange outcomes of meetings between a living body and the others and othernesses in its surroundings. (p. 452)

This view of communication is perhaps closer to the original meaning of to communicate—to share. Communication thought of in this way creates a sharing of relational lived activity, and is what I imagine to be a living inquiry. The following narrative is shared to express the process of my understandings of clothing, the body, and my own artistic practice through a sartorial lived inquiry.

A Living Inquiry of Curriculum Through Art and Clothing

I am traveling in an object of speed and bodily comfort. This technology, known commonly as a car, houses my clothed body as I, as the self, am embodied and move throughout my world. While I am protected, enclosed, and housed, I am also at risk of other drivers and environmental hazards as I move through space in time. Others, however, are at risk of my protective housing speeding down the road. I take in and process information on my journey: signs, movements, and cues. I notice a bumper sticker on a passing car that reads, "Change how you see, not how you look." To understand this message, I negotiate my understanding of "seeing" and "looking"; I try to make meaning of how one sees and how one looks.

The artwork is, to be sure, a thing that is made, but it says something other than the mere thing itself. The work makes public something other than itself; it manifests something other; it is an allegory (Heidegger, 1971).

According to Heidegger (1971) the word "allegory" is "a story, poem, or picture which can be interpreted to reveal a hidden meaning" (p.20). The word allegory comes from the Greek allegoria, from allos "other", + –agoria "speaking". Allegory is the "aim" that Heidegger addresses in order "to arrive at the immediate and full reality of the work of art, for only in this way shall we discover real art also within it" (p. 20).

I created "Change How You See, Not How You Look" in response to the bumper sticker. "Seeing" a message on a bumper sticker is a complex system of events. Change How You See, Not How You Look functions as an art object, as a functional-every-day-object, and as an object of ambiguity that displays both an individuality and a desire to belong to a social community (Barnard, 2002; Crane, 2000; Kaiser, 1997; Maynard, 2004). Just as a bumper sticker was recently "seen" by an artist, this object requires an allegorical seeing to "reveal the concealed" (Heidegger, 1977, pp. 16–19). As I wear this piece, I am aware of my look and how I am seen.

The shirt and art object is fashioned from fabric. "Fabric," from the Latin faber or "something skillfully produced," is curiously related in this case to "fashion" from the Latin *factio*(n) which is from *facere* "do, make." "[T]he human body, as if no different from other manufactured objects, can be used as a commodity to display power, prestige and status" (Finkelstein, 1991, p. 4). Joanne Finkelstein argues that, "the shaping and adorning of the body has become a way for the individual to present his or her desired self-image to others" (p. 5). According to Nancy J. Troy (2003):

Haute couture [literally meaning, high dressmaking] was developed and promoted in the late nineteenth and early twentieth centuries by dress designers who regarded the commercial world with disdain. These men and women carefully constructed their personas as great artists or discerning patrons of the arts for whom the banal and potentially degrading aspects of business were beneath the elite status to which they aspired. (p. 192)

In the words of Joanne Entwistle (2000), "our bodies are not just a place from which we come to experience the world, but it is through our bodies that we come to be seen in the world" (p. 29). My clothing is my skin. Experience is the body. It is this "weaving together" through which I become. The "text" of my shirt relates in this case to the word "textile," that which is woven. Merleau-Ponty states, "[m]y body is the fabric into which all objects are woven, and it is, at least in relation to the perceived world, the general instrument of my 'comprehension'" (p. 238).

In this lived inquiry of "Change How You See, Not How You Look" I have experienced the fashionable object that is fashioned to fashion the body in relation to a social politic. It is an inquiry that is sartorial because of its fit and its construction. But it is a construction that is not created from static fragments, but of organic piecings that remain alterable, opened to retailoring through foldings, gatherings, and tucks.

Bill Atweh, Clare Christensen, and Louise Dornan (1998) assert that student engagement in research activities is not unusual in education and call for student research that "will increase their knowledge about their world and that this knowledge will lead to action" (p. 116). As an art educator, I turn my attention to the artistic investigations of several students. Their artistic, sartorial investigations were completed during the 1999–2000 school year while I was their teacher, and were part of an exhibition entitled *Conceptual Clothing*, which was held in a gallery on the secondary school grounds.

Students used clothing as a method of artistic inquiry, to dialogue with and through their understandings of the world. Therefore, we viewed the curriculum as an unfolding inquiry that surpassed the borders of the classroom and the school grounds. Both everyday dress, as well as symbolic dress, was included in their sartorial artistic inquiry. The projects addressed a broad range of possibilities, including consumption, body image, body functions, violence, gender and sexuality, and human emotions, like depression, anger, and love. Student artists created and exhibited a wearable three-dimensional artwork, took a photograph of their work as another site of understanding or text, and wrote an artist's statement as a reflection of their thoughts, research discoveries, and processes. In what follows I will analyze these students works.

Laurie was curious about the preservation of the body and about the consumption of "needs." Her negotiation between knowing that she wanted to create some type of wearable skirt out of liquid-filled plastic baggies and her own personal struggle with the maintenance of a particular body image led her to create "Liquids of My Life." Her sartorial inquiry recalls the mulitsensory notion of art. Laurie says of "Liquids of My Life," "This skirt is made of various drinks and beauty products that I would find hard to live without but I don't really need. I am putting what preserves me inside on the outside for everyone to know." Exploring Laurie's desire to share or reveal what was on the "inside," to make public or to disclose something hidden, I refer back to my earlier musings of Heidegger's (1977) thesis of revealing the concealed to seek understandings. At the same time, this "understanding"—that Laurie felt that she was hiding something on the inside, perhaps an interest in physical beauty—creates additional questions and possibilities. Like Merleau-Ponty (1968), Laurie maintains a relationship between interiority and exteriority rather than the simple Cartesian duality of interior/exterior difference. She seems to be aware of the relationship between these things she calls liquids, a skirt, and herself as a living body. They become less like objects and more like the "coextensive phenomenon" of her body in and of the world.

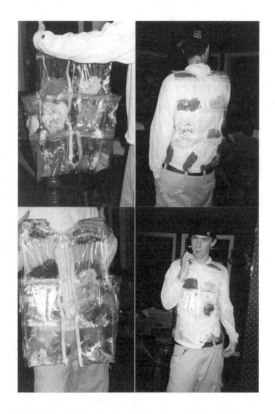

Erik, *Wasted.* Courtesy of the artist and Daniel Barney

Erik created a vest that dealt with his inquiry into waste and hunger, including a call for social activism to remedy these dilemmas. Erik writes:

I chose to make my conceptual clothing deal with the subject of hunger and starvation. Everywhere in the world there are hungry people who are not getting enough food. In some places entire countries go with less than enough food for all their people, other places there are only groups or individuals that are starving. Even here in our town, there are people who are going hungry. Why is it that there are so many starving people, when in the United States alone we produce enough food to feed everyone? I made a vest for my article of clothing. First, I got [plastic] baggies and glued them together. Second, I added a zipper. Last of all, I filled each [plastic] bag with a different food. It wasn't just any food; it was all food from my house that was going to waste. There are all sorts of different things wrong with the various foods. Some of them were getting stale or moldy, some were just old, and others were simply leftovers going to be thrown away. There is so much food going to waste while there are thousands of people who would do anything to just get a tiny bit of it. People need to open their eyes and start working together to get food for all. Nobody deserves to go hungry.

The vest was heavier than expected; it clung to the skin, with individual compartments threatening to burst open, spilling their putrefying contents. Several students discussed the politics of dress. For instance, an understanding revealed through Erik's inquiry is that clothing is not the only thing that is profoundly political in our lives. In Erik's process of creating his artwork, he made relational connections; connections to others' lived experiences. Those brave enough to try on this vest were confronted with the weight and smelled the decaying food. It was not a work that brought comfort or protection, but opened awareness and understanding. Elliot Eisner (2002) suggests that human understanding is enlarged when relationships are noticed. Erik's work implies a shared responsibility, which is unique from an action/reaction, or this than that, model. Merleau-Ponty (1962) discusses a "primordial knowledge" (p. xvi) upon which our everyday encounters with the world are based. Influenced by Merleau-Ponty, Shotter (2004) suggests a "form of participatory thought and understanding [that] can help us to understand the 'inner' nature of our social lives together and the part played by our expressive-responsive activities in their creation" (p. 443). This relational view is demonstrated in the subsequent student narratives.

Michéle describes her art-making process:

I was stumped for a day or two, thinking about what I would do for this exhibition project, when BAM! the idea of paper mache bounced into my head. It's fun, it's messy and the feeling of the wallpaper glue is just utterly fabulous! So off I went to find someone to be my model for the dress's shape. Finally, after much haggling and negotiation, I got my mother into her underwear and covered her with these delightful strips of slimy newspaper. After blow-drying her and tripping the whole house's electricity about five times, I peeled the bodice off. It changed shape somewhat, but nothing that a little wire could not fix. I didn't like the newspaper showing, but still liked the collaged-look of the newspaper. For some strange reason hearts popped into my head…so off I went to the library, (where I am not allowed to join unless accompanied by my mother as well as her immigration papers), and combed their shelves for heart diagrams. Shortly after this, my dear friend, who had most graciously lent me her library card, and I left. I then went to [a photocopy store] where I had to pay the blasted amount of $6.38 for the privilege of having 3 color copies when all I wanted was one. Then the gentleman next to me proceeded to tell me stories of how his ex-wife would eat raw ox hearts and then went on to describe this in great detail while I was ready to faint on the floor beside him. After all these horror stories I went home, slopped the whole thing together and spray-painted the back black, now my kitchen has a rather interesting smell, but I'm sure the family will get used to it.

John created "Tied Down". He says that he chose to make a shirt out of rope, thinking it would be fun and easy. Stating in his own words:

I was wrong. This shirt is made up of 275 feet of rope and was bound together by 33 sticks of hot glue. I made this shirt as a visual representation of how some people live their lives. Often people choose to live their lives without trying anything new. They live without ever stepping out of their comfort zones. They stay tied down and don't go beyond what they're capable of doing.

I remember John sharing his sartorial inquiry with the class. We saw first, his raw, and then later, his calloused hands from working with the abrasive rope. The shirt weighs heavily on the body bearing down upon the ground. Like the proposition that a yellow shirt tells me exactly what a person is thinking or feeling, the understandings communicated through John's "Tied Down" are rife with complexity.

Clothing is an ambiguous demarcation of boundaries. As stated by Dani Cavallaro and Alexandra Warwick (1998), "There is no obvious way of demarcating the body's boundaries. Hair, nails, corporeal waste and secretions, indeed the skin itself, could be seen both as integral to the body's identity and functioning, and as dispensable appendages" (p. xv). We

John, *Tied Down*. Courtesy of the artist and Daniel Barney

experience the world primarily clothed; we, therefore, experience the world, not just in, but also, more importantly, through our clothes.

Stephanie Springgay and Linda Peterat (2002) describe dress as a skin, both as a covering, a protector, and a gatherer of information. We are both our clothes and not our clothes; a "partially-this-and-partially-that" as described by Shotter (2004, p. 453). And yet, as Entwistle (2000) argues, "dress in everyday life cannot be separated from the living, breathing, moving body it adorns" (p. 9). Entwistle continues in the following:

> [D]ress in everyday life is always more than a shell, it is an intimate aspect of the experience and presentation of the self and is so closely linked to the identity that these three—dress, the body, and the self—are not perceived separately but simultaneously, as a totality. When dress is pulled apart from the body/self...we grasp only a fragment, a partial snapshot of dress, and our understanding of it is thus limited. (p. 10)

I extend Entwistle's thesis to objects and others, beyond that of dress. When x is pulled apart from the body/self we grasp only a fragment, a partial snapshot of x, and our understanding of it is thus limited. How does one experience the whole? Perhaps, like the bricoleur or tailor, understandings might be pieced together through a sartorial inquiry. Not as a piecing of fragmented, isolated parts, as so often envisioned in planning a classroom curriculum. Not as some of this and a little of that to be tailored or fitted permanently, but an organic, woven tailoring, a living this-and-that. This entails understanding curriculum inquiry through dress—a sartorial inquiry—as fluid, folded, and lived.

i don't know if i learned anything from this article - poor language (too passive), WAY too many quotes, a incoherent thesis.

Teaching Bodies Who Teach: Men's Bodies and the Reconstruction of Male Teacher Identity in Ireland

Donal O'Donoghue

Introduction

Historical studies of schooling and masculinities analyze how schools have shaped, defined, and given meaning to men's bodies (Heward, 1988; Morrell, 1994). Through their material, social, and discursive practices, schools organize, sort, rank, and regulate bodies while simultaneously gendering them. But bodies are not just objects of social processes they too are agents of social practice (Connell, 2002). In studies of schooling and masculinities, teachers' bodies, and male teachers' bodies in particular, have received little attention. Questions as to who and what shapes their bodies, and for what purposes and with what consequences, are rarely asked. As Diane P. Freedman and Martha Stoddard Holmes (2003) note, students' bodies most often command attention in schools, while the ethnic, racial, sexed, dis/abled, gendered, aging, pregnant, and/or classed body of the teacher tends to go unnoticed and be invisible.

Drawing on research into the masculinizing practices of a single-sex elementary teacher training college in Ireland, during the first half of the twentieth century, this chapter focuses on men teachers' bodies. Following the work of Alan M. Klein (1993), David Kirk (1993), and Mineke van Essen (2000), this chapter examines how, and in what ways men's bodies were observed, monitored, actively constructed, and masculinized as they practiced teaching in practicing schools.[9] This research was gleaned from a close and critical reading of historical documents from the college archive, including college prospectuses, a college rule book, a collection of photographs (of college environs and students) and a complete set of handwritten teaching practice report books.[10] These teaching practice report books written by the Professor of Method and his assistant document and describe the teaching performance and practice of 322 men who were students in the college between 1928 and 1938.[11] The teaching practice reports and the College Rule Book, which hereafter I simply call "texts," are the primary source and data for this chapter.

John Beynon (2002) claims that while "recent critical studies address masculinity directly as a sociohistorical cultural concept, older texts deal with it indirectly, even obliquely, and can be profitably reread against the grain" (p. 144). Similarly, David Morgan (1992) suggests a deconstructive reading of such texts, a reading which involves "reading between the lines," a searching for themes that are not always clearly stated, a reading of "absences as well as presences, to decode the text or to discover hidden or suppressed meaning" (as cited by Beynon, 2002, p. 50). Therefore, while this study draws on historical documents, it is not historical research per se. Using Beynon's (2002) and Morgan's (1992) suggested methods the teaching practice reports were closely read and examined to unpack what was defined, presented, and understood as appropriate masculine behavior for men intending to become elementary teachers in Ireland during this period. Moreover, my research uncovers ideas of what constituted ways of being a man and a male teacher which hide behind (and sometimes not) the language of teaching and learning in these reports. Furthermore, details of student achievement and performance were collated from the reports and the frequency of descriptions of in/appropriate and un/desirable attributes, dispositions, and practices were noted and calculated. They were later matched with specific grades and levels of achievement. From a theoretical perspective, these teaching practice reports, were considered and made sense of through, and with theories of the body, especially Pierre Bourdieu's theory of physical capital, and social constructivist theories of masculinity (Connell, 1995, 2000; Kimmel, 1994a; Lesko, 2000; Mac an Ghaill, 1994; Martino and Pallotta-Chiarolli, 2003; Messner, 1997).

Bourdieu (1978/1985) conceptualizes the body as a form of physical capital as a bearer of symbolic value, produced, presented, and managed to acquire status and distinction across social fields. He demonstrates how different social classes produce distinct bodily forms. Such forms are interpreted and valued differently in and across different social fields and social classes. Furthermore, bodies carry different exchange value across social fields and social classes. According to Bourdieu, "bodies develop through the interrelation between an individual's social location, habitus and taste" (as cited in Shilling, 2003, p. 113). Chris Shilling (2003) provides the following example to explain this idea: "The muscular male body [traditionally associated with the working class] carries particular symbolic weight in certain contexts where strength is valued. However, the overall character of working class bodies (for example, their accent, posture and dress) is not generally as highly valued as are the bodily forms produced by other social classes" (p. 116). Following Bourdieu's (1978) claim that the bodily forms produced by the working classes constitute a form of physical capital that carries a lesser exchange value than that developed by dominant classes, Shilling (2003) argues that social class wields a significant influence on the way in which individuals develop their bodies and on the symbolic values attached to particular bodily forms. However, the symbolic value attached to specific bodily forms, activity, or performance is not fixed. Neither does it relate only to social class. Bodily forms and performances take on different symbolic values in different social fields, and while bodies are implicated in society, they are equally and continuously affected by social, cultural, and economic processes (Bourdieu, 1985). Simply, the body is always an unfinished entity which develops in conjunction with various social forces. Bourdieu's conceptualization of the body as a form of physical capital is useful in unraveling how the body was re/constructed and symbolically valued (or not) in my analysis of the teaching practice reports.

It would be remiss of me to engage in a process of a close and critical reading of these texts without giving due consideration to the social, political, and cultural context within which they were written. The teachings of the church, and the policies of the state resonated in the preparation and training of elementary teachers. The Irish Free State[12] itself, while not a theocracy in the strict sense, was greatly influenced by Catholicism and Catholic moral and social teaching which it adopted in many of its policies. As Diarmuid Ferriter (2005) claims, "much has been written of the Church's determination to impose its control in the New Free State and to make its authoritative voice heard on a range of social, political and religious topics" (p. 330). In the decades preceding Independence, with the advent of the devotional revolution, Catholicism became a significant marker of Irish national identity. Following Independence, the Irish Free State came to rely on the Church for moral leadership and ethnic identity (Taylor 1995). As Anne Byrne, Ricca Edmondson, and Tony Varley (2001) claim, "the outlawing of divorce, the ban on artificial contraception, the imposition of censorship became the cornerstones of an approach whereby the State, even if not acting strictly at the behest of church elites, came to legislate in a way that was extremely mindful of the requirements of Catholic tenets of morality" (p. x). Furthermore, Article 44 of the Irish Constitution 1937 (which was expunged in 1972) recognized the "special position" of the Catholic Church as a guardian of the Faith in the Republic of Ireland.

In the cultural sphere around this time there was a regeneration of Irish manhood and masculinity. The Gaelic Athletic Association (GAA) was founded in 1884 and apart from the obvious aim of reviving certain Irish sporting practices and games, one of its primary goals was to re/establish and re/construct Irish manhood—a manhood that would stand apart from the British or imperial manhood, and shake off the representations of Irishness appearing in the British media (Cronin, 2000; McDevitt, 1997). As Patrick McDevitt (1997) claims, "The athlete's beautiful, healthy and vigorous Irish male body counteracted the Victorian English characterization of the Irish as either simian, drunken ruffians, or effeminate and feckless, child-like inferiors in need of Anglo-Saxon domination" (p. 265). He argues that the founding of the GAA and the subsequent standardization of its games especially hurling and football, "marked nothing less than a nation-wide campaign to resurrect the physical stature of the manhood of Ireland, which was deemed debilitated because of the combined effects of British rule and the Great Famine" (McDevitt, 1997, p. 262). Moreover, the production of an embodied "Irish Manhood" located and represented in the materiality and physicality of the body was forefront in the minds of cultural nationalists at this time. Engaging in any sport, but particularly in the games of the GAA, required an athletic well-built muscular virile body; a body that is worked on, controlled, and obedient. The GAA and its team games provided a site where particular forms of masculinities could be made visible, performed, and negotiated through, with, and between bodies.

Neither the influence of the church nor state (including cultural activities) can be discounted in any study of the preparation of elementary teachers during this period. Even today the Church exerts much control and authority over many elementary schools throughout Ireland. However, this chapter is about how men teachers' bodies were observed, monitored, and actively constructed and masculinized as they practiced teaching in practicing schools as evidenced by the teaching practice reports I analyzed. Yet, it attends to the social, political, and cultural mores of the time, as it does to Bourdieu's theory of physical capital and social constructivist theories of masculinities.

The Training of Elementary Teachers in Ireland at the Beginning of the Twentieth Century

Since the foundation of denominational elementary teacher training colleges in Ireland in the 1870s and until the early 1970s, men and women had been trained separately in single-sex residential colleges. During the period under review in this research study there were five denominational training colleges in Ireland, and one non-denominational college which was co-educational. Three of five denominational Catholic colleges were women only colleges while the remaining two were men only colleges. Students followed a two-year teacher training program in these denominational colleges. The curriculum was broad and varied and prepared teachers to teach all subject areas within the National Curriculum to pupils normally between the ages of 4 and 12. Entrants to the training colleges were normally eighteen years of age at the time of entry.

Before entering these colleges many students, especially those enrolling between 1930 and the early 1960s, would have attended and received their entire second level education in Preparatory Colleges, which in effect were feeder schools for these colleges. Apart from the Church of Ireland Preparatory College, these preparatory colleges were single sex, residential, and denominational. With the exception of Easter, Summer, and Christmas vacations, many future teachers would have inhabited a same sex only sphere from the age of fourteen until the day they first stepped into a classroom as certified teachers, usually at the age of twenty or twenty-one. Even then they could be expected to spend more time with members of their own sex rather than the opposite sex, especially men, should they find themselves teaching in single-sex boys primary schools.

My research focuses on one of these two male teacher training colleges. It was a Catholic College established for the purpose of training Catholic men to teach Irish Catholic elementary children. The opening lines of the 1924 College Prospectus lays claim to this: "Religion holds the first place in this College, and its spirit and practice are made to influence the whole system of education and the daily lives of Students" (np). In its organizational structures including its material, social, and discursive practices the college was similar in many respects to a seminary: It was single sex and homosocial in nature; it was governed and run by religious clergymen; and students had to engage in specific religious rituals and practices. The spirit and practice of religion (Catholicism in this case) was made to influence the whole system of education and the daily lives of students. Daily religious obligations consisted of morning and night prayer, daily mass, and the recitation of the Rosary. On Sundays and Holy days the rosary was recited at sermon, and at Benediction of the Blessed Sacrament. Confession was compulsory and students were to receive Holy Communion on the advice of their confessors. As with the seminary, the college adopted and employed a range of desexualizing strategies, and it enforced a celibate masculinity which was taken as the norm.

Men were rarely in contact with women during their time in the college as the teaching staff and the support staff consisted of men only. The College Rule Book suggests that the body as a sexual entity was feared and denied. Close relationships between men were actively discouraged. Students were only allowed to leave the college in groups of three or more, and not in pairs. Rule 1 in the Special Prohibition and Admonitions section of the College Rule Book states that "two or more students, who may be found in a WC [toilet] together even with the door open, will be considered as guilty of a grave violation of College discipline, for which they will be liable to the penalty of expulsion." Without stating or naming it, the fear of homosexuality here is so significant that men would be liable for expulsion for an act that they might never perform/commit. The fear of same sex intimacy was greater than the act of intimacy itself. In Catholic social and moral teaching the body is proclaimed as being weak and sinful and in need of strict monitoring, control, and regulation. Uncontrolled, untrained, and undisciplined bodies were prone to sin. As Fuller (2004) explains,

> The emphasis on subduing the passions, and thus conquering the world, the flesh and the devil, was an integral part of the ideal Catholic way of life. ...The baser instincts had to be conquered. The sexual instinct was viewed in a particularly fearful and suspicious light. (p. 53)

Apart from fleeting references in the autobiographies, memoirs, and education monographs of former students and staff, there is nothing explicitly written about life in the college, social or academic, during the first half of the twentieth century. What is written, albeit fleeting references, suggests that during this period it was a strongly hierarchical institution within which students had little autonomy. "It was really like entering another world, a former student, (who attended the college from 1918 [to] 1920) recalled many years later" (Greene 2000, p. 105). T. J. McElligott (1986) claims that training for elementary teaching "was conducted in an atmosphere little different from a boarding school and subject to many of the same irksome restrictions" (p. 134).

As part of this two-year teacher training program students practiced teaching in the College's Practicing Schools. Until the introduction of the New Programme for the Training Colleges in 1932, which saw a number of mainstream elementary schools being approved for the purpose of practice teaching (Department of Education, 1931–32), teaching practice was carried out solely in these Practicing Schools which were located within the college grounds. On average, during their two-year teacher-training course, students spent a total of 12 weeks of practice teaching in these schools.[13] Six weeks were devoted to practice in First Year, divided into two three-week blocks. Six weeks were devoted to practice in Second Year divided in the same way. Students were required to teach three lessons each day. The Professor of Method and his assistant visited students on three occasions during each Teaching Practice block. These visits served two primary purposes—one to advise and provide guidance to students while practicing teaching, and the other, to assess students' performance and suitability as a teacher. Students were assessed under the following categories and using these criteria: manner, preparation, and method of teaching. The Professor of Method and his Assistants also recorded some general observations. The assessment criterion "manner" refers to how students presented as teachers, their attitudes, dispositions, and presentation of physical self, including their dress, posture, gait, and other behavioral mannerisms and bodily movements. The quality and extent of the student's preparation was evaluated and assessed by examining his lesson notes and selected teaching resources and his ability to plan teaching and learning opportunities in a variety of subject areas across a range of age groups, and over an extended period of time. The criterion "method of teaching" related to the manner in which the student taught, the methodologies employed, and the manner in which knowledge was presented to pupils and how their learning was extended, evaluated, and assessed.

At the end of each academic year one report was written for each student which documented the student's performance, progress, and achievement. On completion of their training each student would have had two reports. Each report was structured under the assessment criteria listed above: manner, preparation, method of teaching and included some general observations. As noted earlier, it is these teaching practice reports—two for each student—that form the primary source and data for this chapter. Between 1928 and 1938, students were allocated an overall individual grade for their performance under the criteria already listed. There were six grades and each grade matched a certain percentage range. The grades were as follows: Middling (30–40 %), Fair (41–50 %), Very Fair (51–60%), Good (61–70%), Very Good (71–80%) and Excellent (81% and over). Extracts from these reports are cited in this chapter. Extracts are referenced by academic year, year of study, and grade awarded. For example, a reference such as 1928–9 y2 E should be read as follows: 1928–9 is the academic year for which the report was written, it is the second year of study and the student was awarded the grade of Excellent.

How Men's Bodies were Imagined, Addressed, Defined and Disciplined

In the college, men were taught to care for their bodies, to wash, clean, and maintain their bodies, to present them in socially acceptable ways. A number of rules in the College Rule Book pertain to this. For example, according to Rule 6 of the Dormitories Section of the College Rule Book (RB), "Care is to be taken that the bed-clothes, as well as all other clothes for the wash are changed frequently—sheets never passing a fortnight, nor inner clothes a week. Stockings should be changed twice a week" (RB, np). Men were instructed to exercise their bodies, nourish them, and engage in appropriate recreational activities and cultural pursuits. Recreation during the daytime and in fine weather was to be taken "in the lawn to the West of the walk leading to the Practicing Schools; in the evening in the large quadrangle. Inside the house the places for recreation are the Play-hall, and (at appointed times) the Library" (RB, np). Men were not to appear in Practicing Schools "with dirty hands, unpolished shoes, or other marks of untidiness." In the practice schools surveillance of the body was overt. Surveillance was exercised by a number of individuals at any one time—the pupils, the class teacher, the student teachers, and the Professor of Method and his assistant. The gaze of the Professor of Method and his assistant objectified and classified, as did the gaze of others including pupils. The objectifying and classifying gaze of the Professor of Method and his assistant was brought into play in the writing of the reports and the grading of a student's performance.

In so many reports, attention is drawn to the presentation and management of the body. Physical appearance, dress,[14] behavioral mannerisms and bodily performance were constantly referred to. "Careless" and "uncared for" appearances needed constant monitoring and modifying. "This young man requires careful handling, had to be reminded rather frequently about his personal appearance" (1930–1 y1 F). Attention to appearance featured more frequently in the reports of students who were positioned within the Middling to Fair grade bracket than it did in the reports of students described as Good, Very Good and Excellent.

At first heavy, dull and stupid looking. Improved a good deal later— much more manly and convincing…Improved, brighter, cleared but gestures and movements still awkward. Doesn't look quite so depressed. Decent, but still looks "crude" awkward and browbeaten. Peculiar habit of stopping and grunting while he thinks of what is later said or done next. (1935-6 y2 F)

Good appearance but stands and moves rather awkwardly and speaks nervously. (1931–2 y2 M to F)

Funeral, limp, dull, unimpressive delicate appearance. Movements and actions rather awkward…A rather delicate worried appearance. (1930–1 y1 M)

Bodies tended to be observed and subsequently read, appraised, and classified from a naturalistic/biological perspective. Such aspects of the body (its volume, height, weight musculature, etc.) and the way in which it is carried (deportment) and presented were assumed to convey the true "nature" of the man, and his potential as a teacher. "Fine appearance before a class but not used to best advantage…from such a fine commanding appearance much better results might confidently be anticipated, but certainly were not forthcoming (1934–5 y1 M). Put simply, the body not only contained the man, but it was the man.

Bodies which were described as "frail," "weak," "limp," "awkward," "delicate," "nervous," "fussy," "untidy," and "lacking physical strength," and "on the whole uncontrolled and undisciplined" were perceived as a liability rather than an asset for teaching. "Certainly one of the weakest of his year. Has absolutely no redeeming feature except perhaps his appearance" (1930–1 y1 M). Having a body categorized and/described as "weak" "frail," and "limp" was hardly a virtue in the New Ireland, where, as McDevitt (1997) claims, "the banishment of the image of weak Irish men produced by the Famine was a prerequisite for national autonomy, and the advent of the GAA was the first step in this process for many nationalists" (p. 266). Weak, frail-bodied men were constantly made aware of the discrepancy between their real bodies, to which they were bound, and the "socially demanded body" toward which they were expected to strive: "Admits he is conscious of a rather boyish appearance, and is thus unable to show any personality or determination in his efforts." (1930–1 y 1 M). As Bourdieu (2001) argues, "The probability of experiencing the body with embarrassment, malaise, timidity or shame rises with the discrepancy between the socially demanded body and the practical relation to the body that is imposed by the gazes and reactions of others" (p. 65).

The body which "Stands badly. Rather untidy. Stares but doesn't see class. Hands and arms flying around...Awkward build and stance. Swings his arms like a windmill...habit of stooping awkwardly towards class and moves too much to and fro" was repeatedly awarded low grades regardless of competence and ability in planning and preparation. For example, a student's preparation and notes which were deemed "very good as a rule— sensibly brief. Thoughtful and useful" was described as "Very gentle, almost limp. Little colour. Apologetic. Lacks all appearance of masculinity. Fails to assert himself...A very gentle soul that readily recognises his own shortcomings. He was awarded a Middling grade (between 30 and 40%).

Bodies that were "weak," "limp," "awkward," "delicate," and "lacking physical strength," "boyish in appearance," and "uncontrolled and undisciplined" were deemed unmanly. The construct "unmanly" came to encapsulate many of the qualities that real men were not. The man who lacked manliness[15] "speaks too fast" or in "a lame, level, lifeless drawl" and "wears his head down;" he is "indistinct," and is "exceedingly nervous and troubled;" he "stands like a stick and is ill at ease;" he "lacks virility" and is "very unimpressive" and "not particularly energetic;" he "lacks energy and go;" his "general attitude [is] not very manly;" he is "too quiet and apologetic;" he is "not nearly bright or determined enough;" he is "rather shy and backward;" he has "no semblance of manliness or confidence;" he is "boyish and rather unimpressive before a class;" he "forgets altogether about discipline, jogs along in a quiet way with only those in front interested" and he "won't look manfully at class" and is "afraid to face his class manfully or to address children impressively;" he does not "get a very profitable return for his labour;" he "travels along in a very lame and listless fashion;" "Judged by the little use he has made of his opportunities he doesn't seem a very desirable type;" Contrast that with the manly body and the manly way of carrying and presenting that body.

The man who was manly "speaks in a manly and fairly impressive way;" he is "bright and confident" with a "fine deep voice" he is "presentable" and "a nice, decent, gentlemanly type;" he is "industrious lively and pleasant;" he is "distinct," "business like and impressive;" he "is a young fellow with a future;" "he has enough backbone to make a determined effort to correct his own defects;" he is a "fine decent young fellow;" he "doesn't neglect the backward boys;" he "attacks most lessons in a business like fashion, and tries to rouse and enthuse;" he "is not afraid to interfere to secure order;" he is "a very excellent type of young man, very sincere and works more from conviction than from his desire to please anyone;" he "tackles his work manfully. Gets certain definite amount done in time. Reads well, explains simply and effectively, sends his questions around the class, cross examines to winnow the chaff from the grain and he is patient and persistent with the backward scholars;" he "tackles difficulties manfully." Interestingly, the characteristics of unmanliness resonate with Rafford Pyke's description of the "sissy" which appeared in *Cosmopolitan* magazine in 1902. Pyke wrote:

> If manhood is defined by justice, courage, generosity, modesty, dignity, then the sissy was flabby, feeble, mawkish, chicken hearted, cold and fearful. He was a slender youthful figure, smooth faced, a little vacuous in the expression of the countenance, with light hair and rather pale eyes a little wide apart; a voice not necessarily weak, but lacking timbre, resonance, carrying power. (as cited in Kimmel, 1994b, p. 24)

Manly men had all the characteristics of the Victorian and Edwardian masculinity that Beynon (2002) describes: Men in Victorian and Edwardian Britain "were expected to be strong, authoritative, decisive, disciplined and resourceful" (p. 30).

The constructs, manly and unmanly, proved to be symbolically important distinctions between the masculinities valued and devalued in the practice of teaching. Bourdieu (2001) claims that "manliness must be validated by other men...and certified by recognition of membership of the group of real men" (p. 52). Manliness was validated in this case with the rewarding of high grades, and this in turn symbolized recognition of an able teacher with potential and capability, a teacher who was "confident and assertive," "deliberate and decisive," with "backbone" and "courage," and who spoke "emphatically and distinctly," a teacher who was "industrious and businesslike in his approach," and had "a pleasant and encouraging attitude with children;" a teacher who, in short, was a "real man" and not a wimp or a poof or a boy; a teacher who "feels the need to rise to the challenge of the opportunities available to him to increase his honour by pursuing glory and distinction in the public sphere" (Bourdieu, 2001, p. 51). Students achieving a middling grade tended to be described as, "Not nearly manly, bright or determined enough. Impossible to record any favourable features. A pass is a merciful mark" (1930–1 y1 M). Another continues:

> Didn't succeed in creating a very favourable impression. Too dull, melancholy and downhearted. Certainly made efforts to improve, but it was a struggle and didn't always have the desired effect. Appears very decent and honest but not nearly manly or assertive enough when before

a class (1934–5 y1 M). ...Very earnest, nervous—eternally perspiring. Not expressive or decisive enough. (1935–6 y2 F)

Interestingly, promise as a teacher was always guaranteed when some evidence of manliness could be detected, no matter how small. Shortcomings in teaching methods and subject knowledge could be compensated by having the appropriate appearance of manliness:

Evidence of very limited vocabulary in Irish, and the very little fluency in what he has. One of the really weak first-year students. Really doubtful if the trifling progress shown is worth a pass. Might not be so helpless if he had some confidence and manliness. (1932–3 y1 M)

In the absence of manliness, efforts were generally categorized as unpromising.

A high grade in teaching practice also acts as a symbol of acceptance into what Bourdieu (2001) calls a field (champ)—a structured space with its own laws of functioning and its own relations of force—in this case the education field. A student receiving the grade Excellent, for example, was described as "A magnificent type of young fellow. Gentlemanly and refined in his handling of class. Plenty of ability. This coupled with his very good character augers well for his success as a teacher" (1933–4 y2 E). This student "will make himself felt in a school."

In short, the reports reveal that bodily form and bodily performance (which were ultimately taken as indices of manliness, or lack of) played a significant part in determining a grade. And, more important, bodily form and bodily performance appeared to have had a greater impact on a grade decision and allocation than did the ability to conceptualize and plan a lesson or series of lessons. "Increase of confidence and manliness in front of class would improve his work for as a rule his lessons were well prepared" (1933–4 y2 M–F).

As Bourdieu (2001) argues, manliness "is an eminently relational notion, constructed in front of and for other men and against femininity, in a kind of fear of the female, firstly in oneself". (p. 52). This echoes Michael Kimmel's and Michael Messner's (2001) argument that "we come to know what it means to be a man in our culture by setting our definition in opposition to a set of "others," racial minorities, sexual minorities and above all women" (p. 29). In this instance, in this college and during the practice of teaching, in the absence of women, manliness, while constructed in front of and for other men and validated by other men, tended to be constructed against boyishness and boyhood more generally. Historically, of course, manhood has been contrasted with childhood, with manhood denoting full adulthood (Kimmel 1994b).

Boyish looking men were almost in all cases described as unmanly in these reports. The reports articulated that boyish looking/unmanly teachers would encounter grave difficulties in their teaching, as they were "rather boyish and unconvincing, with a thin voice" and "conscious of boyish appearance with senior classes" or "not sufficiently manly to insist on proper discipline." While this logic did not always apply, "very good indeed considering his boyish appearance and size," boyish men however, were deemed "rather unimpressive before a class. Very nervous. Apparently very anxious and willing to do his best, but has not yet gripped fully class instructions."

These reports suggest that college authorities actively constructed manliness in opposition to boyishness. However, "through proper handling" and direction, a boyish student could assume manly characteristics. In other words, manliness could be acquired over time with a deliberate effort to combat "nervousness," "quietness," "shyness," "fussiness," and "nosiness."

> On the quiet side. Not sufficient energy, emphasis or vigour. Very pleasant but not convincing or manly enough…Starts before securing attention…(1934–5 y1 M)

> Still rather reserved and quiet but somewhat more expressive and manly. (1935–6 y2 F+)

> With more manliness and courage efforts could be considered quite creditable. (1934-5 y1 F)

Whether manly or unmanly, boyhood or manhood, identity was always male. Only in one of the 664 reports was woman or female ever mentioned.

> Somewhat nervous and fussy. Yet becomes more distinct and manly in course of the year…Very earnest, but a trifle peculiar. Strikes one as being somewhat old-womanish. Suffers from scruples in relation to points of little importance. (1935–6 y2 F)

An article in the *Irish School Weekly* from this period (April 4, 1936) claimed that the "Ideal Teacher" should "be young enough to remember his boyhood, but old enough to have put aside childish things" (p. 344). An earlier article in the same publication (January 2, 1932) stated:

> As the golden hours of the boyhood merge into the adolescence of youth, a change begins imperceptibly and unconsciously to creep in. When early manhood is attained, the transformation of the heart and soul and mind is nearing completion. The young man has put away the things of the child. The pleasures and pastimes and adventures which made him so happy when a boy, he now no longer cares for. He deems them childish, puny, insufficient. (p. 8)

Here boyhood and manhood are presented as binary opposites; being a boy is presented as the antithesis of being a man, but perhaps in a more developmental sense that of a masculinizing one. The reports strongly suggest that being boyish, and by default unmanly was not a particular virtue when it came to teaching. Here, this categorization did not alone involve the subordination of boyish-looking students, but it also involved the informal policing of manliness. This policing took many different forms, and one of the forms it took was the surveillance of students' voices as they practiced teaching. Couched within the language of developing an appropriate teacher voice, monitoring of student voice was another method of producing and policing the most valued forms of masculinity.

In the reports, several references were made to the quality of voice and especially to voice intonation and modulation. Attention to voice was important in the training of these teachers, as they were likely to be teaching classes of 50 students or more following their training, and using traditional pedagogies that relied on "chalk and talk" and "recitation" strategies (Denscombe, 1985). However, in the reports undue emphasis was placed on student voices. Bodily performance as it related to voice emerged as an agent of classification of manliness and unmanliness. Voices that were "distinct," "emphatic," "confident," "assured," "full and deep" were prized and invariably described as manly. Unmanly voices were "thin, high-pitched, squeaky" and "peculiar" and "unnatural." There was a very noticeable effort to effect change where an unmanly voice was detected. Grades awarded for practice demonstrate that unmanly boyish voices were not valued to the same extent as those which were deep, distinct, and manly. For example, the following statements were taken from the reports of those achieving low grades (Middling):

Voice thin and squeaky and doesn't carry. (1932–3 y1 M)

Thin squealy voice. Fair life and go but not emphatic enough. Improved late but tone still thin…Peculiar squeaky tone—doesn't seem natural. (1934–5 y1 M)

A sloppy speaker. Doesn't utter his words decisively enough—poor use of vocal organs. (1929–30 y2 M)

By contrast the following comments were found in reports of those students who were awarded high grades—Good and Very Good.

Splendid teaching voice, clear and confident. (1933–4 y2 VG)

Active, clear voice, full and pleasant for teaching purposes. (1929–30 y2 G)

The maturing and deepening of students' voices was noted and acknowledged with approval. High-pitched, squeaky, and piercing voices are clearly undesirable probably more so because of their association with boyishness and signs of unmanliness.

While bodies are both objects and agents of practice (Connell, 2002), it is difficult to tell from the available data the extent to which these men were aware that their bodies were being closely monitored, surveyed, and worked on. Furthermore, it is not possible to tell the extent to which the body was an agent as well as an object of this production. But, as Bob Connell (1995) puts it:

> Practice never occurs in a vacuum. It always responds to a situation, and situations are structured in ways that admit certain possibilities and not others. Practice does not proceed into a vacuum. Practice makes a world. In acting, we convert initial situations into new situations. Practice constitutes and reconstitutes structures. Human practice is, in the evocative if awkward term of the Czech philosopher Karel Kosik, onto-formative. It makes the reality we live in. The practices that construct masculinity are onto-formative in this sense. (p. 65)

To what extent were these men and their bodies "situationally present?" Erving Goffman offers that "one of the most evident means by which the individual shows himself to be situationally present is through the disciplined management of personal appearance or "personal front" (as cited in Fraser and Greco, 2005, p. 84). The reports do suggest that many students were willing to listen and to attend to how they presented and controlled their bodies.

A noisy teacher—talks and urges and slaps the desk like an auctioneer...yet all reports agree that he has made an earnest effort to improve even if he did not succeed in teaching much in any given lesson. (1933–4 y2 F)

Decent, earnest, progressive. Always anxious to know and to do the best. Very promising. (1929–30 y2 G)

Do statements such as these suggest that students on the whole subscribed to the constructs of teaching and male teacher identity as presented by the college authorities? Goffman argues that "a failure to present oneself to a gathering in situational harness is likely to be taken as a sign of some kind of disregard for the setting and its participants" (as cited in Fraser and Greco, 2005, p. 84). This obviously appeared to be the case with a small number of students at least. In the report books such students were assessed as lacking in respect for the proper tenets of teaching and learning.

This student is marked too high, not that he is not capable of teaching a reasonably good lesson, but he is careless and lazy and needs too much supervision. Not likely to make an earnest teacher. Told myself openly in class, when taxed with want of earnestness, that he didn't care whether he passed or not. (1937–8 y2 VF)

Complaints received from staff-teachers of refusal to accept directions, and of indifference when not under direct supervision. Will require careful watching evidently in future. Needs all the help and instructions he can get, as none of the teaching efforts shown merited better than the bare pass mark...Difficult to size up this young man. Strikes one as being either intellectually lazy or stupid. On one occasion was actually impertinent to a superintendent in the schools while he offered suggestions. (1937–8 y2 M)

In addition, these comments hint at the failure of the college, the Professor of Method and his assistant to transform these young men into ways prized and valued by the college.

Concluding Remarks

Bourdieu's conceptualization of the body as a form of physical capital, as a bearer of symbolic value, presented and managed to acquire status and distinction across social fields is played out in this site in a complex but systematic manner. The management of the body during Teaching Practice was central to the acquisition of status and distinction as a man, and as a male teacher. Certain bodily forms and bodily performances were recognized as possessing value; some were valued more than others, and certain bodily forms and performances carried a greater exchange value when it came to the awarding of grades. Legitimate and deviant ways of managing and experiencing bodies were identified and articulated. They were further categorized as manly or unmanly. Manliness as manifested in bodily form and bodily performance—one that was based on an integrated performance of the whole body—was fundamental to the forms of masculinities promoted within this site. Manliness was indisputably considered as an essential requisite for male elementary teachers and was actively sought and promoted: "Increased manliness desirable." And "complete lack of manliness" was identified as a "Chief Fault" in the practicing of teaching. On the whole, being manly appeared to be the solution to so many ills associated with poor teaching. Lacking manliness appeared to be the parent of many difficulties in teaching and disciplining a class.

Following Bourdieu's idea of the body as an unfinished entity which develops in conjunction with various social forces the data presented in this chapter demonstrates that students were actively encouraged during Teaching Practice (and, indeed, outside and beyond this) to develop symbolically valued bodily forms and bodily performances—particular postures, gestures, and gait and particular dispositions (restrained, measured, competent, and confident). The ultimate aim was to develop highly disciplined and controlled male bodies that performed in particular ways. The image of masculinity projected as appropriate and desirable for a male teacher was bound up in the moving, managed, and disciplined body.

There is no doubt that the college engaged in a body-building project while men practiced teaching. Men were encouraged and directed to act and speak in particular ways: "Took some time to get this young man to speak and act in a manly fashion" (1936–7 y1 M). A deconstructive reading of these texts, as suggested by Morgan (1992), a reading which involves "reading between the lines," a searching for themes that are not always clearly stated, a reading of "absences as well as presences, to decode the text or to discover hidden or suppressed meaning" reveals many things including:

the construction of teaching bodies; the formation of men; the shaping of Catholics; and the imparting of Catholic teaching (especially with regard to the body); and the disavowal of homosexual practice. College authorities sought to refine these students into gentlemen. Behavior such as "chewing tobacco most strictly forbidden, as being a habit altogether below those who aspire to the profession of teaching" (RB: Rule 3, np). Although belonging to individuals, these bodies were defined and given meaning by the observations of the Professor of Method and his assistant. The body acted as a location for the constructions of multiple and conflicting identities, gendered, sexual, occupational, and so on. It is very interesting that both the physicality of the body, and the manner in which it is presented and managed plays such a significant part in the definition of teacher masculinities when in fact traditionally it has been intellectual labor that has been used to define a teacher's work. The college was not just a place concerned with educating the mind, but it was equally concerned with monitoring and shaping the physical, material bodies of these men who came here to become teachers.

Part III

Public Spaces: Mediating Embodied Difference Across the Curriculum

Life Goes On: Disability, Curriculum, and Popular Culture

Julie Garlen Maudlin

I t seems to me that it was quite by accident that I stumbled upon the realm of disability studies while writing my doctoral dissertation on the relationships between curriculum and the body. As I began reading, I became intrigued by what Lennard Davis (1995) calls the "strange and really unaccountable silence" about the issue of disability in academic discourse. Davis writes:

> The silence is stranger, too, since so much of the left criticism has devoted itself to the issue of the body, of the social construction of sexuality and gender. Alternative bodies people this discourse: gay, lesbian, hermaphrodite, criminal, medical, and so on. But lurking behind these images of transgression and deviance is a much more transgressive and deviant figure: the disabled body. (p. 5)

As I pondered my own understanding of that "transgressive and deviant figure" and became immersed in the literature of disability studies, I found myself feeling as though I might have, at least for a time, found a theoretical home that makes sense to me. Here I found theorists asking questions that resonate with my own confusions, questions like those Martha Stoddard Holmes (2003) asks in her opening to *Fictions of Affliction*:

> What kind of bodies are represented as feeling bodies—stocked with pain, sympathy, disgust, desire, and laughter, not just blood, organs, tissues, nerves, and muscles? Why, and in what contexts, do we read our own or others' physical bodies as slates on which feelings are writ large, or as markers in an emotional landscape? What cultural texts inform those readings, what intelligence guides them, and what power do they wield (and for whom)? (p. vii)

But let me be completely honest about why I am writing about disability. I am obsessed with my body. I weigh myself every day (sometimes twice). I examine my body in the mirror most mornings, but not before mentally preparing myself for disappointment. I exercise and spend hours reading up on different diets and meticulously planning meals. I anxiously web search any new blemish or symptom that appears, and I worry about the possibility that an accident or some dreaded disease might steal my independence, my fragile sense of normalcy. I can't not think about my body, which doesn't make sense to me, because there doesn't seem to be anything extraordinary about this body I inhabit. I don't know what it's like to be gawked at by curious onlookers, to be denied access to a building, or even a whole career because I happen to occupy a wheelchair. But as I tried to sort through some of these confusions about my body, I realized that there must be a connection between my misguided obsession and the ways that society has shaped the way we think about bodies, especially bodies we consider to be "abnormal." My reason for writing about disability, then, is to interrogate the insecurities that drive these fears, to recognize the ways that society has constructed disability by perpetuating a fiction of normalcy, and to understand how that fiction has shaped the way I think about bodily difference.

However misplaced these fears might be, they are a product of my indoctrination in an MTV super-model culture that touts the apparent inherent purity and superiority of able-bodied people who have full cognitive functioning and are considered "attractive." These messages evoke among the able a fear of being abnormal, perhaps even a hatred of difference, a hatred that, according to Davis (2002), "abhors the possibility that all bodies are not configured the same, that weakness and impairment are the legacy of a cult of perfections and able embodiment" (p. 156). This compelling fiction of normalcy has clearly had a profound affect on both my perceptions of bodies and my physical body itself. Drawing on Davis's (1995) use of the term to imply the political significance of disability, I intentionally use the word "normalcy" to describe the fiction of an ideal bodily state. Although this term is sometimes criticized as an uneducated alternative to "normality," I employ it here to defy the lingual standardization of such terms, and to further emphasize the fabrication of bodily "norms." These are the norms of an ableist culture, a society that has allowed disabilities and disfigurements to be read as other, strange, or in Freud's (1963) term, "uncanny." For me, interrogating how our (or perhaps I should say my) culture of ableism has constructed disability forces me to confront these fears and confusions I have about bodily normalcy.

Why look to popular culture? Davis (1995) says "Disability is a specular moment. The power of the gaze is to control, limit and patrol how the person is brought to the fore. Accompanying the gaze are a welter of powerful emotional responses. These responses can include horror, fear, pity, compassion and avoidance" (12). For me, the significance of popular culture is "specular," because it affords an (almost) guiltless gaze not only at the indelible images of the impossibly thin, seductive women and sinewy men that shape dreams but also at the monstrous images of difference that manifest themselves in nightmares. And if my immersion in popular media can speak volumes about my own desires for normalcy, it must have something important to say about my perceptions of disability. Furthermore, if we take seriously the profound presence of popular culture in American society, then we must accept that the media that we engage in shapes our assumptions about disability.

I want to explore popular, particularly cinematic, representations of disability because, as Henry Giroux and Roger Simon (1989) note, "Popular culture represents a significant pedagogical site that raises important questions about the relevance of everyday life, student voice, and the investments of meaning and pleasure that structure and anchor the why and how of learning" (p. 5). I believe that popular culture raises particularly relevant questions about the way that we have constructed disability and excluded bodies from the curriculum based on this otherness. Toby Daspit (2000) asserts, "[c]urricular appropriation of popular culture may assist in reorganizing the prevailing narratives that schooling has perpetuated" (p. 165). I appropriate popular culture to investigate how representations of disability have assisted in organizing prevailing narratives of disability in educational settings and offer critical readings of some particular texts in an attempt to reorganize those narratives.

Writing Disabled Bodies

In order to understand how perceptions of disability have operated to impact our collective decisions regarding education environments, I investigate the ways that popular culture has "written" the disabled body. Martin Norden (1994) points out the significance of popular representations, particularly films that construct and objectify disability:

> By encouraging audience members to perceive the world depicted in the movies, and by implication the world in general, from this perspective and thus associate themselves with able-bodied characters, this strategy has a two-fold effect: it enhances the disabled characters' isolation and "Otherness" by reducing them to objectifications of pity, fear, scorn, etc.—in short, objects of spectacle—as a means of pandering to the needs of the able-bodied majority, and it contributes to a sense of isolation and self-loathing among audience members with disabilities (p. 1)

The narratives of isolation and otherness highlighted by Norden (1994) offer insight into the ways we have organized a disembodied school curriculum further allowing for the exclusion of particular bodies based on the assignment of "disability." I look to gain insight into the culturally and historically situated bodies of the differently abled by investigating contemporary popular films with the same question Holmes (2003) asked of Victorian literature: "What are the longer-term effects of the coding of all of our bodies—through the recurrent stories that shape our social relations—as bodies instructed to feel in limited ways?" (vii). Those "longer-term" effects include the individual and collective perceptions of disability through the embedded curriculum of popular culture as well as the development of the official curriculum that has dominated education in the twentieth century and has excluded disabled students in multiple ways.

Jenkins, McPherson, and Shattuc (2002) observe that when it comes to analyzing the media, the challenge is "to write about our own multiple (and often contradictory) involvements, participations, engagements, and identifications with popular culture—without denying, rationalizing, and distorting them. The best cultural critics speak as "insiders" as well as "outsiders" (p. 7). It is difficult to write about disabled bodies and representations of disabled bodies without inadvertently engaging the same pathologies and voyeurisms in which those representations were constructed because, as Sharon Snyder and David Mitchell (2001) observe, there is no "sensual and sensory language to theorize the body itself" (p. 381). Even the term itself, "disability," a term which itself constructs a binary between the able and "dis" able, does not adequately represent the continuum of physical and/or mental abilities that can be discussed. However, I attempt to meet that challenge by writing as a participant in the social construction of disability (through my internalization of bodily norms) and both as a consumer and a critic of cultural representations of disability (which can encompass a vast continuum of physical and/or mental ability), in order to better understand those involvements, participations, engagements, and identifications from the perspective of the able-bodied.

Disability in Television and Film

Let me begin by highlighting an example of the contradictions posed by contemporary representations of disability. When I began to think about the ways in which people with disabilities have been portrayed in popular culture, I thought of Corky. In the television series *Life Goes On*, which aired on ABC from 1989 to 1993, the lovable lead character, teenager Corky Thatcher, who was born with Down's syndrome, was "mainstreamed" into a regular school with his sympathetic "normal" peers. The actor who played

Corky, Chris Burke, emerged not long after the mainstreaming "movement" in public education had begun to take shape in the late 1980s. In "real" life, Burke actually did have Down's syndrome, and as an actor with disabilities, he was a relative first for American television, and a subject of considerable media coverage. Although Corky marked an important milestone for representations of the disabled and the show presented him as a person with disabilities living the "normal" life of a teenager, it also perpetuated notions of disability as pitiful and innocent. It also minimized the stigma that still characterized the experience of students with Down's syndrome and other diagnoses that labeled them "disabled" and largely continued to force such students into the isolation of separate and often unequal learning environments.

The series was not unlike many other contemporary media, which often seemed to portray disability in a positive light but carried an underlying message about the "otherness" of the disabled. More importantly, the series served to de-emphasize in the public consciousness the (often grim) "reality" of living as a student with disabilities. While the able-bodied community heralded the series as a positive exemplar of the inclusive American sitcom, millions of "real" American students with Down's syndrome and a host of other disabilities spent their days in the isolation of special education "resource" rooms (Winzer, 1993). While the relative popularity of *Life Goes On* seems to express a certain mindset about the need for an inclusive curriculum, the history of American education tells another story entirely, and the isolated past of special education leaves little uncertainty that disabled bodies have been purposefully excluded from the curriculum.

Before I discuss other popular representations of disability, I want to situate these images within a broader understanding of the social experiences of people with disabilities. Like Jenkins, McPherson, and Shattuc (2002) I view these popular texts "not as discrete entities that stand alone but instead exist in relation to a broad range of other discourses, placing media production and consumption within a vast social and cultural configuration of competing voices and positions" (p. 17). Therefore, it is important that we recognize the exclusion of people with disabilities from "mainstream" society (particularly education) for what it was, and in some cases, still is— purposeful and appalling. It is well known that for nearly a century, the needs of students with disabilities were overlooked or ignored by public schools, relegated to the margins, and isolated (Winzer, 1993).

Such disturbing images have characterized the "treatment" of students with disabilities for much of the history of public education. In fact, in spite of the mandate for inclusion put forth by the Education for All Handicapped

Children Act in 1975, it is really only in the last decade that we have seen a significant shift toward fully including students with disabilities in the regular classroom and providing for them the same opportunities that "normal" children are entitled to. By the early 1990s, when *Life Goes On* was reassuring Americans that special education students could take active roles in mainstream society, there was nothing that could really be deemed "integration," in the language of the Civil Rights Movement.

Instead, the practice of isolation and the notion of "correction and prevention" were the prevailing paradigms concerning the "treatment" of children with disabilities, and these trends have perpetuated the hegemony of able-bodied culture. These ideas resonate in what Eli Clare (2001) identifies as four paradigms of disability that have dominated popular perception: the medical, charity, supercrip, and moral models. Clare's (2001) terms represent the prevailing ways that able-bodied American society has responded to disability. The "medical" model presents disability as a pathological condition that must be treated or cured through medical technology so that the person can live a "normal" life. The new ABC reality show *Miracle Workers*, in which patients with serious medical conditions receive expensive "life-changing" medical procedures for free, is good evidence of the prevalence of this assumption. In the tradition of the long-running Jerry Lewis Telethon, the "charity" model emphasizes the need to eradicate disabling conditions through generous giving by others. The "supercrip" model depicts the person with a disability as heroic and courageous for becoming successful or simply living in spite of his or her condition (think Helen Keller, F.D.R, Ray Charles, etc.) and the "moral" model, by Clare's definition, associates disability with moral weakness or depravity (which corresponds with Martin Norden's (1994) "Obsessive Avenger," an embittered character seeking revenge). I would add that the "moral" model might also include the aggrandizement of the individual to a higher moral plane because of his or her disability, as in the staple characters described by Norden (1994), the "Sweet Innocent" (young, asexual, highly spiritual character often endowed with a miracle cure for his or her disability) and the "Saintly Sage" (the wise, virtuous older character who serves as the voice of reason for able-bodied protagonists). From my own analysis of popular media, I add the "spectacle" model, in which the disabled body is viewed as exotic or grotesque, which brings to mind various media that conflate the "otherness" of disability with "horror." This model is closely tied to another representation, the "comic" model, in which disabling conditions are depicted humorously.

These categories, indicative of some of the most common assumptions about disability, are not all-inclusive and, as Clare (2001) is quick to note, they intersect and overlap, but they can give us some idea of the multiple ways that disability is conceptualized through contemporary popular culture. They can also help us understand how these narratives operate to define and limit disability in these popular media. Holmes (2003) observes that they teach us that disability is "alien, terrifying, tragic; that it transforms your life in overwhelmingly negative ways; and that it is normal to feel horrified, relieved, and inspired, all from a safe distance, when we encounter disability" (p. ix). Here, I want to examine some popular films that address issues of disability and define them in the public consciousness.

Disability in Popular Films

Disability has been and continues to be big business when it comes to the film industry; as Davis (2002) notes, three of the Academy Award nominated films of 1997—*Shine*, *The English Patient*, and *Sling Blade*—were all disability films. Not long after films emerged as a medium in America, filmmakers began capitalizing on the comic model to release a number of short silent films that featured disabled characters. As Safran (1998) notes, "Many early movies used disabilities to heighten the effect of slapstick comedies and melodramas, and frequently presented the stereotypes of victim or villain, or as seeking revenge for their disability" (p. 468). In fact, the first short film depicting physical disability, Thomas Edison's 50-second film *The Fake Beggar*, appeared in 1898 (Norden, 1994). The early titles speak for themselves: *The Legless Runner* (1907), *The Invalid's Adventure* (1907), and *Don't Pull My Leg* (1908). As an indication of the popularity of this genre, during this era of the early development of the film industry, the famed D.W. Griffith directed no fewer than 14 films featuring physical and/or sensory impairments (Safran, 1998).

While familiar disabled characters remain largely absent from television, the cinematic fascination with disability has continued across generations into the postmodern era of the digital media. One of the most memorable images from my childhood was that of *The Elephant Man* (1980), with its grotesque representation of disfigurement and underlying message about charity. Since that time, a myriad of motion pictures have depicted a wide range of disabilities: autism in *Rain Man* (1988) and *What's Eating Gilbert Grape* (1993), AIDS in *Philadelphia* (1993), blindness in *At First Sight* (1997) and *Ray* (2004), disfigurement in *The English Patient* (1993), *The*

Man Without a Face (1993) and *Vanilla Sky* (2001), cancer in *One True Thing* (1998) and *Stepmom* (1998), congenital physical conditions in *Simon Birch* (1998) and *The Mighty* (1998) and learning disabilities in *Sling Blade* (1996) and *I Am Sam* (2001). The depictions of people with disabilities in these films are as varied as the conditions they address, ranging from asexual innocence to angry bitterness to deviant sexuality, and while many of them attempt to do justice to disability in their realistic representations, most still seem to embody one or more of the traditional assumptions about disability.

Edward Scissorhands

Within this group of contemporary disability films are two figures that loom large in the collective cultural consciousness and in my personal mental inventory of disability representations. The first is *Edward Scissorhands* (1990), which might easily be regarded as the Generation X's Frankenstein with a sensitive, comic twist. This Tim Burton film was released just as I was preparing to enter the cruel, strange world of high school, a time when adolescent fears of isolation and "otherness" were reaching their zenith. Perhaps it was both this timeliness and later, the film's enduring presence on the network TBS, that made the images of Edward's garden-shear hands, sunken eyes, and wiry mess of black hair so unforgettable. As an "artificial" (manufactured rather than a product of procreation) person, Scissorhands may not, on first glance, appear to portray traditional notions of disability, but as Christopher Smit and Anthony Enns (2001) point out, disability does not have an easily recognized, coherent form. Rather, the disability is defined in relation to what is perceived as a lack of human potential, so that the category of disability becomes a distorted reflection of what society considers "normal" and "human." Scissorhands certainly provides a telling reflection of assumptions about humanity and normalcy. Edward is the creation of an ambitious inventor who died before he could craft hands to replace the set of rotating scissors. He exists happily in complete isolation in the Gothic mansion belonging to his creator, but his problems begin when Peg Boggs stops by on an Avon sales call. Boggs takes pity on him and brings him home with her to 1950s Suburbia. At first, Edward finds himself subject to the fearful and curious scrutiny of the neighborhood, but his shrub and hair-cutting talents quickly elevate him to celebrity status. However, Edward's experience in mainstream society soon takes a negative turn; his love for Peg's daughter, Kim, is unrequited, and an accident in which he unintentionally harms another person is interpreted as a malicious act, forcing him to return to exile indefinitely.

Norden (1994), in his comprehensive history of physical disability in films, gives American film the moniker "Cinema of Isolation" because more often than not, characters with disabilities are set apart, portrayed as outsiders. This is certainly true of *Edward Scissorhands* and many of the other films mentioned here. *Edward Scissorhands* also embodies a number of other traditional assumptions about disabled bodies and what it means to be "normal." Peg feels sorry for Edward, and it is her charity that brings him into Suburbia, based on Burton's own childhood in Burbank, which he describes as "disembodied" (Ansen, 1991). Edward quickly becomes a spectacle, a "freak" to be studied by the curious eyes of the "normal" people, but his unique talents make him a hero (supercrip). However, Edward, longing so much to touch, to engage in normalcy, is unable to control his disability, and his weakness is interpreted by society as depravity. Caroline Thompson, the screenwriter for the film, says of Burton's character in *Newsweek*, "It's the perfect metaphor for how many of us feel. It's more than feeling like an outsider, it's feeling dangerous…yearning to touch and knowing when you do, you destroy" (cited in Ansen, 1991). In the end, we are left wondering if he would have been better off left in isolation, where society felt he really "belonged" in the first place.

In my initial readings of this film, I perceived the pain and isolation that accompanied Edward's otherness, and those feelings appealed to my own insecurities about navigating the murky waters between what I have understood as the isolation of intellectualism and the attachment to mainstream cultural norms. However, I think that *Edward Scissorhands* holds some important insights into the way we construct disability and how those constructions operate in an environment that is similar to Burton's disembodied Suburbia, namely, the school. The neighborhood of neatly situated, tackily decorated tract homes is not unlike the sterile classroom, with its neatly lined desks and pre-fabricated posters. Edward, with his childlike uncertainty, unsteady gait, black attire, and complicated appendages, stands out monstrously against this backdrop of repressed tidiness. Like Edward, students with disabilities, particularly perceived physical and mental differences, complicate the "tidy" environment of the "regular" classroom. Like Edward's human hosts, we are fearful and suspicious of "others" who cannot control their minds and bodies the way that the able do; we may "tolerate" those that are different but, like Edward's friends, our apparent friendship may only be a mask for our underlying fear and misunderstanding. Edward is truly "disabled" in the Suburban environment, with its numerous physical and social barriers. From Edward's demise we learn that having the appearance of accepting difference is not the same as embracing difference and changing the fabric of society to allow for those differences.

Burton, himself a self-proclaimed alienated artist, clearly has something to say about the way American society responds to difference, with his construction of "an uneasy sense that the surface gregariousness of middle-class life can quickly turn threatening" (Ansen, 1991, p. 58). Yet, the viewing audience is left to accept Edward's fate and to understand physical difference as "alien, terrifying, tragic," and to assume that those who fail to embrace the nuances of disembodied normalcy (in which bodily entanglements are kept at a safe distance), those whose differences are beyond their control, should be kept in isolation. We comfort ourselves with the assumption that students with disabilities are better off not being exposed to the selfishness, maliciousness, and fearfulness of mainstream society.

Forrest Gump

Another unforgettable character, Forrest Gump (1994), shared Scissorhands' naiveté about the brutish qualities of mainstream society, but his narrative follows a somewhat different path. This huge box-office hit centers on the life of a mildly mentally (and in the beginning, physically) disabled Alabama man who wanders innocently through the major historical events of the 1960s and 1970s and inadvertently finds personal and financial success. Like Edward, Forrest embodies more than one of the traditional assumptions about people with disabilities. When we first meet Forrest, we find that, in keeping with the "medical" model of disability, he must endure painful leg braces in order to straighten his legs and allow for a "normal" appearance. The braces, in turn, are an outwardly visible sign of his disabilities and cause him to become a spectacle, an object of ridicule by cruel children and adults alike. Nevertheless, Forrest is blissfully unaware of the malice and disgust with which he is regarded, and in contrast to Scissorhands, whose lack of understanding and restraint results in questionable moralilty, Gump is morally elevated as a result of his simplicity, the archetype of Norden's (1994) "Sweet Innnocent." Unlike Scissorhands, whose eyes are inevitably opened to the cruelty of humanity, Forrest remains oblivious to reality, and the other characters go to great length to protect his child-like "purity"; his mother even sleeps with the school superintendent to keep him in a regular classroom. Her desperate act emphasizes her desire to maintain Forrest's persona of normalcy, whatever the cost. In fact, while Forrest is viewed as the epitome of a "good" person because he lacks the ability to impose judgment on others, he never has to make any moral choices like those faced by other characters in the film. Like Peg, it is primarily a mainstream mother-figure, Jenny, who offers charity in the form of friendship, and like Edward, it is Forrest's special "talents" (in this case, his knack for running and ping-pong) that propel him into celebrity (supercrip) status. Forrest also falls in love in the film, and although his childlike adoration for Jenny offers none of the complexities of "normal" adult relationships, he does eventually (although somewhat inadvertently) consummate his relationship with her, resulting in a child (who, incidentally does not share Forrest's disability).

Isolation and Inclusion

When juxtaposed, these two characters construct a telling binary between two major issues in special education: isolation and inclusion. The message that these two films seem to offer is that the inclusion of people with disabilities into mainstream society can work if those people have an outwardly "normal" appearance, are innocent and asexual, require no adaptations, and pose no threat to our own insecurities about ourselves. The two characters, both framed as outsiders, are radically different in the ways that they navigate mainstream society. Edward is acutely aware of the fact that the scissors make him different, and his awareness only further inhibits him from engaging in appropriate social interactions. He also engages in purposeful moral choices, although those choices only lead him to discover the pain of betrayal and deceit, and result in his loss of innocence. Once corrupted, he is no longer "good" in the eyes of the Suburbanites and must return to isolation.

In comparison, Forrest Gump certainly seems to convey the more positive message about accepting difference, but that acceptance comes with a price. In Forrest's case, the success of his mainstream experiences seem to hinge on the fact that although Forrest admits that he is "not a smart man," he believes his mother when she insisted, "You're no different than anybody else is." In that sense, Forrest is as ignorant about his own uniqueness as he is about the larger social context in which he is living. He need not be concerned with the potential obstacles faced by people with mental disabilities because he manages to float easily through life like the metaphorical feather (an important aspect of the film's imagery). Forrest becomes accepted, even celebrated, by mainstream society, but the messages that he embodies are potentially regressive ones. Forrest, parroting his mother, espouses the belief that "You have to do the best with what God gave you" and the ever-famous "Life is like a box of chocolates. You never know what you're gonna get." This leaves the viewer to assume that when it comes to those who society has deemed disabled, apparently the best you can do is throw yourself into society, pretend you're no different, and hope for the best, and maybe, like Forrest, you will be rewarded with fame and fortune.

Examined together, these two films offer important insight into current issues surrounding the education of students with disabilities. Since the Education for All Handicapped Children Act of 1975 specified that students with disabilities should be educated with their non-disabled peers to the maximum extent appropriate, public school systems have slowly moved away from the traditional segregated model toward integrating students with disabilities into classrooms complete with their own disembodied repressiveness and long-standing norms (not unlike Scissorhands's Suburbia). The passage of the 1990 Americans with Disabilities Act (ADA), which Congressional amendments renamed the Individuals with Disabilities Education Act (IDEA) in 1997, added to the urgency of what widely became known as "inclusion." According to the most recent statistics released by the United States Department of Education (2003), nearly half of all students with disabilities (46.5 percent of more than 5 million students) are being educated in the regular classroom for most of the school day (79 percent or greater).

The issues that have risen from this shift are highlighted in the characters of Scissorhands and Gump. Like the Suburbanites, many educators are fearful of the bodily entanglements that often accompany students with disabilities. They want to keep the instructional and social norms they are comfortable with in place. Consider the perspective on the inclusion of disabilities expressed in a *New York Times Magazine* article:

> On children's television, the kid in the wheelchair has become a kind of mascot, beloved by all his gang. But imagine a real-life classroom where all of the children are nondisabled except the one who drools uncontrollably, who hears voices or can't read a simple sentence when everyone else can. Diversity is a noble ideal. But many disabled children would be marginalized and ridiculed in the mainstream. (Staples, 1999, quoted in Smith and Kozleski, 2005, p. 272)

The character of Edward Scissorhands seems to uphold this regressive outlook on disability, the idea that some students are just better off in the Gothic mansions of separate facilities and isolated resource rooms. We use the marginalization and ridicule of students who are "different" as an excuse to keep them at a distance, which keeps us from mussing up our tidy educational environments with something as vilified as human saliva.

If *Edward Scissorhands* symbolizes what is "right" about isolation, then *Forrest Gump* represents what is wrong with inclusion, not the concept itself, but our misconceptions about what it means to be inclusive. Thanks in large part to the persistence of his mother, Forrest participated fully in mainstream society, and he was readily accepted once he left behind the vestiges of perceivable physical disability. Aside from the sacrifices of his mother, no special accommodations were required of American society in order for Forrest to drift through a blissfully ordinary life. Just as Forrest was embraced by society, we as educators are somewhat more likely to accept students whose disabilities do not force us to confront our own bodily inadequacies, students who can otherwise be perceived as "normal." In fact, despite his IQ of 75, Gump was heralded by fans of the film as representative of the "ordinary" person. Perhaps more importantly, Forrest's experience would leave us to believe that if we simply allow students access to the mainstream environment of the general education classroom and tell them, as Forrest's dear Mama told him, "You're the same as everybody else. You are no different," then the students, not realizing that they are different, will be successful and everyone will be happy. Unfortunately, it seems that this perspective has characterized "inclusion" in many cases; the constitution of general education classes have changed with the addition of students with disabilities but the instructional and interpersonal norms have remained the same (Baglieri and Knopf, 2004). We may have removed the logistical barriers that prevented students with disabilities from accessing the curriculum, but the socially constructed assumptions about disability, reflected in our popular media, have remained intact.

These memorable film characters, along with the larger cinematic context from which they emerged, provide us with some understanding of how such popular culture texts have written the disabled body out of and into educational practice. Norden (1994) notes that "As powerful cultural tools, the movies have played a major role in perpetuating mainstream society's regard for people with disabilities, and more than not the images borne in those movies have differed sharply from the realities of the physically disabled experience" (p. 1). As Holmes (2003) notes, these narratives teach us that it's okay to feel horrified, relieved or inspired, whether we encounter disability in films or in our everyday lives. Holmes (2003) observes, the "objection here is not with any of these feelings, per se, but with the fact that there are so few others suggested by the textual and visual narratives that train us how to picture, talk about, and enact the relationships to our own and others' bodies shaped by the able-disabled binary" (p. ix). In the case of the films discussed here, the representations of disability have become a part of the broader cultural system; these films provide a safe space in which we can explore our bodily fears from a safe distance. As Michael Ryan and Douglas Kellner (1988) note, they play an important role in shaping social reality, in this case, the able-disabled binary:

> Films transcode the discourses (the forms, figures, and representations) of social life into cinematic narrative. Rather than reflect a reality external to the film medium, films execute a transfer from one discursive field to another. As a result, films themselves become a part of that broader cultural system of representations that construct social reality. That construction occurs in part through the internalization of representations. (pp. 12-13)

Thus, the process by which we construct the "otherness" of disability occurs through simultaneous acts of construction and internalization.

Films featuring people with disabilities have not only shaped social reality, but the economy of the film industry as well. In contrast to the Oscar buzz that has been generated over numerous portrayals of disability (most recently *Million Dollar Baby* (2004), *Ray* (2004), *The Hours* (2002), *A Beautiful Mind* (2001), *I Am Sam* (2001)), primetime television hasn't exerted a great deal of effort to feature actors or characters with disabilities. Davis (1995) notes, "although considerable effort has been expended on the part of activists, legislators, and scholars, disability is still a largely ignored and marginalized area. Every week, films and television programs are made containing the most egregious stereotypes of people with disabilities, and hardly anyone notices" (p. 159). In fact, with a little online research, one can find a lengthy list of television shows that have addressed disabilities in some way, and discover that few characters are in leading roles, and many of them are single, impoverished, oppressed, or worse, fodder for comedy skits. For the most part television has not successfully created many memorable characters that can be seen as ordinary people with human needs.

Life Goes On

This brings us back to Corky. Looking back on the history of film and television portrayals of disability, *Life Goes On* seems to stand out as a marginally successful attempt to disable "otherness" through a lead role. Although the series, with its upbeat theme song and saccharine tone, was not entirely practical when it came to the realities of mainstreaming in America, it did portray some of the social challenges Corky faced in his interactions as a student, and later, as a husband. Yet, the title of the series *Life Goes On* suggests a theme much like *Forrest Gump*: You do the best with what God gave you. Life goes on in spite of being different. And in Corky's case, life largely went on without him as the show shifted the primary focus to the titillating storyline involving the characters portrayed by Kelly Martin and Chad Lowe. This is what we say when we have to face tragedy: life goes on, because it has to, because there are some things that are beyond our control.

Rosemarie Garland-Thomson says, "We want to redefine, to re-imagine disability—not make it go away. But also not have it remain with its stigmatic force. So we want it to go away in a way that we want it to go away" (cited in Brueggemann et al., 2005, p. 13). Similarly, I want to redefine and re-imagine this *Life Goes On* portrayal of disability. For as long as we maintain the "in spite of," the able-disable binary persists. To say that life goes on in spite of being different implies that it is a tragedy to be overcome, like the death of a loved one. Sometimes being different is tragic, but it is not inherent to the body of the person who falls short of what society calls "normal"; it is in the specular gaze, the socially constructed perceptions that have been reified overtime. To say that life goes on is to say that our lives are beyond our control, and certainly there are things that a single body cannot change, but we need to recognize the power we have to construct disability. We have to recognize that "disability" actually has more to do with the way we have constructed "our" society based on what works for the able. Chris Burke, like his character, was imbued with self-confidence, bolstered by supportive parents, and professional success, which carried him through the complexities of mainstream life, while Forrest Gump was satisfied simply believing he was "no different" and being unaware of the oppression that formed the context of his experiences (the Civil Rights Movement, Vietnam), but expecting people with disabilities simply to believe in themselves requires no effort on our part. As with the example of inclusion, we cannot simply open the door and expect equality to magically materialize. We have to change the way we think: about difference, about disabilities, about bodies.

Before we can expect to see genuine change in the way that we approach the education of those whose minds and bodies do not conform to standards of normalcy, we have to begin thinking differently about disability; we must question the hegemony of the normal and begin to see ourselves as being "differently abled." In all our rhetoric about equality, about tolerance and acceptance, we might think that to do so would not require a conceptual leap. But Davis (1995) tells us otherwise: we have only begun to rethink the disabled body; in cultural studies we have romanticized transgressive bodies, but disabled bodies have not yet begun to participate in "the erotics of power, in the power of the erotic, in economies of transgression...There has been no rhetoric tied to prostheses, wheelchairs, colostomy bags, cane or leg braces" (Davis, 1995, p. 158).

Thus, when it comes to interpreting and engaging in popular culture, we need to bring disability more fully into our critical pedagogies. We have a responsibility as members and educators of a vast audience to interrogate representations of disability and seek out the ways they operate to shape our social and educational realities. As Stump (2002) poignantly notes,

> There is far too much fear, hatred, and misery in this world, much of which is brought about by a lack of understanding and sympathy for people or groups of people who are different from ourselves. It is important that we, as the motion picture audience, become literate filmgoers, able to recognize even the subtlest projection of discrimination or prejudice in the films we watch and react to accordingly. (p. 192)

It is easy to allow films or television shows to wash over us and validate our own sense of normalcy, but interrogating our own readings, seeking multiple readings in order to deconstruct normalcy is a challenge. Daspit and Weaver (2000) explain, "It means we purposely seek out those voices that do not fit our world view or our readings of popular culture texts" (p. xix). Likewise, Davis (1995) asserts that we can bring these multiple readings into the classroom by

> highlighting narratives, lyrics, and representations of disability in literature courses, teaching the politics of disability in courses that deal with social and political issues, making conscious efforts to include people with disabilities in the media, and so on. Important as well would be the attempt to teach disability across the curriculum so that this subject does not remain ghettoized in special courses. This aspect of inclusion involves a reshaping of symbolic cultural productions and ideology. (p. 159)

If we imagine a reconceptualization of disability, it must involve this reshaping of the symbolic ideology represented by popular culture. The initiation of these multiple readings should not occur because we feel sorry for people who are challenged by our models of mental and/or physical normalcy, but because whether or not we like to admit it, "ability" is situational, transient, and artificial. Instead of hypostatizing normalcy through traditional interpretations of disability, we need to resituate our readings in terms of the continuum of human ability.

Although I am "able" in terms of the barriers I face in my life, constructions of normalcy have profoundly shaped my thoughts, my actions, and my body. I have to assume that my immersion in the competing media of films, television, music, magazines, literature, and the World Wide Web has something to do with my bodily neuroses, so the desire to rewrite normalcy is personal for me. I have engaged, and still engage, in "body-centric thinking" that reflects a culture constructed by the able, for the able, a paradigm that needs shifting. However, to overturn the hegemony of the normal, to rethink the body, does not mean erasing difference. As Brenda Brueggmann (2005) says, "I think somehow our social goal is not to erase disability, not even to normalize it, but somehow to make it just one of the many aspects of who we are" (p. 15). This is what *Life Goes On* represents for me. Life does not go on in spite of difference. Life is difference.

A Tail of Two Women: Exploring the Contours of Difference in Popular Culture

Aisha S. Durham and Jillian M. Báez*

Introduction

T he absorption of indigenous minority cultural formations in the popular speaks to the unyielding appetite for audiences to consume difference at the same time it recalls the ways fetishized spectacular bodies recuperate hegemonic discourses of the racialized and ethnicized Other. Both bodies of Beyoncé Knowles and Jennifer Lopez figure prominently in contemporary visual culture because they crisscross the cultural landscapes that transnational corporate systems necessitate. They are—in a word made popular by Knowles and recently defined in dictionaries—Bootylicious.[16] Their brown voluptuous bodies bump up against and embrace white Western notions of beauty and femininity, signify subalterneity, and highlight identity as performance. Performing as black leather-clad Kill Bill-like karate sidekicks in a two-minute, $20 million Pepsi advertisement televised in 170 countries outside the United States, the bottoms of the two women received top billing in U.S. entertainment news circuits in 2005 when it was rumored that the rumpshaking Beyoncé slid into her costume perfectly, while the already-curvy catsuit for Jennifer Lopez had to be further altered to fit her ever-protruding booty. That the definition, size and movement of their bottoms garner separate media attention typifies the hypervisibility of specific racial and ethnic female body types. The media attention also calls attention to the sexualized representations of women of color in U.S. popular culture within transnational media. In this chapter, we examine the contours of these two iconic figures in a Pepsi global commercial and reconfigure the sensationalized media commentary about them to discuss the deployment of these national minorities abroad. We suggest the discourse surrounding their bodies—their booties especially—is an extension of the overall commodification, paranoia, and policing of the sexuality of women of color.

To better understand the significance of Lopez and Knowles weaving through Hong Kong traffic in the Pepsi *Samurai* commercial, it is necessary to contextualize converging processes of cultural production. First, we identify the rearticulation of the historical freakish body[17] in contemporary advertising campaigns as a trope of Bootylicious where the butt serves as the commodity sign imbued with notions of USA excess and access to so-called cool, hot bodies in late capitalism. We contend the Pepsi promotion of Latina and African-American icons has less to do with celebrating multiculturalism as it has with marketing "new ethnicities" (Hall, 1996b) and appealing to a burgeoning Chinese market in an ongoing imperialist project called the cola wars. The intertexuality necessary to register both Knowles and Lopez as diasporic and/or hybrid "American" icons is also needed within the commercial itself to read their other performances of postmodernism, postfeminism, and Orientalism. In all, we attempt to theorize the contemporary freakish body from our situated identities as Southern African-American and New York Puerto Rican feminist researchers who are at once spectators, subjects producing embodied knowledge about self-images of the Other, as well as desirable objects consumed in the "global popular" (see During, 1999, p. 211).

Advertising and the Trope of Bootylicious

Advertising has become such a ubiquitous aspect of everyday life that marketers attempt to catch consumer attention by pitching product messages that appeal quickly to commonsense. Commonsense, however, relies on already-circulated and often reductive ideologies about identity and culture (Hall, 1997; Molina Guzmán and Valdivia, 2004). Researchers writing about the female body have thoroughly deconstructed the image of the white middle-class homemaker who symbolizes femininity, the nuclear family, modernity, and the nation-state in mass media (D'Acci, 2004; Kilbourne, 1999). While there is an extensive body of literature addressing Black and Latina/o stereotypes, less scholarly attention is paid to the ways specific ethnic body types in promotional culture function within late capitalist consumer-based societies, such as the United States.

Today, we are bombarded with advertising images of the booty. For example, a Nike magazine ad frames a silhouette with the accompanying text: "My butt is big and round like the letter C and ten thousand lunges have made it rounder" (Brennan, 2005, p. 12c). On television, Shakira's hip shaking is so contagious city dwellers watching her cell phone simulcast spontaneously dance in the street. On radio, rappers instruct listeners on how to perfect the "Beyoncé booty dance" (Watson, 2004, p. 24). While these ads do the image work to sell sneakers, cell phone services, and rap albums, they also work to naturalize age-old ideas about women of color that suggest physicality is indicative of hypersexuality. Both Knowles and Lopez—known more for their body part than their artistry (Beltrán, 2002)—appear in the Pepsi global advertisement during the commercial marketing of difference depicting real women with curves.

Our discussion of spectacular Latina and African-American bodies advertised in the Pepsi commercial *Samurai* is informed by the work of Isabel Molina Guzmán and Angharad Valdivia (2004) who examine both the symbolic and material conditions that produce three Latina icons in contemporary popular culture, including Lopez. They argue that the dissemination and representational strategies employed to construct the Latina body are inextricably linked to the flow of capital as well as language, nation, and the signification of the booty in the Western imagery. The Cartesian split dividing the body as the top-rational-civilized and bottom-irrational-primitive is also mapped through place where ethnic bodies originating from warm climates and/or the Southern hemisphere are characterized by having uncontrollable, bestial sexual appetites. Advertisers work to anchor the image of the booty with ideas about the sexuality of specific ethnic bodies by framing them in tropical settings, and in animal poses and prints. We have noted that Knowles and Lopez wear catsuits and perform the role of the femme fatale in the Pepsi commercial, harkening to the animalization that Molina Guzmán and Valdivia describe.

Other than updating Latina popular culture representations, we extend the scholarship of Molina Guzmán and Valdivia by describing the ways discourses about the (global) South operate within a U.S. context and intersect with African-American female iconicity. For example, southern cities such as Miami are portrayed as having a more authentic Latino/a culture because of the continual migration of people from the Caribbean and Latin America; other places such as Atlanta (coined Hot-lanta for hip hoppers) are depicted as "essentially" Black in the African-American imagery because of the importation of African bodies brought to Southern colonies as chattel during the Transatlantic slave trade. The link to so-called African-ness is reified through the construction of the black female body where the protruding, moving booty marks the "African" in the construction of African-American identity. Similarly, within Latinidad the booty also functions as a signifier of African-ness, evident in the celebration of the hypersexualized mulata (Aparicio, 1998). Knowles, who hails from Houston, Texas, reiterates the imperialist spatial and gendered discourse of the racialized body by suggesting her curvaceous shape and "wild" on-stage dance performances come from Africa (Touré, 2004). For researchers and educators, her admission warrants an acknowledgment of hegemonic rather than oppositional self-representations of the subaltern in dominant popular culture. Both Knowles and Lopez use their "booty" as a negotiated site to construct complex ethnic and brand identities. In the following section, we attempt to unpack discourses of the lower half, the South, and marked Southern bodies that Molina Guzmán and Valdivia describe, and contextualize the ways the two icons figure into the global popular through the trope of Bootylicious.

The Trope of Bootylicious

Contemporary popular culture representations frame Black and Latina women as freakish bodies within the trope of bootylicious. These bodies are framed as freaks because their physicality falls outside the parameters of the thin white beauty ideal, and their sexuality—read through the shape, size, and movement of the booty—falls outside white virginal or frigid femininity (Durham, 2005). They invite and take pleasure in the backward(s) gaze—identifying the unsightly booty while drawing on this site of repulsion to lure onlookers. The deployment of the term backward(s) references the directed rear gaze and the framing of the lower half of the Black and Latina body through colonial discourses. We suggest, this dual process of reading the Black and Latina body describes a kind of push-pull performance of simultaneous sexual un/desirability that is made commonsense in the popular, and is legitimated and given value through organized capital in the cultural circuit. At a time when advertising has become fundamental to the (re)production of wealth in late capitalism, it is precisely the marketability of the booty that catapults Knowles and Lopez to international spotlight, and makes them hot commodities in the Pepsi commercial.

Divorced from consumer capitalism, the spectacular performances by Knowles and Lopez would be devalued and pathologized. The booty—although not a reproductive organ—continues to serve as a visual sign of fecundity and sexual proficiency in advertising. Collapsing sex, sexuality, and sexual reproduction, women of color have been constructed as sexual deviants historically. For example, proponents of the population control for so-called deviants or social undesirables have supported eugenics policies and state-sponsored sterilization programs targeting poor Black and Latina women in the United States and Puerto Rico in an effort to control sexual reproduction (see Roberts, 1997). U.S. news media representations of the welfare queen stereotype framed poor African-American and Latina women as "baby factories" that drained state funds in the 1980s. In a sense, poor African-American and Latina sexual reproduction was not productive to state-capitalist growth. (Cheap, gendered labor performed by poor women of color notwithstanding.) It is precisely because of the hypervisibility of the Black and Latina body in music from West Coast and Southern rap, dancehall, and reggaetón—together dubbed "booty music"—these derided cultural forms become profitable outside their spaces of production. When plastic surgeons record a tenfold increase in $9,000 butt augmentations for middle-class women who request a Lopez-Knowles booty to fill out trendy Brazilian-inspired low-rise jeans, their celebrity "junk" gains currency as Bootylicious (see Finan, 2004; Thompson, 2005). It is precisely when the booty could be harnessed for virtual consumption that Lopez and Knowles morph into icons—icons that carry the ideological weight of otherness in their backside.

While we point to the contemporary freakish body, the trope we describe is an old one. Black feminist scholar Michele Wallace (2004) argues, to look at contemporary popular culture is not to look at the contemporary at all; rather, it is to examine all those "repeatable images" and discourses that work to create and facilitate them (p. 267). Examining the representation of African-American tennis player Venus Williams, Janell Hobson (2003) looks back to the milieu that gave rise to the most famous Venus of the nineteenth century, Saartjie Baartman—dubbed the Hottentot Venus. Dutch owners advertised Baartman's body to European audiences attending sideshow exhibits as a freak of nature. In the popular, the image of Baartman's booty found its way in French cartoons, English vaudeville plays, and Victorian high fashion where the bustle exaggerated the backside of wealthy White women (Gilman, 2003; Green, 1998, p. 26; Hobson, 2003, 2005). Long after Baartman's body was dissected, displayed, and buried, the image of the Hottentot Venus is revived in two new sexual icons best known as: Beyoncé and JLo (Barrera, 2002).

The Pepsi Market and Multiculturalism:
"New Ethnicities" Fighting Cola Wars

The Pepsi market and market strategy of multiculturalism influences how Knowles and Lopez are represented in *Samurai*. First, the cola wars describe intense competition among corporations to monopolize a multibillion-dollar soft drink industry. Shifting capital under globalization has squelched that competition leaving two U.S.-based corporations accounting for the majority of the world's cola consumption: Coke and Pepsi. Pepsi and Coke rely on an arsenal of strategic ad campaigns to sell their cola products as well as American tastes and values abroad. It is one reason why under Communism, China closed its markets to U.S.-based brands. But consider, in 1982, China opened its markets to Pepsi. By 1994, the Asia division president for Pepsi announced a 12-year plan for China (takeover). After buying key distribution and production plants, China is Pepsi's fastest and largest growing market outside the United States in 2006 (Anonymous, 1994; Wilbert, 2006). The choreographed fight by Knowles and Lopez echoes a need by Pepsi to sell its U.S. brand in a location where it already owns the infrastructure. Their fight also illustrates the latest advertising campaign waged by Pepsi in a 112-year-old cola war (Ward, 2005).

The Pepsi Market and the Market of Multiculturalism

Following the February 2005 debut of the *Samurai* commercial, Pepsi reigned as the world's leading soft drink company where once Coke claimed king. Pepsi profited $98.4 billion (Ward, 2005), monopolized China's soft drink market, and the *Samurai* commercial co-starring international soccer sensatio, David Beckham became the one most "written about" ads in 2005 (Anonymous, 2005). The growth of Pepsi can be attributed to its Asia division, to the popularity of non-cola products, and to its strategic advertising campaigns. Overall U.S. cola sales have waned in years due to national health campaigns blaming colas for the American obesity epidemic. Despite health concerns, Pepsi continues to advertise soft drinks in U.S. urban centers densely populated by ethnic minorities (Wentz, 2003), and produce new soft drink advertisements such as *Samurai* to generate cola profits from other communities outside the United States.

To sell cola, Pepsi also has to sell its brand. Using the tagline "Generation Next," the corporation's market strategy within and outside the United States emphasizes "multiculturalism" to code its brand as progressive. Rather than emphasize ethnic segmentation—or, specific ads targeting individual ethnic groups—marketers suggest they create multicultural ad campaigns around style that cut across diverse populations, such as urban life and music. In the United States, African-American, Asian, and Latina/o consumers account for more than 40 percent of the Pepsi market (Wentz, 2003)—targeting particular urban, economically vulnerable, and ethnic communities. *Samurai* secures a sizeable U.S. minority market. As familiar ethnic brand identities in music, film, and fashion, both Knowles and Lopez call up U.S. diversity and the diversified portfolio Pepsi marketers want to capitalize.

"New Ethnicities": Consuming Hot and Cool Abroad

Pepsi sells the ideas of hot and cool through the image of Jennifer Lopez and Beyoncé Knowles as "new ethnicities" in the global marketplace. The term "new ethnicity" does not suggest African-American and Latina identities have never existed, but these identities form new meanings within a specific historic conjuncture (Durham, 2004; Hall, 1996b). Both Latina and African-American women have been characterized as "hot" to recall the myth of hypersexuality and to call up the cultural spaces in which both women participate: hip-hop, R&B, pop, salsa and reggaetón. News-entertainment discourses surrounding the "Latin explosion," and the popularity of salsa and "black" rap music coded as cool, reconfigure how audiences might read female bodies: Bottom upward. Cola consumption not only depends on audience investment in new popular culture trends, but colonial fantasies of Others marked as "new" as well.

 Samurai replicates another Pepsi multicultural global ad a year earlier when Knowles teamed with pop singers Britney Spears, Pink, and Enrique Iglesias (as the Roman Emperor) to perform the "New Gladiator." While Knowles, the postmodern identity play, and post-feminist girl power remain in *Samurai*, the location shifts to Hong Kong and the cast changes to feature Lopez and Beckham specifically because of their iconicity in Latin America, Europe, and Asia. The cast, plot and setting for *Samurai*, then, does not necessarily emerge from an advertising strategy of multiculturalism, but as a response to supply-demand processes of cultural production in a global market. Both Knowles and Lopez represent an already-captured U.S. minority market repackaged as new to consuming audiences buying Pepsi's cola and buying into U.S. American taste of what (and who) is hot and cool.

Reading the Textual Experience

Textual analyses combine several methodological approaches to understand how signs gain meaning. While we rely on racialized discourses and semiotics honed in textual methods to address representations of Knowles and Lopez in *Samurai*, we emphasize ethnography as an essential component to reading the cultural body. The researcher body is a sensuous site of knowing (Conquergood, 2003, p. 353). As image-makers and viewers, we bring personal experience to interpret the images we consume (Sturken and Cartwright, 2001, p. 56). Isolated texts do not exist. They are not arrested in time. Signs shift and move, and are as complex and contradictory as the bodies that read them (Shohat, 1998). We read signs from our relationship to them, real bodies and ideologies.

Reading the researcher body in relation to the textual body is dialogical, wholly contextual, and historically specific. Our interpretation of Knowles and Lopez as commodified freakish bodies could change based on our personal experiences and other performances by Knowles and Lopez. We make sense of their representations through our situated identity as Puerto Rican and African-American women raised in the U.S. South (VA) and North (NY), and from our participation in the cultural spaces where the two women are located. Elsewhere, we describe how sexual spectacles of the Black and Latina body are made meaningful and shape our everyday interactions (Durham, 2003). The convergence or collision with the real, situated body and textual body frames our understanding of hegemonic representations in popular culture. It is the emphasis on the sensuous body and embodied knowledge of the self and the Other that we claim textual analysis as a textual experience (Dow, 1996).

The researcher body is the instrument to examine texts. In the Introduction to *Paper Voices*, Stuart Hall (1975) outlines the process of textual analysis. We use his interpretation only as a model to highlight a dialogical relationship between cultural bodies. Hall suggests the researcher initially absorb as much as possible through what he calls a "long preliminary soak" (p. 15). A full reading encompasses a critical analysis of the content, structure, attitude values and assumptions of the text (Grossberg, 1993). The full reading is an active ongoing process of negotiation between the hegemonic elements of the text that relies on the situated researcher experiences. After performing a full reading, Hall suggests the researcher consider why the text is popular and then place it within its cultural and social setting (see Grossberg, 1993). Thus far, we have suggested the icons represent visible signs of difference, and are popular because they perform a type of subalterneity for audiences in the United States and abroad. In the following section, we analyze the reproduction of the freakish body in *Samurai* and address three points of difference that recuperate colonial discourses of the Other.

Staging *Samurai* and Choreographing Difference

We divide the commercial into three scenes: dojo, bar brawl, and the (en)counter. The commercial opens with a pan of the Hong Kong skyline that cuts to the dojo, an indoor space where the black-masked, kimono-wearing Knowles and Lopez practice kendo. A screen showing the face of an Asian man interrupts their duel. Similar to the messenger who delivers orders in the television and film series *Charlie's Angels*, the man greets the two in English as "honorable ladies" and informs them about their next assignment. In the subsequent shot, the two are still masked but with black helmets, knee-length high-heeled boots, and full-body catsuits. The first scene closes when they race through the Hong Kong cityscape on motorcycles to the Pepsi bar where they confront Beckham and his five Asian male underlings.

As Knowles and Lopez cross the bar threshold, a chorus echoes the words "Wild Thang." At the counter Knowles and Lopez each grab a bottle of Pepsi, unaware that Beckham suited in a black blazer in a private room watches them. Beckham taps his chopsticks signaling to his underlings that Knowles and Lopez have arrived. One man grabs Lopez's forearm before she can drink the cola. Knowles strikes the man and the two women fight off unidentified Asian men marked only by all-black attire. Meanwhile, Beckham waits to be served. After they have defeated his underlings, Knowles and Lopez return to the counter to drink their Pepsi where Beckham later approaches them. His movement from the private room to the public bar space introduces the second scene. Lopez says to Beckham who is seated beside her: "You are." Beckham replies, "Yes, I am." Lopez continues, "Sitting on my purse." Giggling, Knowles and Lopez grab their colas and leave. The tagline "Dare for More" with the Pepsi logo appears beneath their booties as they exit.

Choreographing Three Points of Difference

There are three points of difference, or themes, in *Samurai*. First, the trope of same-difference is employed to produce the two icons with similar physicality but with distinct racialization and geographic markers. Movement and costumes are also similar in the commercial. During fight sequences, their movement is choreographed, if not mechanical. When Knowles and Lopez do not fight in matching catsuits and kimonoesque outfits, their actions continue to be synchronized (e.g., walking, driving, and drinking). For example, in the final scene their curves are framed to mirror one another. Their silhouette forms the shape of the Pepsi bottle they carry. The size and shape of their backsides appear identical despite rumors of costume alterations for Lopez. Together both Knowles and Lopez recall the Pepsi bottle and its logo which is split by curvy lines. They are the brand. In a sense, they are the bodies that can be trained to be the same, even as audiences might see these unmasked heroines as different within the Pepsi bar. Their likeness to the bottle and each other is indicative of how female bodies of color are seen as objects and interchangeable within multiculturalist discourse.

The trope of simultaneous sameness and difference lends itself to the contemporary representational strategy of ethnic ambiguity in advertising and popular culture where producers use ethnically ambiguous bodies, such as Lopez, to sell to majority and multiple niche markets (Molina Guzmán and Valdivia, 2004). The sameness the two perform is supposed to render ambiguity, but is distinct in relation to designated whiteness. Hair and complexion become two ways difference is signified in popular culture. Both Knowles and Lopez don dyed blonde hair; however, Knowles's hair is lightened to lighten her skin tone to exaggerate the similarity with Lopez. The straight hair Lopez wears is often associated with whiteness and Asianness, while the wavy, soft curls signify African roots. The fact that Knowles wears wavy rather than tight curls, suggests she can "tame" her black kinks, and by extension her blackness, seen as unmanageable or out-of-control. Hair, in this way, marks both sameness and difference. The light complexion of both Knowles and Lopez allow them to traverse various ethnic, racial, and class lines. For example, Lopez has played a Mexican in *My Family* (1996) and *Selena* (1997), a Native American in *U-Turn* (1997), and an Italian-American in *Out of Sight* (1998) and *The Wedding Planner* (2001). While Knowles has not traversed different ethnic identities to date, her light skin affords her class mobility and black middle-class respectability in the film *The Fighting Temptations* (2003), where she transforms from a poor, cornroll wearing nightclub singer to a gospel singer desired by a man who may inherit thousands. In both cases, physicality functions to mark difference in relation to whiteness and to signify sameness across and within ethnic communities represented in the popular.

Center-periphery

The commercial *Samurai* reproduces Orientalism by centering the foreign bodies of Lopez, Knowles, and Beckham as the social actors traversing through Hong Kong fighting off Asian underlings, and trying out Asian art and style. Returning to physicality, the hairstyles accompanying the kimono are supposed to call up the caricatures of the samurai and the geisha. Lopez's straight extensions worn in the bar brawl scene specifically hark to the Lucy Liu character in *Charlie's Angels*. Heavy black make-up tracing the eye is another performance of Asian minstrelsy. Other than the costumes, the ad title, setting and employment of martial arts flatten Asian identity considering, the samurai is a Japanese warrior, kendo is a Japanese martial art, and the kimono is a traditional Japanese robe. Moreover, Hong Kong is a city made unintelligible through computerized graphics of an ambiguous cityscape. Promotional news coverage reported the commercial as *Kill Bill* (2003, 2004) meets *Crouching Tiger, Hidden Dragon* (2003), and reiterated the Hong Kong, kendo and kimono motif (Scott, 2004). These conflations of Asian culture and identity within the ad and in the commercial circuit illustrate the ways the flattening of difference reiterates Orientalism.

While the postmodern identity play folds difference onto itself, Hong Kong and the interaction among national bodies make difference distinct. Hong Kong is represented as a postcolonial space where signifiers of East and West are invoked constantly. While Asian bodies dominate the material space of Hong Kong, in the Pepsi bar they are foregrounded only to serve the interests of the United States and the United Kingdom. Lopez and Knowles function as agents or ambassadors of the U.S. Empire via Pepsi. (The power afforded to them through the nation-state, however, is problematic provided that Black and Latina women are granted second-class U.S. citizenship.) Beckham, on the other hand, stands in for the British Empire, recalling its colonial ties to Asia. The men who fight with Lopez and Knowles and fight for Beckham recall real Asian bodies that perform low-paid "dirty work" for Pepsi across the world.

Other than the postcolonial space of Hong Kong, East-West binaries are reified through the costumes, music, and martial arts—the transition of Lopez and Knowles from wearing kimonos practicing kendo in the dojo to fighting in catsuits and listening to music in a city bar. In this way, the East and West are juxtaposed and are constitutive of one another with postcolonial identities of Lopez and Knowles traversing both spaces. The dojo, for example, signifies the East and tradition, and functions as a site of discipline where the two bodies train in kimonos with plastic-like breastplates. It also marks Hong Kong as a postcolonial and postmodern space as it is located in a skyscraper and it is equipped with technologies to produce a screen akin to a hologram. The Pepsi bar, on the other hand, signifies a Western urban metropolis where Lopez and Knowles interact with other ethnic bodies listening to English-language music at a commercially owned bar that splices hip-hop record loops with the refrain of Asian strings. The two learn kendo in kimonos in the dojo, but fight in catsuits and stilettos in the bar. In this sense, the Pepsi bar fits into an imperialist project in which Lopez and Knowles extract raw materials of kendo and put them into utilitarian form for themselves by applying the martial art when real danger is present. The use of kendo, the Hong Kong bar branded (by) Pepsi, and the use of Asian, African-American, and Latina bodies to do the physical labor for Beckham and others in the commercial, illustrate the ways culture, space, and identity can be co-opted, and disciplined and constructed as East and West for the purposes of U.S. transnational capital.

Though Knowles and Lopez are placed in the center as ambassadors of the U.S. Empire, they are measured against a white hegemonic femininity even when white women are visually absent. For example, the chorus "Wild Thang" ushers the two action heroines into the Pepsi bar echoing their sexuality as animalistic and savage. This trope of "animalization" is also produced through their dress in catsuits—implying a cat-like, untamed sexuality and recuperating the *Catwoman* heroine most recently performed by biracial actress Halle Berry. Further invoking this trope, Knowles leaps from the upper level of the bar and lands on her feet like a cat. The duo returns to the bar counter where they meet Beckham. At the end of the commercial Lopez disregards Beckham's celebrity status when she says, "you are...sitting on my purse." The purse signifies white, Western femininity and also capital in general as this is where most Western women place their cash, credit cards, and so on. Lopez thus playfully destabilizes Beckham's power as the male patriarch in the commercial, by pointing to a reference of white femininity which she does not actually own. Lopez's satirical performance of white femininity marks her as non-white for not having a purse, and at the same time points to the futility of a purse for any action heroine. This moment also hints at postfeminism[18] across popular culture that celebrates female action heroines such as the television series *Buffy the Vampire Slayer*, *Xena: The Warrior Princess*, and *Dark Angel*. It also points to the ethnic female heroine, in particular, harking to the blaxploitation films of the 1970s. Lastly, the commercial also references Beckham's previous marriage to "Posh Spice," Victoria Adams from Spice Girls in its call for "girl power."

Mediating Difference

Lopez functions as the intermediary between the Anglo Beckham and the African-American Knowles. Both women fight, but it is only Lopez who is a speaking subject within the commercial. Since Lopez speaks only to Beckham, she functions as the mediator between Knowles's and her relationship to the patriarchal, racial authority in the advertisement. In these ways, Lopez is the marked multiracial Latina body in this text (though Knowles is also from a mixed racial heritage as she is Creole), mediating the white-black binary. Her body, and Latina bodies in general, trouble the black/white binary within Western thought and illustrate how these bodies are co-opted in the popular to put black-white-Asian bodies in conversation with one another.

In addition to Lopez's centrality as a speaking subject, she commands much of the visual landscape vis-à-vis camera angles that show her fighting off more foes than Knowles. Through movement and speech Lopez is depicted as more active than Knowles. These differences in representation between the two women are intimately tied to how they function as icons in mainstream media. For example, Lopez is often portrayed as urban or "street" due to her hometown in the Bronx in New York City and her role as a hip-hop singer and dancer. These markers associate Lopez with other representations of Puerto Rican women such as Rosie Perez—as aggressive, sassy, and loud (Valdivia, 2000). On the other hand, Knowles is often represented as a country girl possessing polite femininity. Though both women participate in the mainstream hip-hop sphere, the two are positioned in opposition to each other to highlight difference.

Implications

There are both symbolic and material implications of Knowles and Lopez functioning as global icons in the contemporary transnational marketplace and within curriculum studies. Given the prominence of their butts in media discourses about these women, it becomes imperative to ask how and why their booties represent the national body. What does it mean for the booties of women of color to represent the United States symbolically? As discussed earlier in this essay, much of this process is tied to the multicultural turn across U.S.-based transnational corporations that market globally. In this particular case, Knowles and Lopez have been used as a marketing strategy to sell American cool abroad without seeming too "American." As women of color—black and Latina—the women represent the additive element or the forever hyphen of all ethnicized Americans that mark them as Other, which media industries harness to commodify difference. Selling hypersexual, racialized female bodies is a commonplace, if not overdone, advertising mechanism now exported abroad to so-called untapped markets of communities of color in the United States and abroad. The tagline "Dare for more" that runs beneath Lopez's and Knowles's booties at the end of the *Samurai* commercial points to the commodification of sexuality couched within the language of multiculturalism.

Within the logic of advertising, women's bodies are constructed as instruments of industry in which women are to be desired and consumed. While women of all ethnicities and races are represented as sexual objects the bodies of Knowles and Lopez represent the ways in which racialized bodies are hypersexualized and used as surplus labor in the United States, particularly signified by the "excess" of their booties (Negrón-Muntaner, 2004). Like many people of color in the United States, Knowles and Lopez work within the service industry—specifically, they sell culture vis-à-vis their bodies. Often, racialized peoples are relegated to employment in which their labor is largely physical, as opposed to intellectual work. Knowles's and Lopez's bodies serve as capital within mainstream media discourses that often refer to Knowles's skin as "golden" and Lopez's as "bronze" thus, conjuring up metaphors of money and capitalist exchange in general.

These spectacular representations have implications for the "real world" and everyday for women who are exploited daily in sex trafficking and tourism, the pornography industries and everyday interactions in which expectations of sexualized performances are the norm (Durham, 2003). We note, there is also a disparity between the celebration of Knowles and Lopez as spectacular bodies—albeit in an exoticized (Barrera, 2002) and heteronormative (Beltrán, 2004) fashion—and the everyday lives of women of color. Despite the iconic status of these female bodies of color, ordinary bodies of women of color are seen as deviant, grotesque, and ultimately in need of remaking (Hobson, 2003), and encouraged to discipline themselves whether it be through weight loss, dying hair, make-up, or plastic surgery. These bodies are represented as out of control and hence marked as hyperfertile and a threat to whiteness. This disparity between the spectacular and the ordinary is especially present in the consumption of Lopez's and Knowles' products, which range from CDs to fragrances to clothing. For example, one of the authors recently tried on JLo jeans and was only able to fit in a pair three times larger than her actual size. Though Lopez claims that her clothing line is designed for voluptuous women, it is obvious that these products are only intended for the thin body types. Furthermore, like popular culture in general, the hypervisibility of celebrities such as Knowles and Lopez points to the ways in which representation mask the material realities facing communities of color (Aparicio, 2003; Collins, 2004). Mary Beltrán (2004) argues that contemporary Latina action heroines elide these power relations arguing that "the más macha heroine is both an of-the-moment cinematic role model symbolizing Latina and national progress on a number of fronts, and a smokescreen in relation to inequities that continue to prevent many Latinas from gaining power in real life" (p. 198). Frances Aparicio (1998) similarly argues that these types of representation erase the history of sexual violence against women of color.

By analyzing representations of Lopez and Knowles in *Samurai* we call for a shift in paradigms to better understand the contemporary processes that underpin popular culture. We propose that these shifts be developed in consideration of two levels: the aesthetic and the theoretical. Aesthetically, voluptuous, thin-build, hourglass shaped bodies are highly visible in contemporary popular culture. The trope of bootylicious reproduces the freakish body that needs to be contained within commercial cultural production. Theoretically, a fresh approach to studying representation is needed given that contemporary popular culture is increasingly foregrounding difference. In this chapter, we have begun to sketch a framework for curriculum studies that examine issues of representation across difference. Ultimately, we argue that such an approach to studying and teaching popular culture is imperative to implement in public pedagogy and curriculum.

*Authors would like to thank Drs. Isabel Molina Guzmán and Angharad Valdivia for their theoretical insight and initial review of our comparative project about iconicity. A version of this essay was presented as a featured panel at the International Congress for Qualitative Inquiry, University of Illinois at Urbana-Champaign, USA.

Disrupting Mass Media as Curriculum: Opening to Stories of Veiling

Diane Watt

The powerful influence of the mass media and its narratives in the construction of identities calls for critical engagement in educational contexts. In spite of the fact that social practice varies widely throughout the Islamic world, there is a tendency for many to view Islam—and particularly women's bodies—as fixed and homogenous. In the mass media, the Muslim female is often depicted as inferior to so-called Western versions of womanhood. The Islamic practice of covering for women is regularly represented as a sign of backwardness, religious fundamentalism, male oppression, and terrorism.

Educators concerned with social justice need to contend with the fact that the media plays a decisive role in producing understandings of what Muslims are like, especially given curricular absences. There is an urgent need to develop open views of Muslim women as diverse rather than monolithic. Nina Asher (2002) argues that multiculturalism has evolved into a discourse about the other with little examination of the self at the center of the dominant culture. For this reason, this discourse and practice remains within a frame which privileges patriarchal, Western, Eurocentric knowledge and perspectives and normalizes the split between self and other. Asher thus calls upon educators to interrogate difference and deconstruct processes of othering in relation to curriculum and teaching. She employs the term "hybrid consciousness" to refer to "the awareness that emerges out of the struggle to situate oneself in relation to multiple borders at the dynamic intersections of race, culture, gender/sexuality, class, and nationality, in specific historical and geographic contexts" (p. 85). By juxtaposing my own auto/ethno/graphic stories with stories of Muslim women, I disrupt media discourses surrounding the veil and the women associated with it, discourses which can have violent effects on the identities and lives of individual women in North America.

The issues of veiling and media representations have become compelling for me, in part because of my experiences living in Pakistan, Syria, and Iran, but also due to what I see and hear in the ordinariness of everyday life as a teacher and graduate student, both within and outside of a Canadian university. Many of the stories I have heard from students, friends, and colleagues who are Muslim and female confirm that the narrative of the oppressed Muslim woman is pervasive in our society. Women who wear hijab tell of being involved in struggles with teachers intent on "modernizing" them. Others avoid face-to-face meetings with administrators and potential employers for fear of being treated differently because of the scarf they wear on their heads. It seems that "these women represent something other than themselves" (Cooke, 2001, p. 131). Even those women who do not adhere to Islamic dress codes are not immune from the effects of dominant cultural meanings. Muslim women who choose not to cover report that they are often assumed to be "more open minded" than women who do wear the hijab, or alternatively, not "real" Muslims.

Maxine Greene (1995) proposes that if teachers truly want to provoke their students to break through the limits of the conventional and the taken-for-granted, they themselves have to experience breaks with what has been established in their own lives. Reflecting upon the ways in which the stories of other women and my own encounters with veiling displace hegemonic cultural meanings and thereby create openings for difference to be articulated within education. Following Wanda Pillow (2003), I interrupt a comfortable reflexivity which "invokes the Cartesian belief in a unified, essential self that is capable of being reflected on and is knowable" (p. 181), preferring to render the knowing of myself and the other as "uncomfortable and uncontainable" (p. 188). It is a reflexivity which seeks to know while at the same time situates this knowing as tenuous. As a privileged, middle-class, white, heterosexual woman, I am cognizant of the dangers inherent in speaking for—or even about—the other woman, of reinscribing her as helpless victim. At the same time, I refuse to remain silent, to ignore what is happening around me. Lisa Delpit (1988) asserts that those with the most power, those in the majority, must take responsibility for initiating and sustaining conversations in education. By subjectively situating myself in the uncomfortable position of critiquing dominant meanings in my own culture, I challenge mainstream knowledge about Muslim women. Curriculum theorist Ted Aoki (2005a) suggests that it is by dwelling in such tensioned, difficult spaces that "newness can flow" (p. 319). My participation in complicated conversations (Pinar, 2004) on difference may raise for readers "questions about bodies, places and times, disrupting comfort spaces of thinking and knowing" (Lather, 2000, p. 299). By taking up such decentered knowledge in the classroom, the curriculum, and in educational research it may be possible to resist normative discourses and promote social justice (Sumara, 2005).

Muslims in the Media and Popular Culture

When I ask my adult students how they come to know about other peoples and cultures they often reply: from film, television, and the mass media. Michael Peters and Nicholas Burbules (2004) explain that in our postmodern world traditional spaces have collapsed, "overturning the classroom as a space of enclosure—the pedagogical machine devoted to reading and writing—to open up new spaces no longer disciplined by the teacher" (p. 70). In this move "from enclosed to open spaces, from closed to open systems, the teacher's authority becomes decentered, especially when the 'information level' is higher outside the classroom than inside," and access to media is "often immediate, unsupervised, and continuous" (p. 70). The images produced in our society week after week, year after year, become a taken-for-granted part of the visual culture which surrounds us—an unofficial curriculum of the everyday.

In an article on the challenges of anti-Islamaphobia education, Jasmin Zine (2003) asserts that since 9/11 certain Canadian identities have been called into question. She observes that orientalist constructions of difference permeate representations of Muslims, with images of fanatical terrorists and burqa-clad women being primary markers of the Muslim world. Zine urges educators to deconstruct representations of Muslims in the media and in popular culture. Based on an examination of over 900 films produced in Hollywood over the last century, Jack Shaheen (2003) found that 95% of Arab film roles portray Arabs in stereotypical ways, and compares such stereotyping with a similar depiction of Jews in Nazi propaganda materials. Fazal Rizvi (2005), writing about education for social justice, posits that representations of Islam, "have been couched within the broader discourses of national security, social cohesion, and patriotism" (p. 171), and charges that clear differentiations are drawn between "us" and "them," so that those who are not "us" do not "belong here." In the aftermath of the terrorist attacks in New York, Rizvi maintains that this is how many Muslims have experienced life in the United States.

In 2002, the Canadian Islamic Congress conducted their fourth annual media-watch in which nine major Canadian newspapers were examined, and found that there was an increase in anti-Islamic tone and usage following the events of September 11 (Hussain, 2002). In the introduction to a revised edition of *Covering Islam*, published after 9/11, Edward Said notes that the focus on Muslims and Islam in the Western media has become characterized by and even "more exaggerated stereotyping and belligerent hostility" (cited in Rizvi, 2005, p. 170). Daood Hamdani (2004) warns that anti-Muslim sentiment is on the rise in Canada, declaring that Muslim women are more at risk because some of them are more easily identifiable by their clothing and they also face gender discrimination. Research sponsored by the Canadian Council of Muslim Women (2004) reports that nearly one in three Muslim women has a university degree, compared with one in five among all women, and twice as many Muslim women hold master's and doctoral degrees as all women in Canada. The rate of unemployment (16.5%) among Muslim women is more than double the rate of 7.2% for all women. In spite of their higher levels of education, Muslim women are concentrated in lower paying clerical and sales and service occupations.

Homa Hoodfar (1993), in her research with Muslim women in Montreal, argues that because for many the veil equals ignorance and oppression, Muslim women "have to invest a considerable amount of energy in establishing themselves as thinking, rational, literate students/persons, both in their classrooms and outside" (p. 5). One of her research participants explains:

> I have always been a very good student but always when I have a new teacher and I talk or participate in class discussion the teachers invariably make comments about how they did not expect me to be intelligent and articulate. That I am unlike Muslim women. (p. 14)

Even though the majority of Hoodfar's participants were brought up in Canada and feel part of Canadian society, she was impressed by the degree to which the persistence of the images of oppressed and victimized Muslim women, particularly veiled women, creates barriers for them within Canada.

Despite the potential complexity of the signification of the veil,[19] it serves as a discursive marker of radical cultural difference, "the most potent signifier of Muslim womanhood" (Hargreaves, 2000, p. 373). Signifiers are always located in a discursive context and the temporary fixing of meaning via representation depends on this context. While the principle of visualizing in general does not replace discourse, it makes it "more comprehensible, quicker, and more effective" (Mirzoeff, 1999, p.6). The struggles over female, Muslim bodies have "local and global dimensions relating to specific national, religious and political discourses, to global Islamic issues, and to the nexus between Islam and the West" (Hargreaves, p. 373). Hargreaves describes the bodies of Muslim women as both subject and object, unstable and in progress, tied to political struggle at both personal and public levels. These are bodies linked to state and political ideologies which depend on discourses about women and their bodies for their credibility, both in Canada and elsewhere. A fixed meaning of the veil is potentially enabled because of its positioning within various discourses circulating in society. Elizabeth Grosz (1995) describes the body as "the unspecified raw material of social inscription that produces subjects as subjects of a particular kind" (p. 32). Grosz explains that "[s]exual differences, like those of class and race, are bodily differences, but in order to acknowledge their fundamentally social and cultural 'nature' the body must be reconceived, not in opposition to culture but as its preeminent object" (p. 32).

On Listening and Not Hearing

Hoodfar (1993) writes that during her 20 years of living in Canada and the United Kingdom, when people ascertain that she is Muslim/Iranian, the issue of the veil and the oppression of Muslim women quickly emerge as the main topic of conversation:

> This scenario occurs everywhere, in trains, the grocery store, the laundromat, on the university campus, or at a party. [...] What I have found remarkable is that despite their admitted ignorance on the subject, almost all people I met were, with considerable confidence, adamant that women had a particularly tough time in Muslim cultures. Occasionally western non-Muslim women would tell me they are thankful that they were not born in a Muslim culture. Sometimes they went so far as to say that they were happy that I was living in their society rather than my own, since obviously my ways are more like theirs, and since now, having been exposed to western ways, I could never return to the harem! [...] Frustratingly, in the majority of cases, while my conversants listened to me, they did not hear. (p. 5)

Megan Boler and Michalinos Zembylas (2003) assert that one of the unfortunate effects of popular history, of oversimplified and reductive understandings of difference, is that we fail to see contradictions, and are therefore prevented from inhabiting more ambiguous and less rigid identities and relations to the world. Since differences are often coded by dominant culture through simplistic systems of binary either/or, black/white meanings, there is an absence of space for contradiction and ambiguity, which "makes resistance to dominant meanings very difficult" (p. 121). Muslim takes on a common-sense relevancy, and Muslim women "are seen in simplistic and limited ways as part of the undifferentiated group, Muslim women" (Khan, 2002, p. xxii).

In trying to account for Hoodfar's (1993) experiences, it may also be of interest to note the centrality of the eye in Western culture. We have come to regard sight as providing us with immediate access to the external world (Jenks, 1995). Perhaps because of this belief, visual ability has become conflated with cognition in complex ways:

> On the one hand, vision is lionised among the senses and treated as wholly autonomous, free and even pure. Yet on the other hand, visual symbols are experienced as mundane and necessarily embedded, and their interpretation is utterly contingent. [...] "Idea" derives from the Greek verb meaning "to see." This lexical etymology reminds us that the way that we think about the way that we think in Western culture is guided by the visual paradigm. Looking, seeing and knowing have become perilously intertwined. (Jenks, 1995, p. 1)

Given the hegemony of the visual in Western thought, some suggest a need to emphasize the pedagogical questions of receptivity and listening. Aoki (2005c), for example, seeks curricular spaces which open up to "a deeper realm beyond the reach of the eye" (p. 375). For Aoki, it "seems urgent that we come to be more fully sonorous beings than we are. It is imperative that the world of curriculum question the primacy of 'videre' and begin to make room for 'sonare'" (p. 373). He refers to this as a "polyphonic curriculum" (p. 375). In contrast to the "closedness of synthetic, integrated harmony" (p. 371) which is the goal of multiculturalism, the polyphonic curriculum invites the dissonance of multiple voices to come together and coexist in an open, generative tensionality. As Pinar (2005) explains, for Aoki curriculum conversation is not a conveyor belt of representational knowledge, but "a matter of attunement" (p. 7). In the words of Jacques Derrida (1985), "[E]verything comes down to the ear you are able to hear me with" (p. 4). Conversation becomes not simply an exchange of ideas and information, but an openness toward the other, deeply grounded in lived educational experience.

Fear of the Other

It seemed natural for friends and family members to worry about my family's safety while we were living in the Middle East during the 1990s, in spite of our protestations. For many of us, much of what we know about this part of the world comes largely from what we see on television and in the print media. It may be difficult to imagine that right here in benevolent, multicultural Canada, there are people living in fear. The sedimented layers of my own multicultural complacency were seriously disrupted when casual conversations with veiled women about their lives in Ottawa since 9/11 revealed that some of these women avoided going out because they were afraid. They worried that the negative images of Muslims in the media might be associated with their own covered bodies, and that someone might want to harm them. Similarly, Hussain (2002) reported that after 9/11 some of her female research participants admitted to not leaving their homes for days. They were afraid of being targeted because they were visibly Muslim. Hamdani (2004) found that more Muslim women and men feel discriminated than any other faith community, with nearly one in three reporting one or more episodes of discrimination or unfair treatment (p. 3). Many of the women's stories I hear also express concern for their children at school. Rizvi (2005) calls on educators to consider how events outside of school affect certain groups of students.

Pinar (2004) argues that it is in the sphere of the subjective that students and teachers connect academic knowledge to their self-formation, and therefore the "reconstruction of the public sphere cannot proceed without the reconstruction of the private sphere" (p. 21). Before talking with women about the reality of their lives in Canada I had paid little attention to the visual depictions of Muslims in the media. During this same period I began to read the work of postcolonial scholars such as Edward Said (e.g., *Orientalism*, 1978; *Covering Islam*, 1981). The reading of such texts, in combination with some of the stories I was hearing, uncovered much of what I had taken for granted, and I began to look at media representations more critically. The meaning of a visual image is not inherent in the image but is a process of exchange between the image and the viewer, whose beliefs inform one's interpretation (Jones, 2003). As our beliefs change, so might our interpretations of the visual world around us.

In January of 2005, a close-up photo of an Iraqi woman in chador—a tear in her eye—accompanied a front page article on the Iraqi elections in *The National Post*. A second photo also featured women in chador lining up to vote. I read the article to find brief reference made to these women in the captions that accompanied each photo, indicating only that they were participating in the election. Readers were provided with no information about the individual women or their particular circumstances. We have absolutely no idea who of they are beyond being veiled and Iraqi, and it is unclear whether the foreign photographer even had permission to take these pictures. I found myself asking why, in this particular feature, *The National Post* chose to cast its gaze upon women in chador, rather than on men or on unveiled women. Jenks (1995) contends that the "gaze" and the conscious manipulation of images "are the dual instruments in the exercise and function of modern systems of power and social control" (p. 15). Do these images, then, reinforce the Muslim women as helpless victims whom the West must "free"—legitimizing Western notions of superiority? While being able to vote in a democratic election is certainly a positive development, these photographs paint a far too simple picture of the situation of Iraqi women. I wonder why nobody bothered to interview these women on that day, why they were represented as disembodied objects. Such images of covered women are routinely and casually inserted alongside media reports.

In her research on the visual representation of Muslim/Arab women in daily newspapers in the United States, Ghazi-Walid Falah (2005) confirms that "pictures of Muslim women rarely relate directly to the subject matter in the text, suggesting that the images serve some other purpose than elucidating Muslim women's experiences to a Western audience" (p. 305). The Muslim women I frequently see represented in the mainstream media— the terrorist, the backwards victim, the exotic other—are nothing like the many Muslim women that I have encountered face-to-face in my own life. While I do not question the existence of oppression or female terrorists, to deny Muslim women a voice—as is often done in the mass media—is to commit violence.

Sharon Todd (1997) reminds us that representations "are not simply concerned with telling falsehoods or truths about groups, but are involved in constructing a sense of who 'we' are, and who 'they' are, and how the society in which we live is understood"(p. 151). By understanding that multiple meanings can be generated from any set of images we are able to move away from an overly simple view of representations as being inherently positive or negative. This leads us to question how images function differently, depending upon their social context and their different audiences. For Todd, anti-racist and multicultural education is therefore "about the inquiry into multiple meanings, and not about the rectifying of specific images" (p. 150). How might curriculum open to spaces where meaning is negotiated rather than simply reproduced?

Preoccupation With the Veil

Trinh Minh-ha (1998) writes that "[t]ravelling can...turn out to be a process whereby the self loses its fixed boundaries—a disturbing yet potentially empowering practice of difference" (p. 23). When my husband and I agreed to relocate to Tehran, I accepted that I would have to cover whenever out in public, for veiling is required by law for all women. I and other expatriate women refused to allow such a law to prevent us from experiencing Iran and its people firsthand. At the same time, we were preoccupied with the issue of the veil, seldom passing up an opportunity to engage Iranian women in conversation on the subject. However, the fact that we had questions should not be taken as a sign of our openness toward the other, for we had little interest in real dialogue. For many of us, the veil equaled oppression, plain and simple, which implies that the position from which we asked our questions was one of assumed superiority. In our simplistic dividing up of the world, we imagined that in our own societies we were free while Iranian women were not. While I (along with many Iranian women and men) strongly disagree with the veil being imposed, I wonder now at our arrogance. Ironically, a good number of the Iranian women we had questioned occupied more powerful positions in their society than many of us did in our own.

Readings of the veil may indeed tell us more about ourselves than about the other. Todd (1997) proposes that we strive toward "a new mode of understanding of our selves in relation to others," recognizing that "no self is possible without an other, without an outside" (p. 149). She draws on Homi Bhabha's notion of the stereotype as being not only a relation of power, but also a relation of desire, in which "a sense of 'usness' is at stake when stereotypes are produced" (p. 150). The work of Julia Kristeva (1991) is also relevant in rethinking self/other, us/them, mind/body binaries. Kristeva believes that in order to live with others, we have to learn to see ourselves as other. Difference is not the gap between one individual or group and another, but is a relation. The stranger is in us; it is the unconscious. Just as it is difficult to come to terms with what is foreign and unknown within ourselves, when we come face-to-face with the stranger we are uneasy because he/she resists definition. We need to come to terms with the stranger, to see him/her as an integral part of our own culture. Kristeva also argues that whenever we encounter other cultures we can never leave our own culture behind; we read the other through the eyes of our own culture.

Ambivalence Under the Veil

The experience of being obligated to adhere to Islamic dress codes while living in Iran marks me in my own culture as having "survived" both the veil and an oppressive Iranian regime. It would be dishonest, however, for me to represent my experiences in this limited way. I feel fortunate to have had the opportunity to experience the rich culture of Iran, and the warm hospitality of the Iranian people. In addition, I could never have anticipated the many meanings covering would eventually have for me as a non-Muslim who was forced to cover. The head scarf was part of a costume I donned as part of the adventure of living in Iran, a chance to perform a new identity. Unlike many immigrants exiled here in North America who cannot escape being permanently marked as other, my experience was a temporary identity shift. The chador helped me to gain entry and be welcomed into places I would otherwise have been excluded from, such as mosques and holy Islamic shrines. I never worried about dressing up just to go to the market, nor about the male gaze in crowded bazaars. When my daughter was five or six years old she asked me when she could get her own scarf, to be grown up just like me. For her, it was just a piece of clothing women wore. At times, the veil was a symbol of how well I was fitting in, a sign of adaptation. But when life was difficult, that thin piece of cloth could also feel heavy and oppressive. In short, I felt ambivalence under the veil.

However, the full implications of having to cover did not become apparent until my return home to Canada. As Minh-ha (1999) suggests, "[j]ust as one exiles oneself from one's culture to inhabit it anew, one also returns to it as a guest, rather than as a host or an owner, to hear its voices afresh" (p. 22). Having become accustomed to modest forms of dress for women during the eight years I lived in the Middle East, my sensitivity to cultural norms in my own society had heightened. What I had previously accepted as normal and had hardly questioned in North American culture now struck me as strange. This became glaringly evident on one of our first visits to a grocery store. As my children and I stood in line at the check-out counter I glanced at the row upon row of women's magazines on offer, and was stunned by the words and images on the covers—scantily clad women modeling impossible standards of beauty; the latest fad diets; explicit tips on how to please your man; and so on. In a near-rage I summoned the manager and demanded that these magazines be removed from the shelves. This emotional outburst was a spontaneous reaction to the sudden realization of women's continued degradation in my own culture. Now that I had a daughter of my own these issues took on a new urgency. "[F]eminism has long acknowledged that visuality (the conditions of how we see and make meaning of what we see) is one of the key modes by which gender is culturally inscribed in Western culture" (Jones, 2003, p. 1). We view the Muslim woman's body as a cultural sign, but fail to see our own bodies as culturally inscribed. Recently, in response to the Dutch burqa ban, the following comment was made on a *BBC News* online site: I really cannot understand what all the fuss is about. Why is it always considered ok to wear less, but if someone likes to cover up everyone becomes alarmed?" (Viewpoints, Nov. 2, 2005, p. 5)

For me, it is not hard to imagine why a young Muslim woman in Canada, who has never been required to cover, might make the decision to do so as an act of defiance against what she sees and experiences in her everyday life as a female in this culture. Theories of bodies are experienced by students both in and out of school, but curriculum has largely ignored how meaning is both inscribed onto the body, and made through the body (Springgay, 2005 a/b).

In a Canadian study involving white, female preservice teachers, Ozlem Sensoy and Robin DiAngelo (2006) noticed a common inability of their students to recognize themselves as racially located. They also located sexism outside of themselves and outside the West as a whole, but saw the archetypal Muslim women as truly oppressed. By accessing their popular knowledge about Muslim women, the researchers found that these student teachers deny their own gender oppression, and in doing so, align themselves with white maleness, elevating themselves as white women outside of a gendered location, normalizing Western patriarchy. Sensoy and DiAngelo found that the veil was the single marker that consistently invoked the narrative of the oppressed Muslim women, and suggest that viewing the other women in this way functions to protect the Western women from acknowledging the ambiguities of their own gendered situations. The researchers stress a need for teachers to interrogate mainstream knowledge, which reproduces power relations. Such interrogations may reveal the patterns by which dominant ideologies are reproduced by teachers and how they may manifest in classrooms.

Disinterested Knowledge Discourses

Even though feminist theorizing has seriously disrupted the mind/body split of humanism, Lynda Stone (1994) posits that "schools are still bastions of traditional, masculinist epistemology" (p. 2). Knowledge remains rooted in the binary terror of humanism's natural ability to divide and exclude. Such information discourses assume a unitary subject at the center, and consider logic, stability, rationality, and scientific reasoning to be the path to a singular truth that is necessarily disembodied, tidy, and measurable. Educating for "tolerance" and "inclusion" may therefore involve an approach to curriculum in which ethics are taught in the form of concepts and moral guidelines. Students might also be offered information about other cultures (which are often assumed to be homogenous, stable, monolithic). However, there are problems with such strategies.

Simply adding voices onto those that are already there does not get at the problem of humanism's assumptions about language and representation. As Deborah Britzman (1998) points out, the other might be invited into the curriculum, but "not because they have anything to say to those already there" (p. 87). The liberal strategy of inclusion assumes and perpetuates an unmarked normative order, with the only two available subject positions being "the tolerant normal" and "the tolerated subaltern" (p. 87). Existing power relations remain largely intact.

In addition, the notion that learning about the principles of a disembodied ethics, or learning about the other, will somehow lead to more "tolerant" attitudes, is dependent upon the belief that teachers and students will "rationally accept new thoughts without having to grapple with unlearning the old ones" (p. 88). In this conception of learning, no account is taken of affective investments in a certain point of view. Drawing on psychoanalytic theory, Britzman, argues that "for there to be a learning, there must be conflict in the learning" (p. 5). She views learning as a problem, but a problem that has to do with something other than the material of pedagogy, and therefore suggests that "we might begin to pry apart the conditions of learning from that which conditions the desire to learn and the desire to ignore" (p. 5). Learning is re/imagined as the learning of one's own history of learning, rather than as a repetition of one's own history of learning. It becomes something other than a linear, progressive accumulation of information. "Psychoanalysis interferes with education's dream of mastery. It risks insight from knowledge devoid of social authority and intelligibility" (p. 10). Britzman asks that educators consider how we come to attach ourselves to as well as ignore certain ideas, theories, and people. This is a learning for which there are no experts, a learning that admits "conflicts, disruptions, mistakes, controversies" (p. 19), a learning that lets things emerge. There is a need to abandon narratives of control and mastery, and the quest for a rationality "that can settle the trouble that inaugurates thought," for thought is "not reducible to finding the proper data" (p. 32). Britzman sees education as a site where the learner must confront the fragility of all knowledge and the meaning of the wish for mastery; a site where the unitary subject of pedagogy is unsettled. She searches for ways out of the logic of official knowledge, imagines an education that can open to the world and the possibility of community, highlighting that the only condition of community is difference.

An Ethics of Embodiment: Learning With/From the Other

Springgay (2005a/b) proposes an ethics of embodiment for education, which is a process of responding to the other as an exposure. It encompasses ways of knowing that are not merely cognitive, but relational and intercorporeal, where learning is a relation and not an object. In a similar vein, Sara Ahmed (2000) asserts that when we refuse to encounter, to get close enough to face others, we are left with judging from afar by reading the other as a sign of the universal. She recalls Chandra Mohanty's (1988) charge that Western feminists have read the veil as a sign of oppression because they have refused to engage with the historically specific contexts in which the veil acquires meaning. There is little attempt to get close enough to see the contradictions and ambivalence which structure how the veil is lived at different times and places. A narrow understanding of veiling as a social practice may create limited visions of agency, subjectivity, and freedom (Balasescu, 2003). Lama Unu Odeh (1993) describes a veiled woman as "not necessarily this nor that," arguing that she "could shift from one position to another" (p. 35). In refusing to enter into a relationship with a veiled woman we are failing to recognize the multiplicity of her subjectivity. Ahmed suggests that the other becomes fixed as an object and sign by the refusal to get closer.

Drawing on the thought of Emmanuel Levinas, Todd (2003) also locates possibilities for ethical forms of relationality in the immediacy of one's encounter with the other. She believes that ethics should be freed from epistemological certitude, that it is something other than acting on knowledge. Levinas insists that the other "is what I myself am not" (cited in Todd, 2003, p. 3), and understands the other as infinitely unknowable. For Todd, then, what is ethical or nonviolent, becomes an attentiveness to and the preservation of the alterity of the other. Teaching is therefore about staging an encounter with the other, with something outside the self, while learning is to receive from the other more than the self already holds. In contrast, learning about the other assumes that the other can be understood, and that such learning is pedagogically and ethically desirable. However, for Derrida (1997),

> Justice—if it has to do with the other…is always incalculable…Once you relate to the other as the other, then something incalculable comes on the scene, something which cannot be reduced to the law or to the history of legal structures. (pp. 17–18)

Learning in this sense is not about understanding the other but about "a relation to otherness prior to understanding" (Todd, p. 9). We cannot know beforehand how we will respond to the other, who disrupts one's self-identity.

Todd (2003) explains that when we claim to know/understand the other, we are exercising our knowledge over the other. In this way, "[t]he other becomes an object of my comprehension, my world, my narrative, reducing the Other to me" (p. 15). On the other hand, if we are exposed to the other, we can "listen, attend, and be surprised" (Levinas cited in Todd, p. 15); the other can affect us. Insofar as we can be receptive and susceptible, we can learn from the other as one who is absolutely different from the self. Aoki (2005b) views such relations in terms of translation, suggesting that "a complete absolute translation is an impossibility....Translation as transformation is an ambivalent construction...a signification that is ever incomplete and ongoing" (p. 328). Could curriculum provoke readings of self and other that have no closure, readings infinitely open to possibility, to what is to come?

An Aokian Note

Aoki (2005d) incites us to rethink curriculum so as to sink more often into "the lived space of between—in the midst of many cultures, into the inter of interculturalism" (p. 382). He poignantly reminds us that,

> Indwelling here is a dwelling in the midst of differences, often trying and difficult. It is a place alive with tension. In dwelling there, the quest is not so much to rid ourselves of tension, for to be tensionless is to be dead like a limp violin string, but more so to seek appropriately attuned tension, such that the sound of the tensioned string resounds well. (p. 382)

This is a call for educators to become less enamored with the metaphor of the eye and its modernist associations with the scientific, the instrumentalist, and the technological. Aoki (2005c) is convinced that "in becoming enchanted with the eye, there lurks the danger of too hurriedly foreclosing the horizon where we live as teachers and students" (p. 373). Meditating on the word "crosscultural," which emphasizes getting across from one culture to another, Aoki (2005a) suggests that educators, like tourists and business people, may be spending too much time emphasizing this "crossing"—from one nation to another, from one culture to another. He ponders the usual meaning of "bridge," the way that we give thanks to bridges for "helping us move from one place to another, the speedier the better, the less time wasted the better"

(p. 316). This he contrasts with the bridge one might find in an Oriental garden, "aesthetically designed, with decorative railings, pleasing to the eyes." On this bridge, "we are in no hurry to cross over; in fact, such bridges lure us to linger" (p. 319). This is a "Heideggerean bridge, a site or clearing in which earth, sky, mortals, and divine, in their longing to be together, belong together" (p. 319). Aoki envisions expressly moving away from the identity-centered East and West into a dialogic space between East and West, undoing the instrumental sense of "bridge" and of pedagogy. By holding the categories of "us" and "them" in embodied tension, could curriculum gesture toward bodies that exceed social and cultural inscription?

Teaching Against Homophobia Without Teaching the Subject

Cris Mayo

T he coming out story enacts a dilemma: to at once recount the subject against a dominant subjectivity, but to do so in a way that does not reinstate the problem of the individual subject. But too often coming out stories are told and/or understood as heroic autobiography, rendered into spectacle, and position the audience as passive in their previous ignorance. I will look at these problems of the "coming out" autobiography in the context of anti-homophobia education. My contention is that the coming out story and other forms of pedagogical autobiography may portray each gay person clearly separate from one another in a way that makes sexual subjectivity appear to be idiosyncratic. What anti-homophobia/anti-heteronormative educational projects ought to instead engage with is how subjects are produced and negotiate sexual identity, underscoring the shared negotiation of the gay speakers and the largely presumed-heterosexual audience. Such educational projects move from the simple recognition of supposedly static differences to examining the processes of differences as shifting, interpenetrating, and contingent. The task of this educational approach, I argue, moves from a stabilizing discourse inhabited with certain kinds of identities and recognizable bodies, to a project that destabilizes the subject of homophobia, as well as the subject positions of teller and audience, making it clear that the subject speaking is not the only subject of discourse. In the end, I will argue for a pedagogy of accusation that centralizes the difficulties and relationality of difference.

To begin a chapter against autobiography with an autobiographical tale will hopefully be excused on the grounds that by recourse to a narrative of experience, I hope to show the problematics of such a strategy. When I first began doing anti-homophobia education in the early 1980s, I quickly noticed that my position at the head of the class made me a singular curiosity—my short hair stood out, as did my suit and tie; it was clear I was a visitor. Even when there was more than one speaker, our "exceptionality" stood out. We looked different than the rest of the class even if we didn't really. Just the fact that we were the visiting gay people and occupying the space at the front of the class meant that we were clearly marked out from our educational audience. The boredom of the experience soon set in and my presentation partner and I began to swap stories. He was a gay man and I was a lesbian separatist (so, of course, we were best friends and always joked about our political incompatibility and lack of interchangeable narratives). For the pedagogical and political projects we were involved in, it didn't matter if we exchanged narratives as long as we remembered to change pronouns. The more we knew one another's stories and knew how to pace the cadence and work the dramatic moments, the more we grew suspicious about using tactics from performance for our educational projects.

I have continued to be suspicious of the pleasures of tale-telling I was engaging in and the dubious promise that "now I'm your gay friend and studies show if you have a gay friend, you'll be less homophobic" which I always told classes since that's what the studies they read told them. Of course, part of what I'm narrating is my own experience of the move from lesbian, gay, bisexual, transgender (LGBT) discourses of ethnic-like relations between gays and straights and an understanding that was already moving with that wave of understanding, the queer relations between supposedly LGBT people and supposedly straight people. We always knew, of course, it was more complicated than that. If "lesbianism is the rage of all women condensed to the point of explosion" (Radicalesbians, 1970), well, coming out stories about one's first crush probably doesn't get to the point. I have tried to move myself out of the position of "show and tell exotic of the day" whose story only confirms the audience's position as those who do not know what should be glaringly obvious to them at this point (that there are queer people, that there is homophobia) and to move them into what we all know from queer theory: there are queer people and they are all of us, though that certainly doesn't mean we share the particularity of experiences under racism, sexism, gender oppression, class differences, and all forms of difference that shape queerness. But part of the problem of any sort of education is that students are an audience and no matter how much audience participation, or critical thinking, or queer theory one brings in, if you tell a story, they sit and listen and disengage—or experience pleasure that you wouldn't necessarily want them to experience.

The Pleasures of Minorities

I have a continuing suspicion that the presence of a gay speakers' bureau was the only moment in the class where sexuality was addressed. The fact of the add-on nature of any engagement with any minority is troubling for all us whose intention is not to install another in a series of minoritizing discourses that marked out and separated difference as a replicable, exchangeable series of easily articulated identity positions. While laudable, these invitations call to students' attention that their instructor's authority does not extend to sexuality, that an "outsider" with no particular relation to them (and often another student, one of their peers, not a professional educator) is sufficient to fill in for "what the textbook does not cover." So, not only is autobiography via coming out stories the site of pleasure for students, it is a passive, spectatorial pleasure at that. And because of its "add on" status, these moments of queer pedagogy are not real knowledge. Students know this because they do not have to take notes. It is also not knowledge that is authorized outside the circuit of the instructor doing the authorization. Here I mean that the "exceptional" instructor invites in all these rather odd people who only tell us their life stories, while the rest of the course is bound in text and the universal subject. When the speakers and the teachers inviting the speakers all manage to inhabit an exceptional position, the space between queerness and the class is made all the more distant. The easy answer is to assert one's own authority and authenticity in this exchange as an attempt to trump the lurking universal subject, but that's a game still stuck in the wrong paradigm.

I raise all of this only to say that when we attempt to address homophobia, we inevitably find ourselves either confessing or refusing to confess to an audience, whose only way into the topic often appears to be confession (or more to the point, hearing confession, in which case we are still the fallen and they are the absolvers). Jerry Springer may be helping us as it appears that under every relationship problem there is an unexpected lesbian, so the expectation of visually picking out lesbians or emotionally sorting out one's relationships is fully fraught with immanent gayness. No one on Jerry Springer needs to come out via story, they tend rather to prove it in relation to someone, that is, through action (most often adulterous and bodily). But before I digress too far into what may not actually be a digression, I want to return to what I see as the problems of autobiography as an anti-homophobia tool. The first problem is that of rendering the audience spectator to the life of gay people; even though we don't, of course, presume we're the only gay or gay-supportive people in the room, the fact that we call ourselves into being by giving an account makes us the story as well as the teller. Even when this is tempered by the ever popular "heterosexuality quiz" (Rochlin, 1992)—when did you first know you were attracted to a member of the opposite sex, and so on—we still manage to reassert a gay person as a tricky story leader and really only intend to point out the dullness of the heterosexual (non) coming out. As we all know, though, this process of sexuality is neither dull, fixed, nor finished. One has only to scan the pages of any glossy gay rag or glossy straight rag to know that sexuality is ever in the process of undoing and redoing itself. That, no doubt, is the more interesting issue, hence the popularity of Jerry Springer. But in a society where particular identities find themselves at particular structural disadvantages, whether persons occupy those identity positions for the short term, the long term, or the intermittent term, the project of anti-homophobia education is still, or all the more, useful.

I know that I am doing some very complex work on anti-homophobia education and political autobiography a disservice and I don't mean to do that. I only mean that the position at the head of the class as authentic experiencer of the mysteries of gayness has an awful counterpart in positioning students as quietly responsive in their own story, as if telling a seamless story as an anti-homophobia educator means that we expect there are, in fact, seamless stories, easily recognizable homosexual subjects, and particular kinds of spectacular, authentic bodies that can speak their parts well.

Queers have always had a fascination with the limits of what autobiography can do, even in the midst of writing them. Samuel Delaney begins his *Motion of the Light in Water* by recounting his own confusions about the details of his autobiography—as he starts, the dates are wrong, he couldn't have been talking to his then-dead father, a whole narrative is interrupted and troubled at the start (Delaney, 1988), but then does begin smoothly. In *The Price of Salt,* Claire Morgan's lesbian pulp novel, the heroine starts to tell her love interest about her background but can't imagine why the details of her family background, father's identity, and so on would matter. All of this raises, indeed, a wonderment: why have we so often chosen a particularist recounting of a dull, even if traumatic, coming out story (Morgan, 1984)? What sort of heroic other-overcoming, self-discovery do we presume will explain the obstacles and vagaries of gay life to the decidedly non-gay? I don't say this so someone will respond: but there are more complicated ways to explain this. Yes, and still the coming out story is very popular, it does bring our audience closer; it's always mentioned on end of course evaluations.

Confessing: The Problem

Indeed recent scholarship has suggested that these panel presentations are very effective, a point I will return to in a moment. Here I want to raise two related problems: the problem of the confession, to which I have already alluded, and the problem of a discourse of effectiveness. The problem under all of this is the problem of confession, the route to self-knowledge and self-surveillance that Foucault (1977/1988) has gotten us all so concerned with, particularly those of us whose work involves asking people questions about themselves. Foucault contends that subjectivity, our deep understanding and scrutiny of our identity, was created as an administrative tool through the practices of confession and normalization. Confession is particularly important in this account because it is predicated on otherworldly concerns, one scrutinizes oneself in order that one may be absolved and thus remain able to enter the afterlife. In other words, as an administrative device it removes one from the world, limits one's self-development to an interpretive encounter with authority. Foucault contends this process of confession is a precursor to modern bio power and that with the eighteenth century came a greater incursion of governmental controls of the populace, at the level of reproduction and general administration of categorization and individuation of people, notably through educational institutions. At first glance, individuation may appear to be a way out of a power that attempts to figure a nation as a populace, but with the growth of institutions bent on examining, testing, and regimenting individuals, this move toward individuation places the power both more closely to each person, but also produces each person as a docile, normalized individual whose self-surveillance will largely save the state the trouble (Foucault, 1977, 1988).

In the midst of all of this, Foucault (1990) contends that we are concerned with questions about the depth of our selves, the liberation of our desires, and the freedom of sex that all miss the point that these very things are what keep us constrained. Indeed, he argues that the very search for the truth about individuals, through the medical, educational, and whatever else institution is part of our problem: the social sciences attempt to approach human beings if they were something about which the truth could be known (and thus administered), as opposed to approaching one's life as a work of art.

For those of us involved in any level of educational institutions, maintaining a suspicious regard of confession, individuation, and passive consumption of narratives is crucial. If we approach social justice education using the same tools that institutions effectively use to bolster injustice, we are clearly in trouble. As Megan Boler (1999) argues, confession and multicultural understanding are troublingly woven together in multicultural education. To counter the problematic tendency of students to read, in her example, *MAUS* and then claim to understand what it was like to go through the Holocaust, Boler argues that we need to move individualized empathetic responses into collective responses to injustice. She contends that "the simple identifications and passive empathy produced through...'confessional reading' assures no actual change," whether in the student or the social conditions under examination (p. 177). Her "pedagogy of discomfort" calls for not only critical examination of the social context in which we are all embedded, but action to improve that context (p. 179). While this approach has no guaranteed results, nor does it make the classroom an easy place in which to be, it avoids the trap of oversimplifying the difficulties of injustice, pushing students to see their complicity in relations of inequality and demanding that we all engage in difficult attempts to undo social inequities. The problematic spectatorial empathy that Boler critiques is, of course, effective. It maintains social distances, it reinforces difference, and it allows those with relatively more power to be able to find a way to live with uncomfortable knowledge by converting it into nonthreatening narratives of leveled difference, interesting texture, and emotions to be consumed.

Efficiency Experts and the End of Pedagogy

In contrast to approaches like Boler's that admit the difficulties of our educational endeavors, there is also a trend in educating for social justice, particularly anti-homophobia education, that suggests effective ways to educate about homophobia. Clearly though we know that the coming out story may make anti-homophobia education more effective in some sense but it also effectively installs the pesky subject behind the problem. It reinforces both the subject of the confession and the passive yet actively ignorant audience to the confession who must be coddled in the anti-homophobia lesson. I will first recount some recent "effectiveness" talk and then move to what I prefer over the confession and testimony: the accusation. In discussing the use of "persuasive communication techniques" in anti-homophobia education, Gust Yep (1997) argues:

> Those who react to injustice and differential treatment often do so with anger. Although rage may be justified, it does not always lead to the changes these individuals are advocating in their reactive stance. This chapter proposes a more proactive position in the eradication of homophobia and heterosexism by going back

to the roots of these attitudes /without looking at political roots, but rather attitudinal roots. (p. 61)

Thus politics are not part of this particular view of effectiveness, where the source of the problem of homophobia is "attitudes." This is the opposite number to the singular story as antidote for the broad political problem of homophobia: those who are homophobic are so because of their singular stories. This means that we as educators need to know our students in more homey and intimate detail before we can adequately assess those students' ability to be challenged. Dee Bridgewater (1997) suggests limiting our goals to what we might reasonably expect from our interlocutors, given their degree of bias and attitudes about homosexuality, something we ought to assess before engaging with them. She argues, "The person contemplating disclosure must establish a realistic goal—intrinsic attitude change or extrinsic behavioral containment." And further suggests, "The individual contemplating disclosure must determine if the person to whom she or he might disclose simply has benign heterosexist attitudes or engages in virulent homo/biphobic discrimination" (Bridgewater, 1997, p. 68). These might be reasonable cautions when attempting education in a dark isolated place, but as I move to advocating the accusatory coming out story and the discomfort we ought to be installing in education, these kinds of pre-engagement limitations are problematic. While it may be reasonable that "a confrontation on…deeply held beliefs could be taken as a threat and thus exacerbate the homo/biphobe's acts," (Bridgewater, 1997, p. 72) nonetheless confrontation is part of an educational strategy when active ignorance has kept students blissfully unaware of their part in injustice.

This blissful and concerted unawareness is what limits the "effectiveness" of coming out in the first place. Heteronormativity too easily covers over any momentary interruption in its processes. Without some energetic intervention in the process of asserting ignorance of queer lives, there is little purpose in even probematizing homophobia. Discourses of efficiency simply continue the institutional process of assuring subjects that their knowledge of themselves is outside the purview of critique. What efficiency is most efficient at is taking the subjects of this institutional normalization as the starting and ending point of education. No one need question their subjectivity or their ignorance if they are embedded in practices that reassure them that they will be educated as if they were already who they could be. Reassuring people that they are not involved in processes of critique and change also allows them to continue to see the inequalities that are all around them. And the steadfast refusal of people to see what is before their eyes and within their own experience strongly undermines what many of us have taken to be the promise of being out, rearticulating identity, and using a politics of performativity.

Audience intransigence is behind the false promise of performativity; a theory whose Austinian original subverted itself in reiteration away from Austin's (1975) reliance on the contract between the one speaking the performative and the audience who must in some way understand and be contractually bound to the performative to a troubled re-articulation where speaking is doing, audience understanding or not. Clearly this is also the problem of education where one can "teach" one's heart out and still the class may not be compelled to "learn," otherwise known as the tragedy of education. The options for those of us engaged in taking apart the subject of homophobia range in this tragic mode from tragi-comedy (where we castigate the audience but become their friend), pure tragedy (where we state our case and hope the audience sees themselves in us as they feel sorry for us), and movie of the week (where we are the aforementioned spectacle whose story, while consumable, leaves the audience sleepy enough to get to bed earlier on a Sunday to arise all the more refreshed for the week ahead, armed with watercooler conversation). Jerry Springer may still be better for the persistent suspicion he surely must raise in everyone that their personal lives are much more complicated than even they could imagine (indeed, what better way to trouble the quiet complacency of anyone's life than to invite them to be on stage at Springer—whatever will happen?).

We have at least three options, probably more: one, trouble the presumed heterosexuality of the audience/world with a discussion of the unstable and wavering relations between gay and straight, gender and sexuality, fantasy and activity, and so on. This usually moves requests for confession to the question and answer period where they come up again, but often with quite interesting twists. As one young man in a large lecture class with a day on anti-homophobia education expressed disgust at anal penetration and then penetration in general, his girlfriend roundly accused him for suggesting that he felt such disgust about her. The conversation moved from an examination of why heterosexual males would feel the need to express discomfort about anal penetration to how penetration was figured as passive and feminizing in many cultural representations and practices. This discussion was useful in that it wove together a critique of gender relations with an examination of the difficulty of maintaining masculinity without denigrating femininity. The young man had essentially queered his girlfriend's participation in heterosexuality and she clearly recognized that gesture as both homophobic and sexist. Discussion then moved into a series of students acknowledging how gender norms and heteronormativity limited their own options as well as encouraged them to dislike queers.

In one of the first classes I ever taught Adrienne Rich's *Compulsory Heterosexuality* (1993), I attempted to show that the lesbian continuum was a problematic concept. Like the other responses to Rich's essay, I was concerned that lesbian particularity, especially the simple fact of sexual activity between women, was elided by the continuum and that my students would be too inclined to see themselves as just like lesbians even though they'd never actually had sex with another woman. My plan for the day was to challenge them to see their heterosexual difference from me by asking them to go around the class recounting their first sexual experience with another woman. As no one had come out in class yet, I was sure that I'd have the authentic high ground by the end of the discussion. Every single student recounted a sexual experience with another woman, forever troubling my preconceptions about the straightness of supposedly straight women.

Another option, closely related to the first, is to "queer" sexuality, to open categories of sexual differences until they proliferate well beyond the usual binary, but keeping in clear view the reality of the binary in social, political, and institutional practices of injustice. As a strategy of alliance, "queer" needs to be very careful not to either efface difference as it produces it, or level difference as it becomes exhausted. Too often, "queer" slides right back into white, gay, middle-class and we all give up on it. But "queer's" intention was to provide a big tent, in which the broadest category covered the most minute specifications. So saying one is a lesbian is no longer sufficient to get at the range and nuance of identities, especially as students in elementary, middle, and high school are all increasingly aware of their sexuality and gender identity in complex ways. In one high school student group, for instance, a young lesbian-appearing couple was in fact a transgender butch and lesbian femme. The space of an alliance group provided them with a community in which to work against homophobia and transphobia. These spaces of complexity push understandings of identity, not as idiosyncratic but embedded, negotiated, and political.

The third is to get ourselves out of the business of telling stories and move more strongly into a pedagogy of accusation.[20] The problem with the way coming out stories are received by their audience is that the pleasure and passivity of reception can miss the point of interaction in the world with others. Stories, if taken passively, reinstall an overly simplistic narrative form (so common to so many educational projects), re-reading the past from the present, and they do this under the guise of letting the audience in on a secret they pretend they do not usually have access to. These stories then excuse and expect audience laziness, though their intention may be to, in part, exonerate ignorance, the telling of stories as secrets to be uncovered only by the presence of a clearly marked gay speaker means that the audience need not have troubled themselves to perk their eyes up from their straight-fest world to recognize that they are not alone. Increasingly, of course, they know they are not alone, but all too often they don't advocate and they don't interrupt the homophobia they see around them. And if they are anything like the pre-service teachers I quiz before our foundations class, they don't know how to accommodate diversity or interrupt bias-laden harassment and would feel rude for so doing (Mayo, 2002). After all, a suitable person from whatever minority ought to be in charge of that. Advocacy is trespassing into someone else's authentic struggle or so their reasoning goes.

Pedagogy of Accusation

Moving our pedagogy and even our stories into the realm of accusation centers the structural inequality of heteronormativity as the frame through which our stories and pedagogies need to be read. Further, I hope that accusation underscores the need for us to be aware of one another and understanding the pressing need to challenge ignorance, hold one another to account, and understand that we are all responsible together. Accusation is of course a relational strategy—we are as likely to be accused back as oversimplifying our audience, underestimating or misrecognizing the ways in which race, class, gender, disability, and other forms of difference alter the way we present queerness and alter the way we suggest queer ideas be framed. As we think about the use of autobiography we need remember that the telling of coming out stories in anti-homophobia education alters the purpose of coming out—or complicates what coming out is. For the audience, the story appears to be the speaker's statement of identity, but for the most part, the speaker is already out, in the sense that they are aware of their sexuality. In other words, the variety of coming out stories is muddled in this scene, where someone who has and no doubt continues to interrogate their identity and relations is re-enacting what may appear to the audience as the story.

But this story has a different purpose than self-knowledge or knowledge negotiation. The telling of the story in an accusational mode is to show the audience that such stories are told, but the fact of the details of the story—the desire for narrative from the audience—do damage to the teller's purpose.

An accusational mode reminds the audience that coming out stories are in some ways extortion—if you tell me a good story, I may consider challenging my active ignorance and intervening in heteronormative practices. The reminder that coming out is a strategy also reminds the audience that heteronormativity demands coming out in a variety of situations and that being queer winds up being a very intermittent identity that requires constant intervention. Hopefully by raising the stakes of the interaction into the realm of accusation, the constant need for coming out in a variety of situations will be underscored. The audience isn't there for the initial coming out and may remain untroubled that later comings out are fully for their benefit, in that they refuse steadfastly and obstinately to recognize that people are out—and in—all around them. In other words, accusation pushes the audience to understand that they are, in fact, why this particular coming out scene has unfolded. Accusation is about showing that relations of difference are already there, even if they are not recognized.

Thus, as educators we need to move from what we do as simply coming out (which I know is never as simple as that) to accusation and even recruitment. As Deborah Britzman (1995) argues:

> Pedagogical thought must begin to acknowledge that receiving knowledge is a problem for the learner and the teacher, particularly when the knowledge one already possesses or is possessed by works as an entitlement to one's ignorance or when the knowledge encountered cannot be incorporated because it disrupts how the self might imagine itself and others. (p. 159)

While I don't honestly think that accusation is always a good idea, there is an energy to accusation that demands a response—the audience is forced from passivity into engagement, the person coming out is not asking for understanding but calling for accountability of people whose way of being in the world has unintentionally and intentionally created the situation that allows coming out to be a moment for spectatorship. Direct confrontation shifts the relations of audience and speaker to co-engagers, and it has the added bonus of not making this engagement easy. Encouraging this atmosphere of accusation also opens the space for counteraccusation: if you're willing to accuse someone, you know you've raised the stakes higher and you need to be willing to be accused back. As much as we talk about queering the scene of education, we need to realize that all of us trespass on one another in different ways and to take intersectionality and difference seriously means that we don't get to talk about race, gender, class, sexuality, disability sequentially, separately or calmly.

Cesarean, Celebrity, and Childbirth: Students Encounter Modern Birth and the Question of Female Embodiment

Natalie Jolly

Introduction

In this chapter, I employ an analysis of modern birth to discuss not only current trends toward medicalization but also the implications that these trends have for the ways in which women experience their female bodies. To begin, I review a few of the medical practices that characterize birth today, including surveillance and monitoring during labor, induction and chemical intensification of contractions, and surgical delivery via cesarean section. As these technologies gain cultural purchase in our society, medicalized birth becomes increasingly legitimated. I suggest that medicalized birth practices, like so many experiences tied to women's bodies, are socially influenced and reflect current idioms about the female body. Moreover, I demonstrate that today's interventionist style of obstetrics grows out of a cultural distrust of the female body, and consider the ways in which women internalize both the normalcy of medical birth and the attendant cultural commentary on female embodiment. Because much of this normalization occurs through the channels of popular culture, I situate my discussion within the context of media representations of birth.

Moreover, I draw on my experiences teaching about birth within my Introduction to Women's Studies courses. I explore the curriculum I developed to facilitate critical thinking about birth and focus on the ways in which the discussion was framed to encourage inquiry into media socialization. Using a number of student quotes, I reconstruct the powerful resistance I regularly encounter when I introduce this curriculum. In particular, I detail the layers of opposition, ranging from a universal dismissal of the topic at hand to a more nuanced treatment of the critique of medical birth. By employing a language of choice, students are able to avoid the need for a systematic sociological investigation and instead imply that decision making happens in a cultural vacuum. Ironically, it is precisely this language of choice that prevents students from connecting medicalized birth to the larger project of feminism, and I investigate the mechanisms by which this disconnect occurs—why do students dismiss the critiques of medical birth and how might their rejection be indicative of a larger cultural distrust of women's bodies?

I conclude with a more abstract treatment of female embodiment, focusing on the normative discourses that reinforce women's body skepticism. The subtle but pervasive cultural commentary on the female body makes it difficult—if not impossible—for any woman to have a positive encounter with her body, and leads us all to believe that women's bodies don't work without intervention. As a result of these formative discourses, students are often unable to articulate a clear critique of medicalized birth, or indeed any phenomena that relies on the assumption of an affirmative female embodiment. In fact, their resistance to the critiques of medicalized birth reflects a more general social tendency to medically manage all functions of the female body. I assert that the power of these medicalized discourses rests in their ability to fit within a larger network of narratives that work to undermine women's body confidence.

The Landscape of Birth Today

Birth in the United States has become increasingly medicalized, as evidenced by the growing number of deliveries that are marked by high levels of obstetrical intervention and medical management (Kitzinger, 2005). Labors today are artificially induced, chemically intensified, and increasingly end in surgical procedures (Wagner, 1994). And today, with the overall social consensus being that hospital birth is safest, this rising rate of obstetrical intervention is viewed as evidence of birth security. Particularly when attended by an obstetrician, a safe birth is seen as virtually guaranteed within the high-tech environment of the hospital delivery room. As a result, the vast majority of women continue to choose physician-attended (91.4%) or certified nurse midwife-attended (7.6%) hospital birth over other non-hospital alternatives (<1%). These statistics have remained relatively stable over recent decades. Today, over 99 percent of births take place in a hospital environment, and are subject to the procedures and treatments that accompany medicalized care (Martin et al., 2005).

Most commonly, medical technologies are used to monitor the birthing woman and manage the delivery of the baby. It is routine practice for women to be constantly monitored through the use of an Electronic Fetal Monitor (EFM) (an instrument that measures the heartbeat of the baby) during the course of her labor (Lent, 1999). Over 85% of birthing women, or more than 3.2 million live births, were monitored during labor using EFM in 2003, and this rate has climbed steadily since 1989 (Martin et al., 2005). EFM is the most frequently reported obstetric procedure, and may in fact be used to monitor an even higher percentage of births. In addition to the EFM, it has become increasingly popular to employ Internal Fetal Monitoring (IFM) (where an electrode is attached through the vagina directly to the baby's head) to ensure constant monitoring of the baby's heart rate during labor. Both of these surveillance technologies necessitate that the woman be connected to machinery through wires, electrodes, and sensors. This technology is quite sensitive, and often requires the birthing woman to remain immobile to ensure a stable reading.[21] Labor monitoring is also carried out through detailed charting to ensure that cervical dilation is progressing along expected lines.[22] Slow or stalled labors are thereby quickly noticed, and more stringent courses of medical management are then adopted.

A woman in labor is routinely supervised and her medical caregivers regularly intervene into her labor and delivery. One-fifth of all birthing women will have their labor induced, a rate that has more than doubled from the 9.5% in 1990. This rising rate has been linked to a growing number of elective inductions (inductions with no medical or obstetric indication) and 25% of today's induced labors are the result of these "patient-choice" inductions (Jones, 2000). Labor contractions are also increasingly amplified with a variety of chemical stimulants, and 16.7% of labors in 2003 were augmented in such a way. This represents a 59% increase from the 1989 stimulation rate of 10%. And even when there is evidence that certain medical interventions are in decline—processes such as vacuum extraction and forceps delivery have decreased in recent years, dropping by 41% to only 5.6% in 2003, down from 9.5% in 1994—there is often a more complicated explanation for these trends. This decrease in assisted delivery (vacuum and forceps) has been linked to a drastic increase in cesarean births, making these vaginal delivery techniques unnecessary (Martin et al., 2005).

As of 2003, the U.S. cesarean rate was 27.5%—the highest rate ever reported. Driven by both the rise in primary cesareans (particularly for low-risk women) and the steep decline in the Vaginal Birth After Cesarean (VBAC), this represents a 5% rise from 2002 and a 25% rise from 1996. The rate of women having a vaginal birth after a previous cesarean (VBAC) fell 16% in the last year and has dropped 63% since 1996 (Martin et al., 2005). Because the American College of Obstetricians and Gynecologists (ACOG) as well as the American Medical Association (AMA) have recommended that physicians now discourage women from attempting VBAC deliveries, it is increasingly difficult for women to obtain a VBAC in a hospital environment.[23] Thus, women who have an initial cesarean delivery are generally required to deliver all subsequent babies via cesarean section (Grady, 2004). Also leading to the growing rate of cesarean deliveries is the rising number of women with very low risk pregnancies delivering by cesarean, a trend that has risen 67% since 1990 (Martin et al., 2005). A number of these are elective cesareans—surgical deliveries that were requested and scheduled by the pregnant woman herself rather than recommended by her medical team (Klein, 2004).

The medicalization of birth has not gone unnoticed and there has been much attention paid to the growing number of elective cesarean sections, the rising rate of induction, epidural and episiotomy and concern over a variety of other medical interventions (Cohen and Feig, 2003; Hannah, 2004; Heinze and Sleigh, 2003; Jones, 2000; Klein, 2004; Leeman, 2005; Rubin, 2005). Unfortunately, much of the conversation has remained superficial, and a critical and systematic engagement is still largely absent. There is no doubt that a rigorous analysis is necessary to uncover the relationship between obstetricians and laboring women, the political and economic clout of lobbying groups such as the AMA, the ACOG, and similar forces, the economic pressures exerted by health management organizations (HMO), and the ways in which the litigious nature of medicine today shape decision making. All of these facets need to be explored if we are to begin unpacking the political economy of birth today and understanding the current state of birth in the United States. In this chapter, however, I am primarily concerned with investigating the ways in which our social and cultural narratives are shaped to reflect a legitimization of medical birth

Birth and the Cultural Body

Sociologists have long documented the multiple ways in which subtle social pressures influence individual behavior. Submission to social norms is not mandatory, but social sanction often follows inappropriate conformance.

Feminist sociologists have gone further to assert that these pressures often remind oppressed groups of power hierarchies and re-inscribe inequality (Collins, 1990; Smith, 1987). An investigation of these socialization patterns is necessary, not so much to explain choices and behaviors, but to comprehend the rich complexity that influences individuals to value certain practices over others, to sanction others who may not share "common values" and to more clearly understand how social meaning becomes collectively imagined, articulated, and reformed

While birth is certainly a biological event, it has a sociocultural component that has changed over time to reflect the specificities of various cultural moments (Leavitt, 1986; Michaelson, 1988; Rothman, 1986). At varying times birth has been a private affair undertaken by a woman alone, an intimate experience shared by two partners, and a grand social event involving friends and family. This shift over time can be seen to correspond to changes in the social imaginary; the status of birth is closely linked with dominant views of the female body and to some degree reflects the overall social conception of women at that time. In the context of the United States, the changing nature of birth is apparent. During the 1920s, birth became increasingly medical, moving from the home to the hospital. Many have cited the "assembly line" style of care that attended this move, and birthing women became a major commodity in the healthcare industry (Leavitt, 1986). This shift mirrored women's widespread move from the home to the workplace and captured the overall tenor of the time—commodification of women's labor (Hay, 2002). Thus at a time when society was capitalizing on women's physical labor, the birthing body itself became a commodity.

A similar phenomenon can be seen during the 1950s, when idealized middle-class women were embracing domesticity and were striving for lives of suburban disengagement. During this time, hospital birth became centered on complete pain management. With the advent of "twilight sleep"[24] and other such interventions, birth became a non-event, one that women were literally "put to sleep" for, perpetuating the cultural myths of the time—modesty, privacy, and isolation. Birthing women embodied the detachment that characterized those years. Normative discourses often manifest in the birth practices of the day and in doing so, write cultural conventions onto the bodies of women. How a society conceives of and approaches birth can therefore offer insight into both the ways in which a culture sees the generic female body and how individual women encounter their own particular bodies.

How, then, do we see birth today? It seems clear that trends toward increasing medical interventions and restrictions to hospital birth alternatives speak to a society that is relatively unconfident of and somewhat squeamish about the birthing body. Such sentiments are thinly veiled under a rhetoric of patient "choice" and we collectively assume that birthing practices are solely reflective of the desires of birthing women. Feminists, however, have leveled numerous critiques against the assumption that medicalized birth serves the interests of women and have suggested that medicine and technology has more often served to undermine the normalcy of the female body (Beckett, 2005; Martin, 1987). Women have long been encouraged to "choose" medical and technological interventions to manage their unruly female bodies, and elective birth interventions are part of a larger project that wraps power imbalances and gender inequality within a language of choice (Bordo, 2003). Feminist historians offer further support in their documentation of medicine's long history of pathologizing the female body, particularly during birth (Martin, 1987). These historiocultural analyses have considered both the particular context of medical workers and birthing women in a given cultural-temporal moment (Hay, 2002; Michaelson, 1988). They have inquired into the role of socialization and investigated the multiple ways that cultural norms become internalized and manifest in the practice of obstetrics. This research suggests that the cultural milieu has very real material consequences for how a woman's body is treated during birth.

And because feminists have always known that the popular is political, analyzing birth today through an examination of popular culture provides a unique insight into our current baby story. Take, for instance, the October 2005 issue of *Elle* magazine, where Britney Spears reported that she "[didn't] want to go through the pain" of natural childbirth (Millea, 2005). True to her word, Ms. Spears scheduled an elective cesarean section to deliver her son, thus swelling the ranks of celebrities opting for surgical over vaginal birth—luminaries including Madonna and Elizabeth Hurley. Most recently, Angelina Jolie has joined the lineup, and not without her own commentary on the experience. After delivering via cesarean section, Jolie made the front page of CNN.com with a headline that reads "Jolie: Shiloh's Birth was Terrifying" (CNN.com, 2006). As this "too posh to push" trend trickles down to the less than famous, it is not surprising to see a nearly 50% jump in the number of elective cesareans in the last decade (Meikle et al., 2005). With the dominant icons of femininity (such as Spears and Jolie) publicly expressing fear of childbirth and with surgical birth emerging as a symbol of status, it is necessary to rigorously examine the role that the mainstream media plays in normalizing medicalized birth and perpetuating a culture of fear around the birthing body.

Birth in the Curriculum

Drawing on current media representations of birth, I introduced a number of these issues into my Introduction to Women's Studies courses. It was my intention that we would unpack what was considered "normal" birth and examine the assumptions made about pain management, cesarean section, and medicalization more generally. To do this, we viewed big screen productions of birth such as the science fiction depiction in *Star Wars Episode III*, where birth happens behind a wall of glass and is assisted by robotic nurses. And despite the sterility and technology, birth in this film results in death of the birthing woman—but not before putting her through unimaginable pain and suffering. We then moved to situational comedies and reviewed the ways in which birth has been treated in popular shows such as *Friends* and *Sex in the City*. Not surprising, birth here is depicted as comic and light, with the laboring woman passing the time worrying about appearances. In these shows, the birthing woman is free to move around, handles the pain of contractions easily, and maintains an upbeat attitude throughout her labor. After these sitcoms, we segued into reality television and juxtaposed the comic depictions with actual live births. It becomes quickly apparent that birth today more closely resembles the high-tech scenes of the science-fiction *Star Wars* birth rather than the witty banter that characterizes sitcom deliveries. Women delivering on shows such as *A Baby Story* or *Birthday* frequently confess that they did not believe that the pain would be as intense as it was, that they felt their bodies weren't able to birth properly, and that (though they were otherwise healthy and had normal pregnancies) they required a cascade of medical interventions that often ended in cesarean section.

It was my intention that viewing popular representations of birth would lead to a conversation about the ways in which we are socialized to see medical birth as normal and to rely on technology, medicine, and doctors to rescue women from their birthing bodies (Martin, 1987). Indeed from the beginning of the lesson, we address our collective impression of birth—I have students write down the first word that comes into their heads when they think of the process of labor and delivery. Easily three-quarters of every class cites "pain" in this word association exercise, and we attempt to uncover the reasons why the birth process is associated with so much fear and trepidation in our society. Why is there such a palpable fear of the pain of birth and a strong lack of confidence in women's ability to deliver? Drawing on my familiarity with birth in a local Pennsylvania Amish community,[25] I demonstrate to the students the ways in which this phenomenon is culturally specific and is in no way a universal phenomenon. I then encourage my students to unpack the underlying messages in the film and television clips we've just reviewed, as well as draw on their knowledge of feminist critiques of socialization and the social/political/economic structure of today's world. We conclude by returning to the increased cesarean section trend, particularly the idea of elective c-section, and connecting the themes we've discussed to today's "too posh to push" tendencies.

I continue to be surprised by the intense and oftentimes heated responses generated by this discussion. In a course that deals with socially stigmatized issues such as abortion and welfare, many (me included) would not expect that critiques of medicalized birth meet with more resistance than all other topics combined. Students have become visibly upset during our discussion and raised their voices to both their peers and to myself. It is not uncommon for students to claim that they "Don't buy it." Throughout the semester, they return to the topic and we continue to work through their strong reactions to the content. Many students initially struggle with their opposition to the particular critiques of medical birth that we explore as part of this curriculum. As we move through the semester, I have realized that, in addition to these surface struggles, several students have a difficult time critically engaging the ways in which birth is socially constructed and are particularly vexed by the ways in which this happens through popular culture. Much of this resistance is voiced through student posts to our course weblog (or blog), which serves as a discussion venue for many of our class conversations. Because a blog allows for a more informal tone of communication, students often feel freer to express their personal feelings in a candid and honest manner. As a result, our blog commentary offers a unique insight into student sentiments that have, up until this point, been reserved for face-to-face classroom discussion.

Student responses engender many layers of resistance, beginning with a universal dismissal of the material as being false and untrue and ending with a more nuanced rejection of what underlies the issue at hand. Starting at the surface, many students believe that the information they are reading is simply bogus and has been forged or manipulated in order to prove a point. Consider this student's post regarding a reading[26] which cites data published by the World Health Organization on infant and maternal mortality:

> Although the online article we read gave many statistics where midwives had less infant mortality I believe that you can make statistics to say

anything you want. I don't actually believe that midwives are safer than hospitals with trained docters.

A few students are able to end their engagement with the topic by merely dismissing the entire content as fallacious. Even when students are given material from a variety of peer-reviewed and otherwise reputable sources, many resist further connection with the topic and are able to prevent further engagement by undermining the validity of the argument at hand. For others, the resistance seems to be more ad hominem rather than purely dismissive. Consider the following:

> These midwives have caused a lot of problems for the hospital. They are currently the cause of several lawsuits against the hospital. One of the ER nurses told me about another time when a midwife patient came to the ER in labor. I guess she had already called to let us know she was coming, so her midwife was waiting. Before this woman could get through the ER door, the midwife was outside, ripping down her pants…in broad daylight…in the ghetto. I hope that not all midwives are as incompetent as the ones that work in my hospital.

These superficial dismissals do not characterize the majority of the work done by students—most of whom rigorously engage the material and struggle with the critiques being leveled against our current system of medicalization. Some students question the political economic critiques that suggest physicians are motivated by forces that are less than altruistic:

> Obstetricians seem to be doin their job in my opinion. If there is a problem they are there to help. It's not like they want to use drugs for a C-Section, something that costs thousands of dollars, I think they are just trying to do their job.

Even those students who do acknowledge the litigious nature of medicine today are often hesitant to imply that the authority of medical practitioners be questioned by birthing women. Indeed for many students, a laboring woman's control over her body comes a distant second to the defensive medicine practiced by physicians today. Such a position is clearly articulated in the following post:

> Physicians don't want to get sued; they might not be able to afford it. Also…if the doctor always did what the patient wanted, such as a natural

vaginal delivery, and something went wrong, you can bet your bum that the woman would sue. For a lot. It's in the best interest for everyone if the safest route is taken at the first sign of a problem.

There are a number of students whose resistance to critiques of medicalized birth more closely reflects the popular discourses of the day, particularly those that imply an inherent distrust of women's bodies. The normative discourses of antiseptic hygiene and cleanliness in the hospital environment are regularly juxtaposed against the polluted nature of the woman's body. The sterility of the hospital environment is often cited as necessary, given women's intrinsically unsanitary bodies.

I'm sorry, but soaking in a tub while delivering a baby sounds gross as well as horribly unsanitary. I know it's never talked about, but a lot of women soil themselves, urinate, or even vomit when they give birth. That is the equivalent of delivering a baby in a toilet...which can't be healthy for anyone involved.

Most commonly, students are hesitant to critique today's trend towards ever-increasing medicalization in labor and delivery because they are deeply convinced that a medicated, or even a surgical birth, is every woman's choice. A woman who chooses medical intervention is making an active decision—one that many believe to be free from the social pressures that are, in so many other aspects of life, so influential. So while students are quick to point out the normative forces that encourage a woman to choose plastic surgery or to choose a career in the humanities over the sciences, they are less willing to acknowledge (and many are indeed openly hostile to the idea) that women's choices in birth may be subjected to similar pressures.

I really don't think that people should be so quick to judge a woman if she chose to have an elective c-section, or was pumped full of drugs during the birth.

What continues to fascinate me is the ways in which students (and indeed the rest of society as well) deploy the language of choice—both to imply complete free action and to erase the need for any further systematic sociological analysis. Under these assumptions, a woman who chooses an elective cesarean is acting in a cultural vacuum—she is not influenced by the subtle (and sometimes overt) messages that remind her that good birth is medical birth. Moreover, media messages that glibly suggest an elective cesarean preserves a "honeymoon vagina" (Wolf, 2003) or staves off late term pregnancy weight gain are somehow absent from the analysis. A more careful deconstruction of the elective cesarean section as an issue of choice has revealed that this choice may reflect a deeper social inequality that encourages women to make decisions that privilege others over themselves (Beckett, 2005). Feminist work has long illustrated the ways in which decisions made within a patriarchal society are rarely free and instead reflect the power differential between men and women. A woman's choice to birth via cesarean section to preserve vaginal tautness or to prevent late pregnancy weight gain may reflect just such tendency. Acknowledging the power of normative discourses does not undermine a woman's agency but instead asserts that her autonomy is often conscripted by the cultural milieu within which she is located.

Reliance on a language of choice keeps students from connecting medicalized birth to the larger project of feminism—namely a critique of the structures that perpetuate inequality. More specifically, conceiving of birth within the context of an individual woman's choice renders students unable to see the ways in which discourses of birth can easily be situated within the more general narratives of female embodiment. Cultural meanings have long been inscribed on the female birthing body and research ranging from the history of the forceps to trends in birthing positions to today's current obsession with the elective cesarean all speak to the ways in which cultural norms are regularly expressed on and around the bodies of laboring women (Davis-Floyd and Sargent, 1997). In fact, this transcends the birthing body and manifests in all stages of a woman's life—in a society where girls and young women are encouraged to suppress their menstruation (e.g., Payne, 2006) and where older women are pressured into medicating their symptoms of menopause (e.g., CNN.com's 2002 coverage of the controversy over HRT), our complete and total reliance on science and technology to mitigate the unruly and problematic nature of the female body is unmatched.

Modern Female Embodiment

This cultural distrust of and disgust with women's bodies extends beyond the medicalization of menstruation, birth, and menopause and into the everyday world of women. It influences the cultural female body in subtle and profound ways, physically as well as metaphorically altering the ways in which women experience their bodies. For women, even the literal act of eating (or not eating) has become culturally symbolic and invested with meaning—a female body that eats/takes/consumes to excess is socially reprimanded through an elaborate system of stigmatization and censure. A woman can no longer experience the sensation of bodily hunger or satiation without also hearing a cultural commentary, either congratulating her for denying her hunger (both her physical desire for food as well as her metaphorical desire for power, prestige, etc.) or chastising her for succumbing to the excessiveness of the (female) body (Bordo, 2003). These normative discourses reinforce women's body skepticism, making it difficult—if not impossible—for any woman to have a positive encounter with her body. Every interaction that a woman has with her body is filtered through this cultural commentary, normalizing and desensitizing us all to the subtle but pervasive cultural distrust of and disgust with the female body. It is less surprising, then, that many women become unable to have authentic bodily experiences without this cultural commentary. And as a result of these normative discourses, it becomes hard for women to believe that their bodies could or would ever work properly. Medical birth is just one necessary feature in a society which regularly articulates an inherent distrust of women's bodies. Without a clear conviction that women's bodies can labor without medical intervention, we remain persuaded that the female body is compromised and needs to be fixed—saved by medicine, by technology, by science, or by society.

A curriculum based on a critique of dominant norms including medicalized birth leaves students, for the most part, epistemically bereft—lacking a socially supported body confidence and possessing a personal unfamiliarity with their own unmedicalized body. How then, are they to make sense of material that so profoundly challenges cultural conventions about the female body? My evidence suggests that, while some students are able to express a clear critique of medicalized birth, the majority are unable to do so. Moreover, many students seek out an adamantly polarized position, dismissing the powerful role that media plays in normalizing medicalized birth and championing the choices that today's birthing women have in terms of her access to medical management. In particular, students cite the universal availability of interventions that reduce or alleviate the pain of labor and delivery. As one student reports, "Not everyone thinks pain is empowering."

In fact, very few women believe that any female bodily experience—during birth or otherwise—can have any sort of positive association, let alone be downright empowering. Pain during labor, blood during menstruation, hot flashes during menopause, all are symptoms of a disease that is the female condition and all need to be masked by the miracle of modern medicine.

We are all regularly exposed to normative discourses of medical birth both through the media and through popular culture more generally. The power of these particular discourses lies within their ability to integrate into a larger network of narratives that undermine women's body confidence—medicalized birth makes only a cameo appearance in the screenplay of female embodiment. Cultural meanings have always been both literally and metaphorically inscribed on the female body and continue to shape the ways in which women interact with their own individual bodies. Today, women's relationship with their female bodies is problematic at best and cultural conditioning continues to exacerbate this; from low self-esteem to harmful anorexia, girls and women today relate to their bodies in dysfunctional and sometimes dangerous ways. Because women's relationship to their bodies is articulated through this cultural commentary, few women are able to know their bodies in an affirming way. Instead, female embodiment is characterized by a nearly complete reliance on modern medicine to mitigate the disorderly nature of the female body. As a result, discourses that are critical of modern female embodiment are not only dismissed, but are often vehemently rejected—the critique of medical birth is just one such example. Without a curriculum of female embodiment that supports women's body confidence, it is difficult to imagine that critiques of medical birth—or for that matter any phenomena that is intimately tied to women's bodies—will find resonance within society today.

Part IV

Intersticial States: Performing Bodies

Intimacy in the Curriculum of Janine Antoni

Stephanie Springgay

The contemporary artist Janine Antoni embraces the practices of feminist body art using her own body in much of her work. She translates everyday bodied activities, such as bathing, eating, sleeping, and washing into artistic processes making references to the feminist critique that the "personal is political" (Jones and Warr, 2000). For instance, she gnawed on 600 pound cubes of lard and chocolate and then refashioned the chewed pieces into heart-shaped candy or lipsticks ("Gnaw," 1992). In another performance she dipped her hair into hair dye and then mopped the gallery floor with it ("Loving Care," 1993). Her body is essential to the very fabrication of each piece. While her work can be located in the context of feminist art that critiques issues of body image, and the representation of woman as gluttonous and uncontrollable excess (Smith, 2002) her performative strategies bear witness to the intimacies of everyday life and to the ways that relationships between bodies are nurtured.

Janine Antoni, *2038*, 2000. C print. 20 X 20 inches (50.8 X 50.8 cm)

Courtesy of the artist and Luhring Augustine, New York.

Take for instance, her photograph titled "2038" (2000), in which she is submerged in an old fashioned bathtub and appears to be nursing a cow identified as #2038 by a metal tag in its ear. The image is at once humorous and haunting. Antoni is serene and calm, a look of tenderness on her face. Instead of her milking the cow, the cow suckles her. This symbiotic tension is not unlike that of the often difficult relationship between mother and child. Tender, erotic, hilarious, and bizarre, this performative photograph raises questions about the delicate nature of bodied interactions; of nurturing, sharing, and inter-embodiment. My interest, in examining Antoni's work, is to think about curriculum through the construct "body art." This is not to suggest a curriculum in which we learn about body art or for that matter art that is about the body, but rather I engage in an inquiry into body art in order to pose questions about the intimacies and vulnerabilities of a living curriculum.

While intimacy can be understood as "knowing someone in depth, knowing many different aspects of a person or knowing how they would respond in different situations,"[27] I want to think about intimacy through Jean Luc Nancy's (2000) notion of being-with. To be a body is to be "with" other bodies, to touch, to encounter, and to be exposed. As such, intimacy is not simply about the possibility or impossibility of ever knowing the other fully or deeply, but rather names the meetings and encounters between bodies (Ahmed, 2000). Bodied encounters, I argue, in and through touch, produce intercorporeal understandings and in doing so imagine an intimate curriculum that is vulnerable and hesitant.

Body Art

There are a number of descriptors used to talk about the visual representation of the body. In the late 1960s and early 1970s, artists, in response to a modernist aesthetics that rendered absent both the physical and experiencing body, began exploring their own bodies as the medium of art, attempting to make public that which was previously repressed and hidden. Many of these representations have been termed performance art. Performance art takes place at a particular time and in a particular space. For example, Antoni's work titled "Loving Care" is an example of performance art. To enact this piece, the artist dipped her hair in a bucket of hair dye and then used her hair (and her whole body) to mop the gallery floor. It is a performance art work because it incorporates the body of the artist, it took place in a specific location (the gallery), and at a specific time (the work now exists in documentary photographs) and there was a relationship constructed between the artist's body and the bodies of the spectators. "Loving Care" could also be described as body art.

Feminist art historian Amelia Jones (1998) uses the term body art, as opposed to performance art, in order to emphasize the position of the body, or what she refers to as the "body/self" (p. 13) within experience. Unlike performance art, which encompasses any kind of theatrical production, body art according to Jones, may or may not take place in front of an audience. Rather body art refers to art that "take[s] place through an enactment of the artist's body, whether it be in a "performative" setting or in the relative privacy of the studio, that is then documented such that it can be experienced subsequently through photography, film, video, and/or text" (Jones, 1998, p. 13). Body art is an engagement with the body of the artist as a set of performative practices that interrogate intersubjectivity. Body art makes visible those social practices and mechanisms that construct bodies and subjectivities. Moving beyond a binary frame in which the body signifies an essential self, subjectivities and identities (sex, gender, desire) are performed as effects of specific power structures (Butler, 1993). For Judith Butler (1993) performativity is the stylized repetition of acts that produce the paradoxical nature of identity construction.

Accordingly, Jones (1998) contends that body art "enacts or performs or instantiates the embodiment and intertwining of self and other" (p. 38). The philosophies of Maurice Merleau-Ponty (1968) locate the body as the expressive space by which we experience the world. In his theories of intersubjectivity each subject participates with other subjects, caressing and interpenetrating each other. Bodies bring other bodies into being without losing their own specificity, and each materializes itself without being contained. Rather than an understanding of self and other as oppositional, intersubjectivity becomes imbricated and reciprocal. One is always already both (self and other) at the same time.

Such a conjecture is similar to Nancy's (2000) theories of "being-singular-plural." For Nancy (2000) to be a body is to be "with" other bodies, to touch, to encounter, and to be exposed. In other words, each individual body is brought into being through encounters with other bodies. It is the relationality between bodies that creates a particular understanding of shared existence. Relationality depends on singularity. A singular body, argues Nancy (2000), "is not individuality; it is, each time, the punctuality of a 'with' that establishes a certain origin of meaning and connects it to an infinity of other possible origins" (p. 85). Jones (1998) connects this idea to body art when she writes that "body art splinters rather than coheres the self"

(p. 51). As such there is contiguity and discontinuity. Through body art an opening is created that allows self and other to be thought alongside each other, not as opposites, nor as universal equals, but together in such a way that constitutes difference.

Peter Hallward (2001) substantiates this with: "The singular proceeds internally and is constituted in its own creation. The singular, in each case, is constituent of itself, expressive of itself, immediate to itself" (p. 3). Criteria are not external but are determined through its actions. Nikki Sullivan (2003) provides us with a further explanation: "Each 'one' is singular (which isn't the same as saying each 'one' is individual) while simultaneously being in-relation" (p. 55). Singularity, as a theoretical construct demands that self and other no longer hold opposing positions. Bodies/selves cannot exist without other bodies/selves, nor are the two reducible to one another.

Antoni's interest in everyday body rituals exemplifies this body/self to body/self relation. In "Lick and Lather" (1994), for instance, Antoni cast fourteen classical busts of herself in chocolate and soap. She then licked the chocolate busts and took the soap busts into the bath until her facial features were no longer discernable. Sidonie Smith (2002) writes:

> In all these installations…the artist's body disappears, only to reemerge as bodily processes worked through the psychic mechanisms of desire and abjection. [...] She turns the surfaces and the insides of her body, her unconscious, her dreams, her hungers, her bodily movements, into the tools and the media of her works of art. (p. 151)

The hidden performances in "Gnaw" and "Lick and Lather" co-mingle with those hidden performances of the social and body politic. Says the artist of her work:

> Conceptually it seemed so logical. Chocolate tends to embody desire for the viewer, but lard is the result of succumbing to that desire. When [I] decided to spit out the masticated material, people read it as an overt commentary on beauty, self-worth and the female psyche. *Gnaw* became an illustration for eating disorders, which was the topic of the work and not the content. That was a shock to me. I wasn't naive, but I was thinking about bulimia much more as a metaphor for a culture that was consuming and spitting itself out faster and faster.[28]

However the work is received and interpreted, Antoni's performative gestures shift the "the terms of embodiment and its representation away from the primacy of vision as a model for comprehending the female body to other sensual registers—volume, tactility, taste, and smell—productively mining different ways to speak the corporeal (Smith, 2002, p. 156). Bringing the viewer into the work through bodied processes that are basic to all our lives, Antoni's body art performs a curriculum of inter-embodiment and intimacy.

Focusing on interpretation as an exchange or negotiation, Amelia Jones and Andrew Stephenson (1999) suggest that meaning making itself is performative. They write:

> [A]rtistic meaning can be understood as enacted through interpretive engagements that are themselves performative in their intersubjectivity. Thus, the artwork is no longer viewed as a static object with a single, prescribed signification that is communicated unproblematically and without default from the maker to an alert, knowledgeable, universalized viewer. Instead...the artist...and subsequent viewers/interpreters are caught up within the complex and fraught operations of representation—entangled in intersubjective spaces of desire, projection, and identification. (p. 1)

The performing body in this sense is a process that is fragile, partial, and precarious. Educational theorist David Jardine (2003) echoes this view when he writes: "Interpretation does not begin with me. It only begins when something happens to me in my reading of a text, when something strikes me, tears me open, "wounds" me and leaves me vulnerable and open to the world, like the sensitivities of open flesh" (p. 59). Licked, chewed, and spit up the body as meaning enacts otherness as deeply embedded in every subject. In her writings on pheneomenology and autobiography, Madeeline Grumet (1988) suggests that "the gaps, the contradictions, the leaks and explosions in the text are invitations" (p. 67) to interpretation. Such acts of interpretation, however, are not isolated moments of self-realization, but formed between bodies and subjectivities.

Likewise Nancy (2000) contends that "being itself is given to us as meaning. Being does not have meaning, but being itself, the phenomenon of being, is meaning (p. 2). Such claims direct our attention away from meaning as a thing or as belonging to something or somebody. In Nancy's views, meaning is the undoing of meaning itself. Meaning, he writes, is "where presence comes apart" (p. 2). Likewise meaning is shared. Meaning exists only in the circulation of meanings "through a weblike structure always already plural even as it is shared and shared out among singular bodies" (Perpich, 2005, p. 77). It is important to note that for Nancy circulation is rhizomatic—it goes in all directions at once "from place to place, and from moment to moment, without any progression or linear path, bit by bit and case by case, essentially accidentally, it is singular and plural in its very principle. It does not have a final fulfillment any more than it has a point of origin" (Nancy, 2000, pp. 4–5).

Body art as a metaphor for re-conceptualizing curriculum displaces the idea of curriculum as a thing with the image of curriculum as inter-embodiment, a process that is constantly being negotiated in everyday life. Moreover, body art responds to the difficulties and tensions of a living curriculum that is intimate and vulnerable posing the question: In the curricular texts of everyday life what does it mean to live in relation to other bodies? This reverberates with David Smith's (2003) words that "between the formal texts of life is another kind of life, the life that mediates, that announces, repudiates, or cajoles curriculum formalities" (p. 46). What seeps between, touches bodies, and creates moments of exposure, is a sense of dwelling, living, and being-with.

Incarnate

"Mortar and Pestle" (1999) is a color photograph of Antoni's tongue thrust into the eyeball of her husband. Says the artist of this work: "I wanted to know the taste of his vision."[29] Experience, according to Merleau-Ponty (1968), "is always embodied, corporeally constituted, located in and as the subject's incarnation" (Grosz, 1994, p. 95). Eliciting a tactile and textured response, Antoni's intimate yet uncanny image materializes the notion that it is through proximity and touch that knowledge is produced. "To begin to make sense of something is to come into contact with it, to touch it—literally—and thereby to produce a body" (Perpich, 2005, p. 85). Antoni says of her actions: "There's a kind of discovery that happens when you push your body to the edge."[30] Antoni's works are not destructive or violent, but rather show a wish to seek out the very essence of things, while analyzing along the way the manner in which we perceive and come to know them. On first glance the photograph is unsettling and perhaps slightly monstrous as we witness in close frame a tongue reach out and lick an eyeball. However, on closer inspection the work seems to encourage us to dig for those more intimate questions that are often buried deep in our subconscious. A more familiar image might have been the same lips (without protruding tongue) touching, perhaps in a kiss, a closed eyelid. And yet, this possible image of familiarity and closeness is not unlike the one offered by Antoni. The difference is that in "Mortar and Pestle" the intimate act simultaneously troubles the very notion of closeness, rupturing the unknown while raising complex associations of sexuality and desire. What might initially provoke a humorous reaction gives way to strength and vulnerability, a private act rendered public, and of the constant presence of desire and its ceremonial or ritual possibilities.

Antoni's choice of media, photography, emphasizes intercorporeality. "The photograph—as screen—is a site of subjectification where self and other intertwine in an exchange of a mobile (performative) rather than static process of meaning making" (Jones, 2002, p. 84). Likening the photograph to "skin" Jones (2002) argues that photography "is not just a simulacral, two-dimensional surface but a fleshlike screen, one that presupposes the depth and materiality of the body" (p. 85). Sara Ahmed and Jackie Stacey (2001) suggest that skin is the site of meaning. Skin is felt, lived, read, written, narrated, seen, touched, managed, worked, cut, remembered, produced, and known. It embodies traces of illness, surgery, shame, and violation. Jay Prosser (2001) offers that "skin is the body's memory of our lives" (p. 52). Physically we recall the events that lead to particular scars (I have a cesarean scar which reminds me daily of the gift of my daughter); the performances and constructions of self (through tattooing and other forms of body modification); and metaphorically as a signifying practice (of race and gender to name a few).

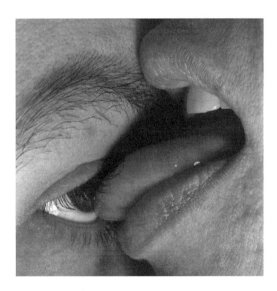

Janine Antoni, *Mortar and Pestle*, 1999. C-print, photographic assistance, David Allison, 48 X 48 inches (121.9 X 121.9 cm). Courtesy of the artist and Luhring Augustine, New York.

Likewise, skin is often viewed as the border between the inside of the body and the outside. It marks a passage and as such takes on the significance of a container or protective agent. Yet, skin also leaks. It seeps and flows attesting to the undecidability of bodies, complicating the processes through which bodies and skins are lived and imagined in relation to others. Skin is not simply surface matter but involves a process of materialization (Butler, 1993). In that sense, skin registers how we touch and are touched by other bodies. "The skin provides a way of thinking about how the boundary between bodies is formed not only through being traversed, or called into question, but the affecting of one by an other" (Ahmed, 2000, p. 45). In this sense skins/bodies do not precede tactile encounters, rather skins/bodies are produced and differentiated in and through such encounters.

In her photograph "2038" and a subsequent installation of cow hides, Antoni develops this corporeal aesthetic. In the exhibition which featured "2038" at the Wanås Foundation in Sweden, stretched from wall to wall and juxtaposed with the photograph of a cow suckling breast, was a raw cowhide. "Bridle" (2000) resembled a drying skin at a tannery, until you get closer to the hide and notice that parts of it have been removed and formed into a leather backpack which is attached to the hide. If a body was to wear the backpack it would also be draped in the entire hide. In other spaces throughout the gallery different hides were stretched and cut out revealing a pair of attached shoes and gloves. The surprising presence of rawhides in the gallery reminds us that we often sacrifice those very beings upon which we rely so heavily, highlighting the delicate balance inherent to a society based upon consumerism. Yet, unencumbered by moralizing Antoni's installation performs images of temporality, delicacy, thoughtfulness, and absurdity, reminding us of the limitations of our own corporeality. The works arouse strong, strange, shivery, pleasurable, and deep memories of tact, smell, and taste.

These synaesthetic receptions interface with the idea of the incarnate body. Antoni's body in repose in the tub points at religious imagery, most notably representations of the Madonna and child. The nurturing milk-giving teat signifies sustenance, pleasure, and anxiety. Eleanor Heartney (2003) has linked Antoni's work to that of the Catholic imagination, demonstrating that Antoni's work embraces such themes as birth, motherhood, and transformation in reference to Catholic doctrines such as the Incarnation, Immaculate Conception, and the Transubstantiation of the Eucharist. For example, in a photograph titled "Momme" (1995) we are confronted with a woman in a white dress sitting on a sofa. Looking more closely we realize that there is another figure/body hidden beneath the dress, nuzzled around the woman's waist. Heartney (2003) likens this image to that of the Annunciation, as the woman, who is in fact the artist's mother, sits bathed in light. On a table nearby is a framed photograph of Antoni's grandmother, "completing the matrilineal line represented in the traditional Annunciation story by Mary and her mother, Anne" (p. 16). In another image, "Coddle" (1998), the artist poses as the Virgin holding not the infant Christ, but her own leg. These disconcerting images explore the meaning of mother love and the vulnerable link between mother and child. So too, both deal with the idea of incarnation, "bringing it back into the human realm, where we are asked to consider how each of us is, like Christ, a spirit made flesh" (Heartney, 2003, p. 16). Incarnate refers to enfleshment and the material manifestation of a body. Heartney (2003) reminds us that Antoni's work challenges the traditional hierarchy of the senses. While Western culture privileges vision Antoni's explorations involve the female-associated senses taste, touch, and smell (Classen, 1998). Likewise her focus on the bond between mother and child emphasizes the first touching which is the connection to the mother's womb. Luce Irigaray (1993) extending Merleau-Ponty's thesis of *Flesh* maintains that tactile sensations begin in the womb, a space of darkness and moisture, filled with a rhythmic contiguous tie to another (the mother). Even the passage into light is marked by touch (the birth canal). Touch is the first sense of knowing. While the maternal-child touch she argues is the primary sense, the "two lips," both from above and below, represent the way in which women's sexed subjectivity is always defined through touch. Thus, touch is fundamentally a sense through which beings come to know their lived experience with the world. Irigaray (1993) suggests that instead of the body as the threshold of experience, mucous becomes a more apt metaphor. Mucous, "which always marks the passage from inside to outside, which accompanies, and 'lubricates' the mutual touching of the body's parts and regions," returns experience to the primacy of touch (Grosz, 1999, p. 160). Irigaray (1993) argues: "the tangible is, and remains, primary in its opening. Its touching on, of, and by means of the other. The dereliction of its ever touching this first touching" (p. 162).

Mucous is neither subject nor object but the inter-determinancy between them, unmediated by external sensibilities (Grosz, 1999). Mucous is a more visceral, pulsating and active body knowing. The mucous can also be understood on the level of maternal-fetal bond where blood courses through and is shared by both bodies. For Irigaray, feminine morphology is never complete: "The birth that is never accomplished, the body never created one and for all, the form never definitively completed" (1985, p. 217). "2038" offers the mother as matter, the female body as "with." Mucous escapes control. It cannot be grasped in its fluidity, or contained. As a lubricant it slips and seeps investing touch with more of a caress than a grasp. It is precisely the fluid embodiment of touch that threatens boundaries, sustains excess, dislocating system and order. Antoni's performing body brings forth an intimate attention to the particular and the sensual—to the everyday bodied activities in a living curriculum (Grumet, 1988).

Intimacy in Living Curriculum

Curriculum in schools often comes with a degree of certainty and familiarity. This is a curriculum premised on standards, rationales, and ordered lesson plans. Instead I want to nurture for my students a curriculum that is open, responsive, and sensitive. I desire a living curriculum that is made up of inter-subjectivities, experiences, and lives. Such a curriculum is intuitive, sensuous, tactile, and felt. Curriculum, in this manner, becomes a way of being—a way of being-with. And yet, it is precisely the intimacy of being-with that troubles me. I am wary of using language that reifies female characteristics—of drawing connections between women and nurturing (see Grumet, 1988). So too I am cautious of universal forms of intimacy, for instance, sharing, that permeate the curriculum.

Lately, I've been trying to teach my 18-month-old daughter about the intimacies of sharing. Hovering over the train table at the public library she often snatches a toy car from unsuspecting toddler hands. "Share" I tell her, as I hand the toy back to the red-faced child. At home she stuffs goldfish crackers into my mouth and looks willfully at me. I'm sharing, mommy.

It is precisely this concept of sharing, put into larger practices, such as curriculum, that fails to account for the complexities of living as bodies/selves intertwined with other bodies/selves. Curriculum often "shares" food from various regions in the world; "shares" aspects of geographical and historical disparity; and "shares" student opinions and ideas in the context of classroom conversation. When sharing takes place by bringing difference into the center and places it side by side, it reduces difference to the same and the common. Megan Boler (2004) tells us that dialogue can be a form of violence against the other. When educators assume that particular forms of sharing-curricula create spaces where all students can "speak," they fail to recognize the social imbalances that privilege some voices while muting others. Complexifying both speech and silence, Boler examines what constitutes a curriculum based on freedom of expression and democratic dialogue. This process involves rupturing and dislocating the boundaries that set bodies apart. Reconceptualizing the intimacies of sharing requires educators to conceive of bodies and knowledges through touch.

To touch the other, to come into contact with her/him, dislocates the moment of consuming her/him into categories of the same. It is to disrupt "a logic that attempts to fix the other, confer an identity on her, an identity that render her body either meaningful or worthless. To touch the other, in both a tangible and intangible sense, is to gain access to her [sic] specificity, to be exposed to it, to be affected by it and to respond to it, but not to subsume it or annihilate it" (Sorrial, 2004, pp. 220–221).

The implications of such a way of thinking are bound up with understanding the relations between identities rather than in terms of describing identities, intensions, or acts of individuals or groups. The possibility, or impossibility, of this curriculum invites us to touch the other not through particularities that are descriptions of a body, but as bodied encounters. Sharing does not presume difference to be something I can list, or belong to a particular body.

"2038" alters our perception of mother and nurture through the idea of "m/Other"—the ambiguous interplay between intimacy and Otherness. As opposed to trying to know the other, to bring the other body into the same, the m/Other relationship is an understanding premised on difference. For instance, Nancy opens up the possibility of thinking about sharing and intimacy "as the fundamental 'being-with' of those singularities, and not as a collection of individual subjects who bind themselves together on the basis of a shared identity" (James, 2006, p. 177). Sara Ahmed claims: "Particularity then does not belong to an other, but names the meetings and encounters which produce or flesh out other, and hence differentiate others from other others" (Ahmed, 2002, p. 561). Re-thinking curriculum through the vulnerability of intimacy enables us to reflect on how differences are produced in the moment of bodied encounters as opposed to differences being contained within a particular body. Likewise, when curriculum ceases to be a thing, "it becomes a verb, an action, a social practice, a private meaning, and a public hope" (Pinar et al. 1995 p. 845).

The complex material, textual, and spatial readings of Antoni's body art opens up maternity to an aesthetics that resonates at the in-between of corporeality, materiality, and difference. At the heart of body art and the questions it poses for curriculum is that knowledge is corporeal; it is produced in and through touch. In highly complex and haunting ways Antoni's performative gestures bring together body/mind, matter/form through processes of multisensory inter-embodiment arguing for the potential to articulate difference differently. By its exposure to intimacy and unity, Antoni's goal, like a curriculum premised on being-with, is not to leave spectators with a product, a final object, but to enable them to experience a collision, a bursting into being, that reverberates beyond its disappearance. Maybe I'd have better luck at the train table if I instructed my daughter to "be-with," m/Othering her/my own becoming.

Embodying Exile: Performing the "Curricular Body"

Barbara Bickel

Multiple Rhythms: An Introduction

This chapter is a multidimensional performance montage that incorporates and embodies intertexts, subtexts, and visual texts. It utilizes both image and text in an effort to extend the rhythm of live(d) curricula of the cultural body with living inquiry. It includes excerpts from field notes, a journey that I spoke aloud as I filmed myself in trance, still video images[31] of a performance ritual, and the voices of artists, theorists and educators in conversation with academic writing.

Trance and ritual are significant in my practice as an artist/researcher/teacher. Through trance I enter a rich and provocative waking dream state that allows me to step outside of my "normal" self, opening up new possibilities. Ritual is the structure that I create, explore, learn, and teach within. The texts of this essay are intertwined and relational echoing the experience of performing ritual as one moves in and out of trance. As each page is encountered, the texts can be read as linear and/or non-linear. I have found that the "curricular body" is not easily accessed or read when perceived solely through a rational, controlling mind within linear space. Each page of this chapter reflects simultaneously the multiple curriculum texts of this inquiry.

Writing the Living Inquiry: Together[32]

I am overwhelmed as I try to piece together the many layers of art, performance ritual, trance, video, text, and theory in connection with the cultural body, curriculum, spirituality, and education. I am forced to write. "[I]n working with words, you have to remain alert to the double empowering and enslaving potential of language" (Minh-ha, 2005, p. 152). I can't write in integrity alone with words. "[I]t is necessary to show the mechanisms of language, the way it functions and operates in the creative process" (p. 152). I write dialectically.

The creative space of the arational[33] (Bickel, 2004) guides me into relationship with my other. Luce Irigaray (2004) calls this "double willing":

> I wonder how to sustain a relationship between us, between two made from body and language, between two intentions participating in an incarnate relationship which is actualized by flesh and words. In this double willing, I and you remain always both active and passive, perceiving and experiencing, awake and welcoming. In us, sensible nature and the spirit become in-stance within the singularity and evolution through the risk of an exchange with who is irreducible to oneself. (p. 22)

How can Irigaray's words seduce me and silence me simultaneously? I'm at once attracted to her relational aesthetic and intimidated by her linguistic sophistication. But I must risk the exchange, and allow the dialectic rhythm to begin. "Rhythm should then be taken in the larger sense of the term, in its aesthetic, social and spiritual dimension" (Minh-ha, 2005, p. 152).

In the aesthetic rhythmic process of writing and re/searching my inquiry has shifted its orientation. In response to my dilemma with words I move beyond rationality and reasoning and return to living inquiry in the moment, to the images and the trance text that together perform each page. I have worked with trance for the past eight years and experience trance as a performative ritual that takes place within an altered state of consciousness. I encounter it as an active form of meditation that is not focused on the concept of stilling the mind, which predominates in most traditional Eastern meditation (Suzuki, 1975). Rather, the active mediation/performance of trance is a place of expanding the mind's imaginary; where "[w]e perform our becoming, and become our performing" (Driver, 1997, p. 114). Within the interstitial space of trance the mind can imagine and hence practice performing the body outside of limiting and "regulatory norms" (Butler, 1999, p. 234). Jean Houston (1987) in her work within sacred psychology teaches trance as an inquiry method of "gaining...knowledge from...states of consciousness that are deeper than your ordinary state...that can avail you of more subtle and comprehensive knowledge" (p. 173).

Trance is the embodiment of a female sentence for me. Within my trances I often meet the other, my double, my ally, my guide. One I can fly with. I offer this rhythmic female sentence in the form of a trance later in this chapter unfettered by punctuation and grammar, flowing from page to page. The trance—I fantasize, lives and expresses the theory that French feminists Helene Cixous and Irigarary embody in their writing. As I read their text I feel that I am reading what has come from my own unencumbered state of trance, from my own performing body in ritual. I let go with Cixous (1997)

> She doesn't "speak," she throws her trembling body forward; she lets go of herself, she flies; all of her passes into her voice, and it's with her body that she vitally supports the "logic" of her speech. Her flesh speaks true. She lays herself bare. In fact, she physically materializes what she is thinking; she signifies it with her body. (p. 351)

My body, which is never static and never a "subject" alone, propels me to extend my writing with images, words, and sentences that refuse restriction and confinement.

The body has multiple locations and representations, the objective body, the subjective body, and the cultural body. I situate the performing body within the cultural body. The cultural body is the body in communion or relation. To isolate the performing body into the subjective or objective realm alone is to send it into exile.

Reflecting on Living Inquiry

The cultural body inhabits, while simultaneously constructing, curricular space. The body requires its own multidimensional "live(d) curricula" (Aoki, 2003, p. 2) encounters to counter/act the tendency to limit it to simplistic abstract, linguistic, conceptual and political binaries, or moralities. To explore this live(d) curricula I draw from an intensive three-week graduate seminar on living inquiry, where I bodily explore the themes of place/space, time, language and self/other (Meyer, 2005). Living inquiry as expressed by Karen Meyer (2005) is,

> [N]ot a philosophy of life, a methodology to be followed, or an analytical tool…it is simply an inquiry into how to live with the quality of awareness that sees newness, truth, and beauty in daily life. (p. 11)

Each day during the course, through video, I document performative flashes of my life. Within this individual live(d) curricula I struggle to place myself as an artist/researcher/teacher within the academe and the world. Through the engagement of my body with the camera, digital film editing, and performance ritual, the moments and gestures of live(d) inquiry become curricular places of learning.

The performance ritual of my lived curricula of the body takes place on the last day of a graduate class within the education building on the university campus. I perform it for my professor and fellow graduate students. This is the first time all of the collected pieces of the living inquiry come together. I have not practiced this. This performance ritual invokes an altered live(d) curricular space, disrupting hegemonic classroom curriculum and space.

As my colleagues/witnesses enter the room their senses are engaged/confounded with the chaos of technology, as computers, projectors, and video cameras are set up and tested by volunteer technicians. Extension cords snake across the floor, requiring careful maneuvering of their bodies as they move through the space. I invite a multidimensional act of witnessing from my colleagues, as my white clad body becomes the screen upon which the edited video material is projected. The presence of my physical body interacting with the technology of multiple digital residual images of the body and places expands the curricular element of this living inquiry. I read aloud as I write words on the floor, the multiple video soundtracks overlap and compete with my spoken voice. The authority of the moving/performing body is the focus in the center of the room.

Performance Ritual Environment

Two LCD projectors and two computers are on either side of the room facing each other. The performance ritual is taking place in the center of the classroom on the floor. Videos project onto either end of the room, on one side onto the chalkboard and wall, and on the other, onto the curtains and wall. Tables and chairs line the outside circle of the room. My colleagues enter the room and sit on tabletops or on chairs. Two classmates film the performance ritual from different locations in the room. Another video camera is mounted on the ceiling. A classmate holds a damp cloth and will pass it to me in the performance ritual.

The Performance Ritual Script

I invite the class to witness the performance ritual with diffused attention and instruct that they can move around the outside of the circle as they witness/attend to the performance ritual. I read the following quote:

> There is so much to attend to that one must look with diffused attention so that meanings on many levels, some clear and conscious, some not, may be absorbed. (Beittel, 1989, p. 17)

I enter the center of the space and kneel down upon the white t-shirt that reads "Art is Vital." One of the video projectors projects onto the front of my body, the other onto the back. These projections include images of hands typing at a computer, the artist reading in the forest, the artist engaged in a performance ritual in a gallery, and the artist drawing. I reach to the floor, pick up the blue marker and write three quotes. I read these three quotes. My spoken voice joins the two sound tracks that are playing on the videos. I spin around on my knees clockwise as I write additional texts in a spiral around my body. The spiral moves closer and closer to me as I write. The quotes are from texts I read during the course.

I complete the writing and move into a sitting meditation for about four minutes while the two videos continue to play and project onto the front of my body and onto the back. These images constitute my daily living inquiry: drawing, ripping notes, in conversation with others, or facilitating a presention at an artist talk. Before the videos end I sit up on my knees and a classmate passes me a damp cloth. I press the cloth to my face before I retrace my movements of spinning counter clockwise on my knees, erasing the written text on the floor with the damp cloth as I spin in reverse. I sit upright upon completion and non-verbally acknowledge the class for attending/witnessing and pass out Kenneth Beittel quotes from a pottery bowl. I listen to responses from the class and we immerse ourselves in a rich dialogue.

Live(d) Curricula: A Spiritual Way

In the theoretical exploration below I draw from a variety of sources whose art and theory integrates the live(d) spiritual, cultural, and curricular body: contemporary women performing artists; curriculum theorists (Pinar, 2004); feminists (Cixous, 1976: Irigaray, 2004; Minh-ha, 2005) and, art educators (Beittel, 1979; Springgay, 2003). I weave together texts from these artists, theorists, and educators to create a bridge for the exiled curricular body to travel across.

As a spiritual feminist my understanding of culture is embedded in historical and contemporary cultural traditions and practices of religion and spirituality. Likewise as a curriculum scholar I find myself most at home amidst curriculum as aesthetic, phenomenological, gendered, and theological texts (Pinar et al., 1995). The spiritual-political dimensions that William Pinar (1975) wrote of in his early writings on *currere* and its emancipatory agenda has called for and continues to call for "[t]he study of identity [that] enables us to portray how the politics we had thought were located "out there," in society, are lived through "in here," in our bodies, our minds, our everyday speech and conduct" (Pinar, 2004, p. 30). Similarly, Dwayne Huebner (1999) reminds us that our ability to be open to the evolution of spirit in society is the "fissure" that has the potential to transform our institutions and society. He states that:

> The condition for experiencing the spiritual is openness and receptivity. This experience requires acknowledging one's fundamental vulnerability and accepting that one can be overpowered and transformed. This openness and receptivity is a fissure, a "fault" in our knowledge and current forms of life. (p. 345)

Openness and vulnerability are qualities that I strive for in my practice as an artist/researcher/teacher. My art practice is one of learning through exposing my self/body as part of an "aesthetic and spiritual process." I am further encouraged to deconstruct notions of power through my study of American visual and performance artist Hannah Wilke. Feminist art writer Joanna Frueh (1989) wrote exquisitely of Wilke's art:

> Wilke believes in physical, psychic, and emotional self-exposure as aesthetic and spiritual process. [Her] performances are unfoldings, undressings of the soul. Wilke's movements are excruciatingly slow, heightened erotic tension, maximizing the strength and grace needed to "dance" her way through the emotional ambiguity of each piece, all of which exorcise, but not to oblivion, the agonies of being a victim, as a woman, as a lover, as a consciously sensual body. Wilke's movements may seem rehearsed, deliberate, ritualistic, but they are spontaneous. Expressionist gestures impelling and alive in a naked woman. Through gesture, Wilke uses her body as a literally and figuratively moving site of revelation. (pp. 17–18)

Wilke's art continued to evolve over the years through performance and "undressing of the soul" until her death through cancer. The deterioration of her body was as much a locus of inspiration and inquiry as was her beautiful, youthful, and healthy body. The impact of her work on my art has been the permission to take the creative risk of being seen and vulnerable without shame.

Through a spiritual, feminist, arts and body-based practice one allows oneself to be overpowered and in that sense transformed and empowered. My living inquiry performance ritual may have seemed rehearsed, but similar to Wilke's performances, it was simultaneously revelatory and ambiguous. Wilke wrote in an exhibition catalogue of the significance for women artists, "to insist on the feelings of flesh, its inspiration, its advice, its warning, its mystery for the survival and regeneration of the universe" (cited in Frueh, 1989, p. 141).

A more recent influence on my art practice and knowing is the provocative and emotionally charged work of indigenous Canadian installation and performance artist Rebecca Belmore. She views performance art as being a medium that crosses traditional and modern elements—"a medium both indigenous and international" (Bailey and Watson, 2005, p. 8). Her bodily presence in her performances carries a powerfully charged energetic, often magnified body made present through physical exertion. Her "work calls forth a sense of loss for something absent [without nostalgia], while creating an energy of resistance" (Bailey and Watson, 2005, p. 8). In an interview, Belmore speaks of her use of the arational domain and altered states as,

> [T]he state of dreaming and what our minds are capable of…when we are not stopping ourselves…I like the idea of seeing "sleeping" as a site of where there is tremendous possibility…Perhaps that is where I would like my performances to exist. I'm fully aware of what I am doing, but at some point I am dreaming. Maybe. (as cited in Bailey and Watson, 2005, p. 25)

Both of these artists challenge the notion of docile and silenced female bodies regulated within a rationalistic, chaos-avoidant consciousness. My own use of trance and art ritual processes equally subverts while opening new possibilities. Through performing vulnerable and powerful gestures with their bodies they call us to question and resist what we are told is "truth," the "truth" that stops us from being fully aware and present in our lives.

The Cultural Body as Sacred: Embodying a Female "Sentence"

My years of working with the body as an artist, both representationally and performatively, has led me to understand and acknowledge the body as sacred. By sacred I mean honoring, receiving, and holding reverence for the spirit of mystery. Ritual theorist Ronald Grimes (1995) clarifies that: "Sacred" is the name we give to the deepest forms of receptivity in our experience" (p. 69). Elizabeth Grosz (1994) maintains: "If bodies are objects [subjects] or things, they are like no others, for they are the centers of perspective, insight, reflection, desire, agency" (p. xi). I would add sacredness to her insights on the body. We are intimately connected to our body and at the same time experience it anew each day. Likewise, sacredness allows the body "to extend the frameworks which attempt to contain them, to seep beyond their domains of control" (Grosz, 1994, p. xi).

The premise of my art practice is that humans have evolved into a place of being in exile from their own bodies, and in that, exiled from a body-based knowledge. I have long struggled for a voice from a body-based knowledge as a female and an artist in this world. I am dedicated to visually reading, writing, and ultimately embodying a female "sentence." This sentence is articulated with, in, and through the body. The intention behind the art I create is to illuminate the body as a sacred source of text and knowing. As well, I am interested in the body as a battleground, and as a site for re-imagining what it means to be a woman. Irigaray (1991) articulates these connections when she writes, "It is important for us to guard and keep our bodies and at the same time make them emerge from silence and subjugation" (p. 43). My deepening challenge is to confront the traditional "sentence" structure that has held the feminine body in exile from itself, rendering Her silent.

Shana Fried (2003) in writing on the work of poets Adrienne Rich and D.H. Lawrence suggests that

> [F]ilm provided a strategic move for subverting language and the limits placed on it...Limits on gender and sexuality as constructed in language were undoubtedly challenged, deconstructed and redefined in each of their writing. (p. 151)

Digital film allows me to deconstruct and redefine the performing body and thereby utter a new sentence, one filled with resistance, agency, and the body. A significant portion of my living inquiry is the act of filming and editing the digital video of the performance ritual. In the spirit of subversion, the digital filming and editing of the performing body is also a catalyst for retranslations that extend the voice of the body, generating new translations.

In an effort to address the confines of language that I continue to experience as a female artist/researcher/teacher in traditional academic writing, I turn to my field notes that reflect my ongoing battle with language and the embodied sentence.

Notes on the porch in the morning sun: It is not often enough that I have space for this in the morning. I love the luxury—so much of life is a luxury. I work hard—I get caught up in the anxiety and I keep moving—doing my best to let go of the anxiety as I move on. But my body does hold the memory of the places/spaces I have been in, and it makes the final command to stop and empty.

Language Is the Surface Structure

Language is our expression of our alienation between each other
Language is so inadequate—How do we express?
Language comes to us as it disconnects and distances.

And so I write for these language field notes. I am completely uninspired to do anything creative around language. Maybe I will rip up words. Just spend the time ripping up words. That is what my artist does. That is what is most appropriate. "Be skeptical of all 'texts' (verbal expressions); they are distortion of experience and 'require a depth hermeneutic'" (Beittel, 1980, p. 50).

Living inquiry is one of the six renderings[34] found in the practice of a/r/tography (Irwin and de Cosson, 2004; Springgay, Irwin, and Kind, 2005). Stephanie Springgay (2004) describes "renderings a[s] performative gestures of meaning making" (p. 43) that "allow for the complexity of meaning; they un/ravel in un/certainty and ambiguity" (p. 42). At the same time they offer locations of pause for reflection or assessment while engaged in the inquiry. A/r/tography engages the roles of the artist/researcher/teacher in a self-reflexive inquiry that is led by the making of art and writing. The back slashes between the letters signify the interrelationality of the three identities. Springgay (2004) writes that the lived a/r/tographic sensibility is a "life open to inquiry that is aesthetic and embodied" (p. 43) where art is related to "constitutive, intercorporeal encounters that produce and transform knowledges as a process of exchange" (pp. 117–118). A/r/tography offers a location for me to challenge the limiting classical and modernist aesthetics of form, order, and beauty and to engage an art aesthetic that is in relationship with self and others—a practice that follows the art process and is curious about the space between, around and inside the: mind/body, rational/arational, secular/spiritual, writing/art, and ritual/education. A/r/tography as ritual draws the practices of the artist/researcher/teacher into the sacred frame of ritual. Reverence and respect, along with an attunement to rhythm, are significant features of ritual.

> The term [ritual] usually refers to a coded social performance such as a ceremonial practice established by tradition or a religious service. ...But that's only one dimension of the ritual. Making a video, for example, is to engage in ritual—both the rituals of new technologies and those of creating and structuring images. ...In other words, rituals serve as a "frame" whose stabilizing effect, experienced through repetition in cycles and rhythmic recurrences, allows us to see things with a different intensity and...to perceive the ordinary in an extra-ordinary way. (Minh-ha, 2005, p. 135)

A/r/tography as ritual makes visible and is responsive to the arational and aesthetic relationships between the body, art, space/place, language, time, self/other, ritual, and education. Research supports the significance of ritual as a site of learning and transformation (Driver, 1997; Shorter, 1987; Zigler, 1999). I locate my a/r/tographic practice as ritual within "a sacred, existential epistemology [which] places us [as artists, researchers, teachers] in a noncompetitive, nonhierarchical relationship to the earth, to nature, and to the larger world" (Bateson, 1972, p. 335). This sacred epistemology stresses the values of empowerment, shared governance, care, solidarity, love, community, covenant, morally involved observers, and civic transformation (Denzin & Lincoln, 2005).

Parker Palmer (1983) in his book on education as a spiritual journey clarifies how:

> Objectivism tells the world what it is rather than listen to what it says about itself. Subjectivism is the decision to listen to no one except ourselves. But truth [sacred epistemology] requires listening ... to each other, responding to what we hear, acknowledging and recreating the bonds of the community. (p. 67).

 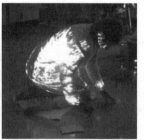 

Ritual is the sacred container that holds and supports the individual and the community in the inquiry/excavation processes of self and Other, creating a stabilizing ground for risk-taking, challenges, and new knowledge to emerge within.

Embodying Exile: Together

I wonder how to sustain a relationship between us, between two made from body and language, between two intentions participating in an incarnate relationship which is actualized by flesh and words.

(Irigaray, 2004, p. 22)

The education environment created in the living inquiry curriculum is based on an invitation to expand notions of being, knowing, and doing. Inviting a practice of sacred awareness into learning environments is the "sacred, existential epistemology" that Denzin and Lincoln encourage to assist in the formation of live(d) curricula and community. Resistance and fear often accompany deep inquiry into self and Other. The presence and embodiment of the witness in the performer/teacher as well as in the co-learners in the community is essential to moving beyond barriers of resistance and fear.

The discussion that took place after the performance ritual is charged with an intensity that ruptures the link between the experience of witnessing and performing. As the performer/teacher, a surge of energy took over my voice and body as I spoke aloud and spun my body on the floor. This energy source I recognize as not solely my own but connected to and magnified by those witnessing the event. The responses from the witnesses below offer insight into the exchange that took place during the performance ritual.

I did not realize how forceful it was seeing images on your body. That was incredible—pow—very strong. ...I was not prepared for that.

In my travels and in my interest in the sacred and place I am aware it isn't just a place. Sometimes it is something we bear witness to. It isn't tangible but it touches us in that same way and I felt that in my body. It touched me.

I found myself really frustrated that you had the two beautiful images and you were blocking the pictures, but then I realized you were the picture. It was coming off of you and I could see what I was supposed to see there. It was actually on you. I had to journey to that realization.

Hearing the multiple sound tracks with your voice magnified the experience of watching.

In performing a curricular body within a sacred aesthetic context, the struggle between flesh and words is both exciting and troubling. Analogous with the live performance ritual in the classroom, I transform the space/pages in this essay to accommodate the rhythmic intertextual dynamics of this inquiry that embodies the longing for an altar/ed engagement with the Other. The "risk of exchange" (Irigaray, 2004, p. 22) the performing body/text enters between self and Other is a "moving site of revelation" (Frueh 1989, pp. 17–18). The curricular body, in a spiritual context, is not a self-centered body. It is a relational transforming body.

I utilize the state of trance and performance ritual to subvert regulatory norms in search of live(d) curricula that is multi-modal. Upon reflection, I acknowledge that this approach sets up a tension. The performance ritual is inevitably vulnerable and self-exposing, flying on the edge of chaos, yet ritually contained. In throwing my body between the projectors and projected surfaces, I physically interrupt the clear reading of the data. I make impossible a single reading of the experience. How can this be embodied curriculum?

Performing ritual as an educator fosters a relational knowing that can lead to forming a community of learners able to locate knowledge inside rather than outside of themselves. As Pinar promotes, and as Huebner suggests, educators and students are thus willing to enter the fissure or "fault'" in current knowledge systems to transform our institutions and society. Through performance ritual "curricular places of possibility, absence, and disruption [are] realized" (Fels, 2003, p. 173). Live(d) curricula requires that we be willing as artists/researchers/teachers to enter the multiple and often exiled realms of time, place/space, language, self/other through the lived curricular space of our bodies. Reframing the pedagogical risks of entering and exploring these domains is essential to contributing to a (re)newed vision of live(d) curricula in our art, research and teaching practices of today. In what follows I offer my embodied female sentence, an utterance of live(d) curricula.

Living Inquiry Trance

3 bell rings
I find myself at the top of a path with stairs below me looking down into the gully at the trees I walk down the stairs that lead to the ocean feeling my feet and the balance of each step as I go down breath wandering down the steps walking under a tree a fallen tree coming down to the flat area I can hear the waves of the ocean as I get closer I come out to the clearing and stand up on a log and look out deep breath I walk across the rocks with my bare feet feeling the stones I'm walking into the water till my feet are touching sand deep breath I am at about my waist in the water I see some seals that are not far in front of me to the left watching me deep breath I dive into the water swimming out my legs thrusting me forward my arms pulling me forward swimming swimming the seals are motioning me to follow them I follow the seals as they swim and turn and go up and down I follow their each movement deep breath its great being able to stay under as long as they do not needing to come up for breath just swimming under the water free then I pop my head out and I look around me the sky is beautiful a fuchsia pink the shore is way in the distance I rise myself out of the water straight up and I'm now swimming in the air moving towards that fuchsia sky I say farewell to the seals who are watching me and I head towards the mountains propelling quickly through the sky there's a cave that I'm heading towards that's in the mountainside deep breath I keep propelling myself towards that cave it gets closer and closer the circle gets larger its the entrance I'm inside the cave there're candles set up as mine are in my home there's a woman sitting in the midst of the candles I'm standing at the entrance watching her she's meditating she knows I'm there she allows me to come in I come in and as I sit back to back with her inside the circle of candles I light the candles that are on my side of the circle each flame igniting each wick we sit back to back with the circle of flames around us I can feel her open clear mind and the vastness of it we just sit together in this vast space inside this cave inside this space there's some kind of root connection where we are sitting to deep down into the mountain deep breath she has not moved through my whole time of being here she's solid I'd like to stay but I know I need to head back I leave part of my self here I slide myself up straight up in the air so as not to disturb her or the candles I silently say farewell to her in this space and I head out of the

cave back out to the ocean flying skimming above the ocean I see the seals below I'm back at the edge of the water and I land getting my feet wet I keep moving towards the trees and the pathway that leads me back up in my mind I hold all these memories of my journey I head back up the stairs each step brings me back closer to current time as I wind my way up till I reach the top deep breath and I bring myself back to my circle of candles back to the present
3 bell rings.

> [S]he is the erotogeneity of the heterogeneous: airborne swimmer, in flight, she does not cling to herself; she is dispersible, prodigious, stunning, desirous and capable of others, of the other woman that she will be, of the other woman she isn't of him of you.
>
> (Cixous, 1975/1997, p. 358)

Breathing Curiously: Queering the Curriculum Body

James Sanders

Breathing

queer theory

queering bodies

queerly re-membering

and questioning

prohibitions

denial

of bodies

longing to know

a touch unspeakable

a look that dare not

speak its name

aesthetikos

sensing by feeling

mind(full) body (re)unions

historically severed

by positive(ist)

diagnoses

sexy

sensations

that question

prohibitions of passion

revolting bodies

demand

art

aesthetics

popular culture

curriculum and pedagogy

cultural studies that gesture

toward tenuous transitory tenets

unthinking and reimagining

the disembodied voices

of researching bodies

touching, feeling

smelling for

truth

An Autobiographic Exploration of Embodied Inquiry

Suturing pieces of published, performed, and neglected reflections, I re-examine personal pedagogical practices and research through my cultural body. Gesturing toward a more complex reading of cultural studies, I will undress and expose those underlying theories embodied in my research performances and interventions, seeking to re-eroticize curriculum and recognize the sacredness of both sexuality as a performance, and the body as a medium through which we might know the divine (Snowber, 2002, 2004). Interspersing autoethnographic narratives across my discussion of queer bodies, I attempt to open up spaces where challenging subjects might be seen, sensed, and studied in school. Touting and troubling those varied tactics, strategies, technologies, and encounters that have (re)shaped my thinking about embodiment, performance, visibility, and voice, I consider my experiences and insights within/against those definitions and tenets recently published by queer, feminist, and critical theorists. Through a self-reflexive process I challenge readers to reconsider the potentialities of redeveloping research, curriculum and pedagogical performances in and through the body—performances that mindfully employ those technologies socially signified as art, and that work toward the ends of social justice and human rights.

During the late 1960s and early 1970s my classroom teachers and professors were well aware and regularly supported student articulations of free speech and protest. Some put their bodies and careers on the (picket) lines—teaching social and literary studies, drama, art, and statistics—not for the sake of high-stakes tests, but in responding to the high-stakes futures facing all male students conscribed into warfare, and women being tracked into low-wage labor. Unlike the carefully controlled spin of early twenty-first century technology-based slaughter, the visceral coverage on the nightly news pictured bodies maimed in the name of another generation's values and notions of freedom. Media bodies incited action, and with military conscription came our resistance; actions tutored by educators speaking out against social injustice and war. But today, a different kind of ideological warfare silently stifles the socially conscious educator.

Banishing media representation of fallen warriors' return from carnage, today's televised (mis)coverage of the specters of war produce classrooms and critical cultures of complacency. The current political regime re(mis)directs the energies of educators to the demands of No Child Left Behind's (NCLB) tyranny of high-stakes testing. Privileging technological skill acquisition over critical or creative curricula, the logic of contagion (Singer, 1993) around issues of national security and global competitiveness now seems to close off critique. Media spin of official NCLB education discourse and publication of state report cards become the intimidating technologies that today disciplines teaching bodies into docility. In this slumbering state of critical inaction, what might it take to reawaken a passion for democracy and human rights? What type of touch might arouse an interest in reopening curricular spaces for social justice?

Our bodies connect us with the worlds we encounter, allowing us to touch that which is invisible—to experience that which we, at times, have yet to commit to language. "The nature of one's body concept is learned, beginning in the earliest years, and is variable depending on life experiences" (Barthalow-Koch, 1992, p. 257). How we recognize and communicate these experiences is a social and political challenge, and one that demands the development of new pedagogical theories. "Theory both enables us to...go beyond individual, personally liberating solutions to a socially liberated situation. ...A theoretical approach systematically considering the range of cultural phenomena, can produce the means for examining...political effectiveness" (Barry and Flitterman-Lewis, 2003, p. 54). A curriculum of the body's experiencing of cultural phenomena may thus be well suited for developing pedagogically practice and political interventions involving students in redressing those social subjects at the heart of curriculum theory (Willis and Schubert, 1991).

Having shifted from a curriculum committed to acquiring bodies of information, to the Reconceptualists' preeminent concern with understanding (Pinar et al., 1995/2004), how might we now begin to embrace those hot and slippery bodies of multiple understandings writhing within a world where borders are repeatedly broached and collapsing? Bill Pinar and Marla Morris (2005) call for international studies that might investigate our interdependencies. But if, as Morris suggests, we are in a period of (post)reconceptualization—what role might the body play in its study? How do we open up discourse on international laws regarding sexualities amidst an abstinence only sex education curricular culture that denies desiring student bodies longing to know that which we are told not to name? How might it be possible for educators to present a queer pedagogical body for embrace amidst a state manufactured curricular culture of contagion? To explore these questions, I reflect on my experiences as a student creating art works that challenged historic narratives and the bodies of oppression.

1971

The ripped and trampled pink cardboard littered the frozen blanket of parched gray grass at the shadows edge of the Twin Towers dormitory. Pushing against the chilling winds that wintry morning while walking to my first class, I was crushed to find my first 3-D design project strewn across the field between the Fine Arts Building and the Post Office. My hot-pink 16' triangular homage to the countless homosexuals murdered by the Nazis had been destroyed in the night by what I would later learn was a gang of junior varsity football players worked into frenzy by a homophobic coach. Taking what skeletal remains I could find to the dumpster for burning, I solemnly marched on to Western Civilization—a class where nothing queer in history was imagined, spoken or discussed.

Fast-forward twenty-two months. A sculpture instructor documents three fiberglass female figures I installed in the open two-story lobby of the Fine Arts Building. The fiberglass bodies' hands were clasped together over their heads, their wrists lashed by a single heavy rope laced through the second story banister. This eerily glowing group of green naked bodies hung balanced and bound together—mouths frozen in seeming screams, as Christmas carols played in the background. Intentionally disruptive, this 1972 Monument to the Daughters of the Bilitis (a groundbreaking lesbian liberationist group) was not destroyed, but dismantled on demand of the Fine Arts Dean the next day.

While meeting a less violent demise, this queer sculptural intervention was considered excessively disruptive for its time. The dean's refusal to permit its installation, like the acts of violence that destroyed earlier artwork, fed and fueled my passion for political activism. The reactions of peers and persons in positions of power produced my even more politically resolute standpoints. Repeating my incite-filled experiences here, I call for a recognition and embrace of the productive specters of dis-ease. Such a practice might challenge students to grapple with destruction, death, and demise of bodies and artworks (their own and others'), serving as a strategy for pedagogically inciting cognitive growth and political agency. While not suggesting teachers destroy student work, I am interested in the ways guided dis-ease can help inoculate inquiring students—producing those radically resilient practices required to affect social change.

> A queer pedagogy is not concerned with getting identities right or even with having them represented as an end in themselves. The point is to read—in radical ways—the insufficiencies of identity...and to examine and to refuse "cases of exorbitant normality"...whether that reading concerns the reader or the read. (Britzman 1998, p. 94)

Building on queer embodied experiences, my critical cultural curriculum has refused the normalities of traditional technical training in the arts. As such, a queer critical cultural curricula performs an "ethics of power, where power is conceived as a determined capacity for action...a critical history of the present which seeks to understand what we have been, what we are now and, on this basis, what it is possible for us to become" (Gatens, 2003, pp. 468–469). Such performances continually enjoin students in questioning how historic renderings and written words reiteratively (re)write the body and cultural policy—challenging them to develop new practices of reading history against the grain. Through careful examination of the embodied encounter and its impact on psychic and cognitive development, political standpoints, and ethical commitments, one may reclaim experience as an act of agency.

Unlike Cartesian modernist mind/body splitting, Spinoza controversially theorized the mind and body as one in the same. In Proposition Two of *Book III of Ethics,* he rendered both reason and imagination as embodied and ethically charged (Curley, 1994). Following this lead, I consider my queer body not merely added on, but integrally a part of each course I develop. This recognizes, as do Rizvi and Walsh (1998), that "[t]o view difference as simply an external factor to be taken into account in the construction of curriculum…is to fail to see how those institutions within which curriculum is constructed may themselves be culturally biased and exclusionary" (p. 9).

I forefront my queer identity during each course I teach, calling attention to the ways sexuality is embedded in every subject. This self-naming is both a political act—one that refuses the invisibility experienced by non-heterosexuals—and an integral part of a critical curricula that seeks to relentlessly challenge the silent constructions of heteronormativity. Addressing my queer body, I recognize its role in my intellectually promiscuous pedagogical practice, and challenge students to consider the ways their sense of self and sexuality shape their readings of the world and performances of cultural practice and curriculum development.

Throughout my formal education, the relationships between political action, curriculum studies, and the cultural body articulated with(in) and through visual art/culture, popular media, film, theater, dance, and aural technologies have been inextricably linked. My embodied explorations have intentionally impacted the subjects, communities, and disciplines I study and at times trouble. While failing to immediately impact shifts in social understandings, the production, presentation, and even destruction of my work transformed my self-understanding. Before I had language to discuss theories, philosophies, and methods of arts-based research, the art I made helped me work through the estrangement I felt as a gay man and political activist in a hostile and repressive cultural setting. The faculty with whom I studied engaged me in dialogue about the installed gestures, drawings, and the independent films I created. They encouraged my work through multiple grants and scholarships, providing far more support of my open sexuality than did the closeted local gay guys. I doubt any of the English and Art Departments' faculty thought of our work together as forms of cross-disciplinary epistemological and ontological inquiry in and through the body—but not having fully articulated theories for what we experienced did not hamper the production of tangible educational outcomes.

Now in a position of power and authority as a professor in a large research university, I find myself continuing to conduct my epistemological inquiries through the body and performance—working with students to consider how shared explorations might lead to the development of new policy practices, ways of teaching, and curricular developments. I am privileged to work with a large cadre of international (under)graduate students with backgrounds in music, dance, theater, literature, visual art, business, sociology, and comparative studies, whose varied political, social, and (a)religious understandings inform our explorations of policy and curricular possibilities. Considering students' multiple cultural contexts, and sensing their varied concerns and educational objectives, I find myself continually adapting the body of knowledge my syllabus states I will cover, and uncovering questions that might crack open spaces where they too can construct and claim meaningful learning experiences.

Public valuations of art and cultural production continue to be contested notions; it seems thus only appropriate to work toward developing disquieting encounters that might better prepare students for those challenges they will face in the future. One disturbing didactic I developed involves a queering of arts education assessment. While students are studying state and national arts curriculum standards, I provide them with stacks of historic art images, asking that teams develop an imagined curriculum from them and align their lesson with one or more of the objectives at a given grade level. What may, or may not be immediately apparent (since not all image cards dealt them include information on the artist or their work) is that almost all of the images are either created by or depicting gay, lesbian, or queer subjects. I am fascinated by the big ideas students generate, and their ways of framing of the lessons, and rationalizing the works selected. I am even more engaged by the discussions that follow—usually involving questions of age appropriateness, religious attitudes toward homosexuality, and the value of securing parental and school administrators' support before introducing challenging lessons. At times, groups may be outraged that they were asked to be a part of "teaching homosexuality," but most come to acknowledge that they regularly reinforce heterosexual practices without even thinking about it, or openly addressing that hidden curriculum. Such provocations seek to produce significant, but not paralyzing tensions and dis-ease—discomforts that might incite students' reclamations of agency.

Developing personal solutions to self-identified pedagogical and policy challenges, each student may explore how to survive and thrive amidst constant change. Recognizing that those in our charge are not empty bowls to be filled, but are subjects entering our institutions with (anti)bodies ready for interaction, I seek to inoculate (without killing) their spirit—readying them for reentry into a world where they might spread a commitment to social justice and human rights. Inoculated, heartened, and hardened for cultural warfare, a critical cultural body curriculum aims to serve students in stopping the spread of xenophobic religious intolerance, corporate cultural cloning, and deceptive political practice.

1975

As an intellectually promiscuous graduate student, Southern Illinois University-Carbondale enabled my explorations of identity and human interaction through clay, dance, photography, and fibers—working not alone, but in a community of artist-researchers. The war in Southeast Asia had ended, I had fallen in love, and our energies were directed toward personal liberation struggles and erotic expression. Over the course of 27 months I organized four collaborative projects, including a guerilla theater dance duet with Douglas Bush, in which he wore a black leotard and me, a yellow prom dress as we danced on 2,000 freshly thrown ceramic vessels installed in Pulliam Hall.

Collaborating with metal smiths-as-musicians, dancer/choreographers, and musical assistants, our group produced two evening-long productions. "Peace for Gloria," a memorial to friend strangled by her lover's belt, explored ephemerality and the cyclical nature of creativity (playing within a hermeneutic circle centered on the aesthetic act). The second work was my 1976 Thesis Exhibition, a production involving 200 audience members led in a Kouros (male youth) processional from my Faner Gallery installation of textiles through four other architectural spaces—at each stopping to witness dances based on Cycladic and Greek classical depictions of the body and balance.

Graduate studies seemed a series of collaborative questioning performances, joining feminist painters in interrogating the absence of women in our art history courses and the encyclopedic museum holdings we studied. With musicology majors and modern dancers, I fingered fine arts slide library files, curating poetically painted pieces that would serve as projected backdrops for lyrical choreography set to Satie and Debussy.

Cross-analyzing aesthetic sensibilities, compositional technologies, and the body's presence across each discipline, choreographing performers collaborated with me to build new works and discover new ways of saying that which we knew through our bodies. Searching for new performing possibilities amidst increasingly conservative nationalist discourses birthed on the occasion of the U.S bicentennial, I longed to represent our visions of historic accuracy—asking the University to permit my collaborators nude performances of Dionysian dances, and requesting funding to document the evening's wonder. Neither request was supported.

Again, as in my undergraduate experiences, the faculty at SIU-C was supportive, arguing the edgy interventions' value to administrators reluctant to disrupt academic serenity. Today, in a new role, I advise groups and students on how to navigate the politics of academia and those larger behemoths of state and national government. Deconstructing social and cultural policy, learning its history, and the ways race, class, sexuality, gender and ethnicity are performed in the arts constitute the core of my curricula, but in itself, it is still insufficient. A curriculum of the culturally dis-eased body is the challenge I argue must be faced if students are to be prepared to create those new worlds we ask them to imagine. I seek to encourage students' development of personally meaningful curricula—lessons that move beyond consumption of cultural practices and simply unpacking or questioning them, and toward envisioning equitable alternatives and learning how to effectively lobby for their vision's materialization. Such a curriculum may require pedagogically performing in ways that might not yet be imagined—ways emerging from our experience of the world—a curriculum emerging from our bodies.

The body, bisected by late nineteenth century medical and psychological interest, may be reunited through performative inquiry—journeys toward self re-cognition, and travels that move toward the re-integration of art and science, social critique, and political action. This journey responds to Cixous' (1976) challenge, "Write yourself. Your body must be heard. Only then will the immense resources of the unconscious spring forth" (p. 883). Writing toward consciousness calls for reexamining the body and the gaze. Examinations drawing on visual theory and bodies of feminist and poststructural thought of the 1970s and 1980s (Cixous, 1976; deBeauvier, 1970; Foucault, 1972, 1977; hooks, 1984; Irigaray, 1985), and black feminist theorists of the 1990s (Hill-Collins, 1990; hooks 1990, 1994, 1995), can help ensure the reuniting journey attends to the intersections of gender and race. Traveling still deeper into identificatory territories of gender, sexualities, and class (Allison, 1994; Badgett, 2001; Kumashiro, 2001, 2002, 2004; Raffo,

1997), acts of queering the body (Britzman, 1998; Butler, 1990, 1997, 2004; Sedgwick, 1990) might be of service in navigating this round-about. Returning to the body as a site for reworking experience, I approach Barry and Flitterman-Lewis's (2003) challenge of a "radical reconceptualisation of the personal to include more broadly social and even unconscious forces [that] has made a more analytical approach to these personal experiences necessary" (p. 53).

1990

Amidst heated culture war skirmishes, I found myself in a chilly waiting room thumbing through magazines in anticipation of a meeting for legislative aid in Senator Jessie Helms' office on Capitol Hill. Having submitted a National Endowment for the Arts grant request supporting a Southeastern Surface Design Association Conference exploring intersections of cultural identity, patterning, and design, I was dutifully contacting elected political representatives from my State, never anticipating any backing from this belligerent bulldog I had voted against. A perky twenty-something blond haired woman bounced into the room. "Come on in," she bubbled, I just don't know why people think Jessie don't support the arts...its blasphemous homophobic trash he hates! Not art!!"

Initially each artist-designer had been selected for the quality of their work and their works' patterned references to Native-American, Asian, Latino, Jewish, and multiple African-American, and Caucasian racial and ethnic heritages. What had not been discussed, nor was fully disclosed or recorded until the final featured artists' panel discussion, was that six of the nine participants were self-identified as gay, bisexual, or lesbian. As that Sunday morning's dialogue unfolded, conference participants chuckled at being told, "There's nothing three women in a pick-up truck can't do." They laughed at the admission that one "had never met a decent designer that wasn't a woman or gay." Tears fell as a gay digital artist told tales of a divorce court decree disallowing his visitation rights with his children. Applause followed testimonies valuing academic affirmative action hiring policies, while murmurs accompanied the questioning of colleagues' conflations of race, sexuality, class, and disease in tech-typing queer artists' difference. The cross-cultural creators' insistence that cultural identity is constituted by more than meets the eye was an insight that audience members could feel in their own largely white middle-class women's bodies. The transcripts, reports, and recommendations from the assembly attended to the multiple and intersecting cultural identification written on the bodies of each artists' works—documentation that, save trade journal coverage, was never widely circulated.

Flash forward two years to the Craft and Ethics Symposium co-produced by Sawtooth and three national groups following the 1993 Year of Craft in the Americas, where again gay and lesbian designers were present during a four-day working meeting designed to chart the future critical work of the craft community. Unlike the majority position queer panelists enjoyed at the earlier gathering, this time they were a silent minority. As the conference host I was asked by a gay peer to raise queer concerns to the forefront—a request I entertained, but never acted upon, insisting that the issue be raised from the floor, not imposed from the podium. Half of the group attended the HIV/AIDS benefit that was taking place on the gathering's third evening, with a quarter more going out to a local gay club for even more dancing. But in the official assemblies that followed on the final day, no one spoke of anything gay.

In reflexively researching my professional experiences I recognize I chose when to interject my own queer body into (un)comfortable discursive spaces. Inconsistently attending to the complex intersections and dynamic between discourses of knowledge, subjectivity, and the politics of culture, in reopening my damaged inquiries—I publicly irrigate psychic wounds with salted words that refuse to comfort or ease the excruciating throb and stabbing insight's memory. My now fully dis/eased body performs toward the ends of enabling defenseless acts of disclosure, struggling against mortality to grasp self-understandings that might be of service to others. Publicly looking at my body, the gaze transforms the act. An act, that bell hooks (2003) notes "has always been political. ...There is power in looking. ...[In] courageously looking, we defiantly declared, 'not only will I stare. I want my look to change reality'" (p. 94).

Likewise, Peggy Phelan (2003) problematizes the political risks of increasing visibility, remarking:

> The current contradiction between "identity politics" with its accent on visibility, and the psychoanalytic/deconstructionist mistrust of visibility as the source of unity or wholeness needs to be refigured. ...[T]he binary between the power of visibility and the impotency of invisibility is falsifying. There is real power in remaining un[re]marked; and there are serious limitations to visual representation as a political goal. (p. 109)

The representation of my queer experience, while unreliable as a source of power, is nonetheless recharged with each critical reexamination. Such self-reflexivity responds to Trinh T. Minh-ha's (2003) warning that "to demand the right to Difference without analyzing its social character is to give back the enemy an effective weapon" (p. 165). The question now is how to maintain a well-functioning weapon.

Deconstruction has been vital to queer theory, "demonstrating that supposedly natural norms of gender and sexuality are power-effects produced within the institution of compulsory heterosexuality" (cited in Pinar, 1998, p. 9). Dennis Carlson (1998) queers these effects in calling for a new multicultural "politics of the self that disrupts the underlying binary logic that govern identity formation in contemporary culture" (p. 108), and in seeking ways to work within and across affinity groups. Stephen Murray (1996) further challenges the assimilationist's view that only private sexual practices distinguish lesbian, gay, bisexual, transgendered and queer subjectivity. Refusing the globalizing discourses of neo Marxists claims (Habermas or Althusser) to totalizing educational narratives, Steven Seidman (1993) suggests that postmodern queer theories identify "multiple, local, intersecting struggles whose aim is...the creation of social spaces that encourage the proliferation of pleasures, desires, voices, interests modes of individuation and democratization" (p. 106). But even in coming to terms with these multiple standpoints, as Pinar (1998) notes, "we remain in a defensive position; trying to teach tolerance, trying to teach the truth, trying to find ways to decenter and destabilize the heterosexual normalization that so constructs the students we teach, indeed the public world we inhabit" (p. 6).

My earliest attempts at decentering the heterosexist spaces I occupied were informed by drag queens of St. Michaels Square I visit on weekends in Chicago. Their camp effeminacy echoed the outrageously destabilizing performances, filmmakers in the 1950s and 1960s worked toward— performances now considered part of a queer aesthetic. Kenneth Anger's (1963) *Scorpio Rising*, Jack Smith's (1963) *Flaming Creatures*, and Andy Warhol's (1966) *Chelsea Girls* are among dozens of films recently reexamined by Chauncey, Gregg, and Puetz at a 2006 University of Chicago film/study series "Recovering the Significance of Postwar Queer Underground Cinema, 1950–1968" (Craig, 2006). Each of these filmmakers were examined by Gregory Battock (1967) in *New American Cinema*, however, their provocations are now taking on new meaning with the rise of queer media theorizing (Butler, 1990; Cleto, 1999; Dyer, 1992; Keller, 2002; Russo, 1987). Whether or not one can definitively claim a queer aesthetic, its camp sensibilities have been discussed since Susan Sontag's (1966) essay, "Notes on Camp." Characterized by sharp social critique, humor, and disruption of the raced, classed, and gendered body, I consider a queer aesthetic gesturing toward the disruption of binaries, including those between the body's representation and commitments to political change. Queer, as the reclamation of a derogatory naming has always been political. So too is my intent in placing a broad array of culturally creating bodies under the rubric of queer.

The sexual politics of Mapplethorpe's hyper/homosexual photos, and (not gay) Serrano's queering of religiosity in "Piss Christ," ignited the culture wars of the 1990s. This cultural warfare was further flamed by the National Endowment for the Arts' controversial denial of grants to Holly Hughes and Tim Miller—giving rise to a "decency oath" legislated by Congress. While Mapplethorpe's fist fucking and golden shower photographs made the private pleasures and acts of gay male subcultures public, more frequently, camp humor has been used to slice through the multiple layers of sociosexual overdetermination. Holly Hughes's *Clit Notes* (1994), and Tim Miller's *My Queer Body* (1994), both provocatively entertain audiences' embrace of queer insight. "*Superstar Vaginal Creme* by Davis...appropriate[d], terroristically, both dominant culture and different subcultural movements...[produces] identities that have been rendered toxic...but are, through Davis' fantastic and farcical performance, restructured (yet not cleansed) so that they present newly imagined notions of the self and the social" (Muñoz, 2003, p. 219). Both publicly visible and hidden, these queer social critiques were likely informed by earlier moving images.

Independent filmmakers provocatively attending to the intersections of race, gender, class, and sexualities—at times have merged poetry and politics in performances that make the social construction of desire intelligible—as did Marlon Riggs and Essex Hemphill, when *Tongues Untied* (1989) aired on public television. Intelligibility, as Kate McCoy (2000) contends, is that which seems "natural, and consequently, unquestionable" (p. 237). Queerly questioning the racist imagery published by gay porn and the internalized racism of "snow queens" longing for white bodies, the duo of Riggs and Hemphill remixed newsreel footage, staged performances, and poetry readings in a pastiche I would characterize as a queer aesthetic suturing self-stylization.

Even earlier, cult followings launched John Waters's career, flocking to witness irreverent queer provocations in films like *Mondo Trash* (1969) and *Pink Flamingos* (1972). It was his towering drag queen Divine's caricaturization of feminine beauty in *Female Trouble* (1975) that Butler (1990) references in calling attention to the artifice of genders' cultural construction. Queer cults following the early erotic work of Todd Haynes

(*Poison*, 1991; *Swoon*, 1992) enabled his more broadly appealing later films socially scrutinizing subjects of sexuality, class, and race (e.g., *Far From Heaven*, 2002). The self-absorbed satirical or surreal queer subject now seemingly researches its own humanity, psychology, and emotional resonances, through the later works of Pedro Almodovar, *All About My Mother*, 1999; *Bad Education*, 2004), who resides in a land of his own where he constructs moving tales featuring gay, cross-dressing, transgender, and transvestite characters naturally interacting with nuns, stage starlets, and seemingly straight folk unperturbed by those marching to the beats of different drummers. Whether such seemingly serious examinations suggest an aesthetic shift from the quintessential camp construction to a new queer introspection that claims itself a feeling as well as performing subject is a discussion meriting more attention, but suffice to say that the queer sensibility certainly seems to have shifted since Duchamp donned the drag of Rose Selávy.

Sexual experiences—while simultaneously socially overdetermined and unimaginably varied—are capable of communicating multiple meanings across racial, language, political, economic, and religious boundaries. The sexual promise withheld or the performance realized—whether for procreative or recreational purpose—is pervasively present across cultures. Advertising industries pimp it, churches rally around its recreational demonization, politicians plunder its appeal, and artists' imagery, gaze, and metaphor rely on its power—and yet rarely is its presence openly discussed in the classroom. Sex is seemingly the elephant in the corner that no one dares acknowledge, for fear of unleashing its power in classrooms filled with students whose experiences often exceed that recognized by parents, teachers, or school administrators.

Paul Duncum (2005) has called for "an aesthetic of embodiment [that] reintegrates aesthetics with vulgar, crude, and sensationalist experiences," considering this a "necessary theoretical construct for dealing with many cultural sites of corporate, global capital" (p. 9). While resonating with critiques of corporate greed, I suggest he fails to deeply question the underlying moralist discourses he recirculates in vilifying the sexualized body. The performances of Miller (1994) and Hughes (1994), photographs of Mapplethorpe, films of Waters (1967/1972), Haynes (1991, 1992), and Almodovar (1999, 2002) all attend to the powerful lessons of the sexualized body—but without the sex-negative (Piontek, 2006) biases that Duncum divulges. The theoretically asexualized surety of critical visual culture studies proponents may remain fixed with glazed gaze on televisual commercial products and corporate interests, while neglecting the desirous and sensing appeal of the artist's sexual production—reducing them to bile-logical scat performances and "cultural sites of corporate, global capital" (p. 9). Until such critics are willing to peel back the heavy wraps of neo Marxist capitalist critique, it is doubtful they will find an entry into those moist interstitial spaces where erotic bodies and their longings' production, consumption, and profit might be studied.

The objectified silencing of erotic bodies is repeatedly enacted with each insistence on the impossibility of its being addressed in schools. In silence, contradictory messages are sent to students, intimating to the uninitiated that sex is a vulgar and nasty subject, and concurrently claiming it an act so sacred, that it can only be secretly shared by heterosexuals pledging lifelong devotion. What hope is there for student understanding if they are sent such mixed messages?

I seek a re-eroticizing of the curriculum—not a nasty aesthetic of vulgarity that is crude or sensationalized—but one that recognizes the sacredness of both sexuality as a performance and the body as an instrument through which we know the divine (Snowber, 2002, 2004). The Kama Sutra instructs such erotic worship; rites of passage comparably communicate culturally specific social beliefs and values, and yet in a nation boasting separation of church and state, the only guidance our schools are told to offer is abstinence and prohibition. Unfortunately, the cultural specificity of erotic performance and religious practice has long been declared the research turf of psychologists, anthropologists, ethnographers, and hermeneutists. These are, however, spaces that I contend artists have always occupied, and ones to which educators could reenter to the psychosexual benefit of their students. Students' bodies are the concern of all subjects in schools. A cross-disciplinary attentiveness to their needs might gesture toward the reunified understanding of mind, spirit, and body. By continuing to unthink disciplinarity and redress erotic omission, a reconceptualized curriculum of the cultural body might be possible. Until that time, it is important to recognize the interstitial spaces extant in arts studies.

Exploring the possibilities of queer intelligibility specifically in and through the visual arts—future researchers might continue to discuss what challenges exist and benefits might result from organizing image archives by artists' sexual identification(s). Grounding this dialogue in the specific context of U.S. public education settings, today's pre-service educators might begin by considering those testimonies of artists, lgbtq adolescents, and teachers in (anti)oppressive learning spaces to guide their way. I contend pre-service educators need to be prepared to challenge those school policies disallowing pursuits of queer knowledge, by arguing that such defiance is ethically necessary to ensure the safety of all students. While anticipating resistance to this challenge, even current curricular content contains openings for initiating dialogue.

Regularly replicas of the Venus of Willendorf are trotted out in classrooms as an artifact of fertility, with little discussion of what that term or the statue signifies. Rarely is the naked availability of Botticelli's Venus broached in classroom discussion, nor are Yorba mothers' calabash care, or cross-dressing mother worshiping son's performances explored beneath their decorative surface. How might attending to the social, medical, and spiritual role of Berdache impact students' reading of Zuni peoples? Could scrutinizing the Warren Cup's intercrural couple lead to a discussion of safe sex practice? The arts open interstitial spaces for studying the sexual body—openings that erotic aesthetic curricula could fill if one was willing to touch and take on the subaltern subject. The arts breathe curiously.

Art educating communities that broach queer concerns are cautioned to not construct intelligibility as exclusively related to the overt representation of genitalia, outrageously explicit innuendo, fluid proof, and/or public/legal documentation of an artist's imprisonment (e.g., Leonardo DaVinci, Caravaggio, or Oscar Wilde). While calling for an eroticized curriculum, I cannot claim to have the definitive answer for how or where queer conceptual boundaries might be finally marked. Nonetheless, the invisibility and/or inaccessibility of queer representations and data (especially in public schools) constitutes a miseducation of those who might most benefit from this knowledge (Letts and Sears, 1999).

Creating access to knowledge about queer artists' lives is filled with legal risks, especially with hordes of homophobic heirs working diligently to straighten out their elders' sexual history. The film *Unconditional Love*, a hysterically humorous insightful examination of private and public bodies, addresses just this theme. And it is perhaps just such visual cultural comedy that might be needed in the classroom to open interstitial spaces for those willing to discuss the risks and benefits of archivists, curators, and art historians' (re)assignment of identities on those artists verifiably engaged in same-sex relations. In doing so, one must remain mindful of the historic and cultural constructedness of sexual norms—values and practices that while complex may deepen students' understanding of sexualities, social history, and change. The complex issues surrounding queer intelligibility is not exclusively one involving those who have died. The standpoints of politically "out" queer artists who are nonetheless reluctant to be "ghettoized" by a queer categorization must also be considered (Sanders, 2004).

We need to theorize race and gender not as meaningless but as meaningful...in need of constant decoding and interrogation. Such analysis may not finally free us of the ubiquitous body-biology bind...but it may be at once the most and least we can do to reclaim difference from the moulds of mass production and the casts of dominant culture. (Ducille, 2003, p. 346)

Cultural studies must continue to grapple with the moral and ethical dilemmas of "outing" or claiming as gay or lesbian, those who lived closeted lives, and correspondingly, our "inning" of artists who are or were openly queer and evidenced it in their work. Opening up dialogue with queer artist-colleagues and urging their participation in self-namings that do not foreclose multiple readings of their work is a project that I encourage others to share. Through such dialogue we might someday be able to define intelligibilities that could indeed be queer.

My life(s) work has been committed to exploring ways of reunifying and *reeroticizing* the mind/body split in academe (Sanders, 1999, 2000, 2005) through (re)searching my body and its cavities for spaces where I might reread the world and ruminate on its remaking. Regurgitating experiences of my performative arts-based interventions, like a heron I spit-up my mo(u)rning catch for the nourishment of those with whom I teach and learn. This autobiographical performance is itself an almost autofellatious machination, one simultaneously seeking to sustain desire while ignoring my own voracious loneliness and wrestling with mortality; a cultural-bodily exhibitionism experienced as an episteme-idea-logical exploration.

The seemingly sanitized safety of academe has opened itself to arts-based inquiries, presently a warm and comforting space that tolerates my embodied curiosities. I must acknowledge, however, that despite the safe spaces seemingly provided by the ivory tower, I have still not dared to air all my dirty laundry or subversive strategies in print. These omissions comprise both internalized fears, and the potentialities of power producing performances not quite ripe enough to open. Researching my performative inquiries has enabled my reoccupation of autobiographic interstitial spaces—some emitting new curricular theories and pedagogical practices that gesture toward the redress of psychic wounds. But while trusting my sensing by feeling (the Greek aesthetikos) may serve as a check and (re)balance to a modern era's privileging of mind over matter, it is necessary that I repeatedly reexamine all postionality, and those socially over-determined situations that may mask discomfort and dissuade my will to action. In calling for an embrace of bodily mattered mindfulness, I have argued that only with and through the body may one meaningfully question the tyranny of disembodied dehumanizing disciplinary discourses—those that deny the inextricable interconnections involved in cultural power dynamics, operating in our multiple experiencing of the world, and in our productions of knowledge, subjectivity, and agency.

In thinking we are always alone, and in writing (the body), one is never quite capable of entering the Other's reading/sensing experience. I recognize that my sense(ation)s long to confidently know a shared cultural bod(il)y experience. Re-searching with colleagues, students, and cultural patrons one can share fluid concepts and question(ing)s—at times exhilarated by what we might perceive are our findings—and yet we can never be confident that our experienced meanings can ever be fully felt or effectively communicated in alphanumeric translation. Re-searching through the cultural/body—publicly sharing our externalizations of that which is experienced alone—we may only pray for a spark of (self)recognition or some reassuring sensation along this nomadic journey that suggests we might have finally reached home. Might have at last sensed in our sharing, that we have exceeded our bodies, and briefly come to know the Other's body/spirit/mind.

I see and sense the body as both site and medium through which a broad array of pedagogical possibilities are practiced and presented. Through shared moving, poetic, and filmic creations we recreate our (self)understandings and (re)position ourselves to encounter our own otherness in and through a cultural bodily (self)recognition that may only fleetingly be known through an aesthetic experience. Believing or knowing through the body—feeling the ever present threat/promise of death— illuminates that mysterious absence where all that remains is memory and artifact(s) indefinitely recording an excess(ive) curiosity, and a constant longing to escape the unitary experience of isolation. For me this continues to be a queer and (dis)comforting journey, one that struggles to acknowledge sexualized differences experienced in shared social and political commitments, estrangement, stigmatization, and yes, pleasure.

Notes

Introduction

1. http://www.bodyworlds.com/en/pages/home.asp.

Body Interfaces in Curriculum

2. I express my appreciation to Hui-Chun Hsiao for bringing her Eye-Toy®
   to the first class session of my courses for three semesters, and to
   Maryellen Murphy for her analysis of one semester of students' written
   ideas of the potential use of EyeToy®. I also thank the pre-service art
   educators in my courses for their creative and critical ideas and dialogue
   regarding body interfaces in curriculum.

Silent Voices, Silent Bodies

3. This phrase is inspired by Anjie Krog's highly reflective and reflexive
   narrative on her journalistic role in reporting on the Truth and
   Reconciliation Commission (TRC) hearings (1995–1999), that gave
   voice and presence to victims of apartheid after its demise. It is an
   inversion of the title of the book: *Country of my skull: Guilt, sorrow, and
   the limits of forgiveness in the new South Africa*.
4. I have used the term "reflexive narratizing" to draw attention to the
   active role of narrative-making, living, and being, as opposed to
   "narrative" as passive object. It is a continuous process of living, writing,
   being, and becoming in narrative, rather than distinct processes (see
   Swanson, 2005).
5. I have developed the concept of the "pedagogizing of difference and
   disadvantage" elsewhere, (see Swanson, 2004), which draws on
   Bernstein's (2000) "recontextualizing principle," and on the concomitant
   relationship between discourse and practice (see Dowling, 1998). It
   refers to the way in which socially constructed difference becomes
   recontextualized in pedagogic practices in (mathematics) classrooms, so

that these social difference discourses are reproduced within practices and they position subjects in context accordingly. Pathologizing practices refer in the same way to social difference discourses that situate students and their communities in terms of deficit discourses, and that reproduce and pedagogize these discourses in context.

6. I have dealt with this in more depth elsewhere (Swanson, 2004), that Western/Euro-centered mathematics has become the universal norm. Because of its dominance in the curriculum and its "esoteric nature," school mathematics is one of the most divisive subjects on the school curriculum, so that the marginalization and inequalities reflected in society are most often reproduced and supported by school mathematics discourse and practice in diverse pedagogic contexts throughout the world.

7. In the light of a definition of proceduralism as it affects differentiating mathematical practices in the classroom, the work of Dowling (1998, 2001) in particular is helpful. Dowling's work allows for an analysis of how subjectivity is realized in pedagogic texts. His work, among other objectives, brings in an extension and refinement of Bernstein's concept of classification.

8. Those bloody buggers of grade seven children...out of the bloody classroom again!

Teaching Bodies Who Teach

9. Students gained experience of teaching in what were then called practicing schools. These schools which were located on campus varied in size. One school was a one-teacher school where the class teacher taught pupils from the time of entry to the school at the age of four until they left the school at around the age of 12. This teacher was also the Headmaster of the school. The second school was a two-teacher school with each teacher teaching 4 class groups each. The two-teacher school closely resembled schools in rural Ireland at the time. The third school was a much larger school with approximately 16 teachers teaching within it. A school of this size would be likely to be found in large towns and the cities of Ireland. Here teachers taught a single class group.

10. These documents comprised the entirety of archival documents that the college held for the period under study.

11. The Teaching Practice Reports of students who entered the College in 1928, 1930, 1932, 1934, and 1936 are those consulted and referred to in this chapter.

12. The Free State, consisting of 26 of the 32 counties in Ireland, was established following the signing of the Anglo-Irish Treaty in 1921.
13. In cases where students were noticeably weak in practicing teaching the period of practice was extended and therefore such students spent more than the prescribed time practicing teaching.
14. While not stated in the reports, it is likely that students had a specific dress code while on Teaching Practice. Photographs from an earlier period of students in practicing schools do show student teachers dress to be formal—shirt, suit, and tie. Indeed the College Prospectus for 1924 lists items of clothing that students are required to bring at the beginning of each academic year and this list includes items of clothing deemed formal.
15. These extracts were taken from reports of men who were described or categorized as unmanly.

A Tail of Two Women

16. For commentary about the dictionary addition, see Cox (2004) and Lenoir (2004). The term "bootylicious" fuses the words booty and delicious, and denotes a shapely, sexually attractive woman. It is a slang term coined by rapper Snoop Dog, and later used by the female pop group, Destiny's Child on their third album *Survivor* (2001). The title track was produced and co-written by Beyoncé Knowles, a member of Destiny's Child. On *The Oprah Winfrey Show*, Knowles defined bootylicious as "beautiful, bountiful, bounceable" (Shanahan, 2003, p. 26).
17. Janell Hobson (2003) deploys the term freak as the abnormal black body commodified in popular culture. She suggests the booty (or batty) can be oppositional site to dismantle colonizing discourses marking black women as Other.
18. Postfeminism in this context refers to the shift in popular culture that "assume[s] that feminism was no longer needed and therefore that women were beyond (i.e., 'post') the need for feminism and feminist activism" (Valdivia and Projanksy, 2006, p. 26).

Disrupting Mass Media as Curriculum

19. For example, see Alvi, Hoodfar, and McDonough, 2003; Cooke, 2001; El Guindi, 1999; Lewis and Mills, 2003; Shirazi, 2001; Yuval-Davis, 1997.

Teaching Against Homophobia Without Teaching the Subject

20. This idea is built on Megan Boler's "pedagogy of discomfort." See Boler, *Feeling Power*,(New York: Routledge, 1999).

Cesarean, Celebrity and Childbirth

21. Because of the growing evidence of false positive reports of fetal distress as a result of EFM, greater attention has been focused on curbing women's movement during labor and encouraging their immobility (Lent, 1999).
22. It is a common obstetrical assumption that women will dilate according to the Friedman Curve, which stipulates 1.2 cm dilation for each hour of labor. Though many women do dilate in such a manner, as many as 20 percent of otherwise low risk women do not progress at this rate (Wolf, 2003).
23. Recommendation made by the AMA and ACOG influence the practice of medicine and shape not only hospital procedures but also the coverage that medical liability insurance providers offer.
24. Gaining popularity during the early to mid-twentieth century, women were given scopolamine (an amnesiac) together with morphine (an opiate) to numb the body to the pain of childbirth. The resulting state was popularly known as "twilight sleep." This narcotization of birth fell out of favor as evidence was produced demonstrating its negative impact on mothers and babies (ranging from women's nightmare birth recollections to infant and maternal death) and as medicalized birth advocates championed the reclamation of unmedicated birth (Leavitt, 1986).
25. I have served as an assistant midwife to several communities of Amish women for the past two years. During this time, I have participated in prenatal visits and postpartum care as well as played an active role in the labor and delivery of their babies.
26. See (Suarez, 1993) or www.purplepanthers.com/mwart.htm.

Intimacy in the Curriculum of Janine Antoni

27. http://en.wikipedia.org/wiki/Intimacy, 2006.
28. http://www.risd.edu/views/wnt01/immaculate_conception_wnt01.htm, retrieved June, 2006.

29. http://www.risd.edu/views/wnt01/immaculate_conception_wnt01.htm, retrieved June, 2006.
30. http://www.risd.edu/views/wnt01/immaculate_conception_wnt01.htm, retrieved June, 2006.

Embodying Exile

31. The images in this essay are stills taken from the documentary video entitled *Living Inquiry: A Video Montage*. Video and still image editing: Barbara Bickel. Video camera work: Joanna Szabo and Barbara Bickel.
32. I do not write alone. The voices/texts of many others inform my writing. I would like in particular to acknowledge the invaluable editing assistance of R. Michael Fisher, Karen Meyer, as well as the reviewers, and the editors, Debra Freedman and Stephanie Springgay.
33. The arational is recognized as the nonrational in a philosophical definition of mysticism but does not merit its own definition within the *HarperCollins Dictionary of Philosophy*. The arational (drawing from Swiss philosopher Jean Gebser and mystical traditions) is a form of knowing that includes the body, the emotions, the senses, intuition, imagination, creation making, the mystical, spiritual and the relational, alongside the rational. The arational can be found in the practices of art, meditation, psychoanalysis, the body, the senses, and so on.
34. The remaining five renderings are contiguity, openings, metaphor/metonymy, reverberations, and excess (see Springgay, Irwin and Kind, 2005 for more details).

References

Ahmed, S. (2000). *Strange encounters: Embodied others in post-coloniality*. London, UK: Routledge.

———. (2002). This other and other others. *Economy and Society, 31*(4), 558–572.

Ahmed, S. and Stacey, J. (2001). *Thinking through skin*. London, UK: Routledge.

Allison, D. (1994). *Skin: Talking about sex, class and literature*. Ithaca, NY: Firebrand Books.

Alvi, S. S., Hoodfar, H., and McDonough, S. (Eds.). (2003). *The Muslim veil in North America: Issues and debates*. Toronto: Women's Press.

Anonymous. (1994, January 29). Coke v Pepsi (cont): China's fizz. *The Economist, 67*.

Anonymous. (2005). The 10 most written about ads. *Campaign, 59*. Retrieved April 29, 2006, from ProQuest database.

Ansen, D. (1991). The disembodied director. *Newsweek, 117*(3), 58.

Aoki, T. (2003). Locating living pedagogy in teacher "research": Five metonymic moments. In E. Hasebe–Ludt and W. Hurren (Eds.), *Curriculum intertext: Place/language/pedagogy* (pp. 1–9). New York: Peter Lang.

———. (2005a). Imaginaries of "East and West": Slippery curricular signifiers in education. In W. F. Pinar and R. L. Irwin (Eds.), *Curriculum in a new key: The collected works of Ted T. Aoki* (pp. 313–319). Mahwah, NJ: Lawrence Erlbaum Associates.

———. (2005b). Language, culture, and curriculum. In W. F. Pinar and R. L. Irwin (Eds.), *Curriculum in a new key: The collected works of Ted T. Aoki* (pp. 321–329). Mahwah, NJ: Lawrence Erlbaum Associates.

———. (2005c). Sonare and videre: A story, three echoes and a lingering note. In W. F. Pinar & R. L. Irwin (Eds.), *Curriculum in a new key: The collected works of Ted T. Aoki* (pp. 367–376). Mahwah, NJ: Lawrence Erlbaum Associates.

———. (2005d). Taiko drums and sushi, perogies and sauerkraut: Mirroring a half-life in multicultural curriculum. In W. F. Pinar and R. L. Irwin (Eds.), *Curriculum in a new key: The collected works of Ted T. Aoki* (pp. 377–387). Mahwah, NJ: Lawrence Erlbaum Associates.

Aparicio, F. (1998). *Listening to salsa: Gender, Latin popular music, and Puerto Rican cultures*. Hanover, NH: University Press of New England.

———. (2003). Jennifer as Selena: Rethinking Latinidad in media and popular culture. *Latino Studies, 1*(1), 90–105.

Argyle, K. and Shields, R. (1996). Is there a body in the net? In Rob Shields (Ed.), *Cultures of internet* (pp. 58–69). Thousand Oaks, CA: Sage.

Arnheim, R. (1957,1997). *Film as art*. Berkeley: University of California Press.

Asher, N. (2002). (En)gendering a hybrid consciousness. *Journal of Curriculum Theorizing, 18*(4), 81–92.

Atweh, B., Christensen, C., and Dornan, L. (1998). Students as action researchers:

Partnerships for social justice. In B. Atweh, S. Kemmis, and P. Weeks (Eds.), *Action research in practice: Partnerships for social justice* (pp. 114–138). New York: Routledge.

Aumont, J, Bergala, A., Marie, M., and Vernet, M. (1992). *Aesthetics of film*. Austin, TX: University of Texas Press.

Austin, J. L. (1975). *How to do things with words*. Cambridge: Harvard University Press.

Badgett, M. V. L. (2001). *Money, myths, and change: The economic lives of lesbians and gay men*. Chicago: The University of Chicago Press.

Baert, R. (2001). The Dress: Bodies and boundaries. *Reinventing Textiles, 2*, 11–22.

Baglieri, S., and Knopf, J. (2004). Normalizing difference in inclusive teaching. *Journal of Learning Disabilities, 37*(6), 525–529.

Bailey, Jann L. M., and Watson, S. (2005). Introduction. In R. Belmore (2005), *Fountain* (pp. 7–11). Kamloops, Vancouver, BC: Kamloops Art Gallery and The Morris and Helen Belkin Art Gallery.

Balasescu, A. (2003). Tehran chic: Islamic headscarves, fashion designers, and new geographies of modernity. *Fashion Theory, 7*(1), 39–56.

Balsamo, A. (1999). Forms of technological embodiment: Reading the body in contemporary culture. In J. Price and M. Shildrick (Eds.), *Feminist theory and the body: A Reader* (pp. 278–289). New York: Routledge.

Barnard, M. (2002). *Fashion as communication (2nd ed.)*. New York: Routledge.

Barrera, M. (2002). Hottentot 2000: Jennifer Lopez and her butt. In K. M. Phillips and B. Reay (Eds*.), Sexualities in history: A reader* (pp. 407–417). New York: Routledge.

Barry, J., and Flitterman-Lewis, S. (2003). Textual strategies: The politics of art-making. In A. Jones (Ed.), *The feminism and visual culture reader* (pp. 39-53). London: Routledge.

Barthalow-Koch. (1992). Integrating cognitive, affective, and behavioral approaches into learning experiences for sexuality education. In J. T. Sears (Ed.), *Sexuality and the curriculum: The politics and practices of sexuality education* (pp. 253–267). New York: Teachers College Press.

Barthes, R. (1983). *The fashion system* (Ward, M. and Howard, R., Trans.). New York: Hill and Wang.

Bateson, G. (1972). *Steps to an ecology of mind: A revolutionary approach to man's understanding of himself*. New York: Ballantine Books.

Battock, G. (Ed.). (1967). *The new American cinema*. New York: E. P. Dutton.

Baudrillard, J. (1983). *Simulations* (P. Foss, P. Patton, and P. Beitchman, Trans.). New York: Semiotext(e).

———. (2005). *The conspiracy of art: Manifestos, interviews, essays*. New York: Semiotext(e).

Bazin, A. (1967). *What is cinema: Vol. 1* (Hugh Gray, Trans.). Berkeley: University of California Press.

BBC News. (November 2, 2004). *Viewpoints: Europe and the headscarf.* Retrieved January 27, 2006, from http://news.bbc.co.uk/go/pr/fr/-/1/hi/world/europe/3459963.stm

Beckett, K. (2005). Choosing cesarean: Feminism and the politics of childbirth in the United States. *Feminist Theory, 6*(3), 251-275.

Beittel, K. R. (1979). The teaching of art in relation to body-mind integration and self-actualization in art. *Art Education, 32*(7), 18–20.

———. (1980). Great swamp fires I have known: Competence, and the hermeneutics of qualitative experiencing. In E. C. Short (Ed.), *Competence: Inquiries into its meaning and acquisition in educational settings* (pp. 105-122). Lanham, MD: University Press of America.

_____. *Analysis, critique, reassessment.* A report at a conference held May 18–20, 1980, under the auspices of the College of Education, The Pennsylvania State University [ERIC document D229337.]

———. (1997). *Zen and the art of pottery.* New York: Weatherhill. [Original work published 1989.]

Belmore, R. (In conversation with L. Blondeau and L. Bell). (2005). On the fightin' side of me. *Fuse Magazine, 28*(1), 24–33.

Beltrán, M. (2002). Jennifer Lopez as Latina star body: The construction of an ambivalent Hollywood "crossover". *Quarterly Review of Film and Video, 19*(1), 71–86.

———. (2004). Mas macha: The new Latina action hero. In Y. Tasker (Ed.), *Action and Adventure Cinema* (pp. 186–200). New York: Routledge.

Bender, D. M., Wood, B. J., and Vredevoogd, J. D. (2004). Teaching time: Distance education versus classroom instruction. *The American Journal of Distance Education, 18*(2), 103–114.

Bernstein, B. (2000). *Pedagogy, symbolic control and identity: Theory, research and critique.* New York: Rowman and Littlefield.

Beyer, L. E. (1998). Schooling for democracy: What kind? In L. E. Beyer and M. W. Apple (Eds.), *In the curriculum: Problems, politics, and possibilities* (pp. 245–263). Albany, NY: SUNY Press.

Beynon, J. (2002). *Masculinities and culture.* Buckingham: Open University Press.

Bickel, B. (2004). *From artist to a/r/tographer: An autoethnographic ritual inquiry into writing on the body.* Unpublished master's thesis, The University of British Columbia, Vancouver, British Columbia, Canada.

Boler, M. (1999). *Feeling power: Emotions and education.* New York: Routledge.

———. (2002). The new digital Cartesianism: Bodies and space in online education. In the Philosophy of Education Society (Ed.), *Philosophy of education* (pp. 331–340). Urbana, Illinois: Studies in Philosophy and Education.

———. (Ed.). (2004). *Democratic dialogue in education: Troubling speech, disturbing silence.* New York: Peter Lang.

Boler, M., and Zembylas, M. (2003). Discomforting truths: The emotional terrain of understanding difference. In P. P. Trifonas (Ed.), *Pedagogies of difference: Rethinking education for social change* (pp. 119–136). London: Routledge Falmer.

Bolter, J. D., and Grusin, R. (1999). *Remediation: Understanding new media.* Cambridge: The MIT Press.

Bordo, S. (2003). *Unbearable weight: Feminism, Western culture and the body.* Berkeley: University of California Press.

Bourdieu, P. (1978). *Sport and social class.* Social Science Information, 17(16), 819–840.

———. (1984). *Distinction: A social critique of the distinction of taste.* London: Routledge.

———. (1985). The social space and the genesis of groups. *Theory and Society, 14*(6), 723–

744.

————. (2001). *Masculine domination*. Cambridge, UK: Polity Press.

Brennan, C. (2005, August 18). In Nike ad campaign, big isn't just better, it's celebrated. *USA Today, 12c.*

Bridgewater, D. (1997). Effective coming out: Self-disclosure strategies to reduce sexual identity bias. In J. T. Sears and W. L. Williams (Eds.), *Overcoming heterosexism and homophobia: Strategies that work* (pp. 65–75). New York: Columbia University Press.

Britzman, D. P. (1995). Is there a queer pedagogy? Or, stop reading straight. *Educational Theory, 45*(2), 151–166.

————. (1998). *Lost subjects, contested objects: Toward a psychoanalytic inquiry of learning*. Albany, NY: State University of New York Press.

Brueggemann, B, Garland-Thomson, R., and Kleege, G. (2005). What her body taught (or, teaching about and with a disability: A conversation). *Feminist Studies, 31*(1), 13–33.

Brydon, A., and Niessen, S. (Eds.). (1998*). Consuming fashion*. New York: Berg.

Burkitt, I. (1999). *Bodies of thought*. London: Sage Publications.

Burnett, R. (2004). *How images think*. Cambridge, MA: MIT Press.

Burns, M. and Martinez, D. (2002). Visual imagery and the art of persuasion. *Learning and Leading with Technology, 29*(6), 32-53.

Butler, J. (1990). *Gender trouble: Feminism and the subversion of identity*. New York: Routledge.

————. (1993). *Bodies that matter. On the discursive limits of "sex."* London: Routledge.

————. (1997). *The psychic life of power: Theories in subjection*. Stanford, CA: Stanford.

————. (1999). Bodies that matter. In J. Price and M. Shildrick (Eds.), *Feminist theory and the body* (pp. 235–245). New York: Routledge.

————. (2004). *Undoing gender*. New York: Routledge.

Butler-Sanders, L., and Oliver, K. (2001). The role of physical activity in the lives of researchers: A body-narrative. *Studies in Philosophy and Education, 20*, 507–520.

Byrne, A., Edmondson, R., and Varley, T. (2001). Introduction to the third edition. In C. M. Arensberg and S. T. Kimball (Eds.), *Family and Community in Ireland*. Ennis: Clasp Press.

Canadian Council of Muslim Women. (2004, November 25). *Press release*. Toronto. Retrieved November 18, 2005, from http://www.ccmw.com.

Carlson, D. (1998). Who am i? Gay identity and a democratic politics of the self. In W. F. Pinar (Ed.), *Queer theory in education* (pp. 107–120). Mahwah, NJ: Lawrence Erlbaum Associates.

Carnig, J. (2006). Scholars to examine queer aesthetics in films. The University of Chicago *Chronicle, 25(*8). Retrieved January 19, 2006 from http://chronical.uchicago.edu/060119/queercinema.shtml.

Castelfranchi, C. (2004, October*). Reasons to believe: Cognitive models of beliefs*. Ms. ISTC-CNR, Roma. Invited lecture, Workshop Changing Minds, ILLC Amsterdam.

Cavallaro, D., and Warwick, A. (1998). *Fashioning the frame: Boundaries, dress and body*. Oxford: Berg.

Cixous, H. (1976). The laugh of the Medusa. *Signs, 1*(4), 889.

————. (1997). The laugh of the Medusa. In R. R. Warhol and D. P. Herndl (Eds.), *Feminisms: An anthology of literary theory and criticism* (pp. 347–362). New Brunswick, NJ: Rutgers University Press.

Clare, E. (2001). Stolen bodies, reclaimed bodies: disability and queerness. *Public Culture, 13*(3), 359–365.

Clark, M. C. (2001, Spring). Off the beaten path: Some creative approaches to adult learning. *New Directions for Adult and Continuing Education, 89,* 83–91.

Classen, C. (1993). *Worlds of sense: Exploring the senses in history and across cultures.* New York: Routledge.

————. (1998). *The color of angels: Cosmology, gender, and the aesthetic imagination.* New York: Routledge.

Cleto, F. (Ed.). (1999). *Camp: Queer aesthetic and the performing subject.* Ann Arbor, MI: The University of Michigan Press.

CNN.com. (2006, June 17). Jolie: Shilo's birth was terrifying. *CNN News.* Retrieved from the http://www.cnn.com/2006/SHOWBIZ/Movies/06/17/jolie.interview.ap/index.html

Cohen, E. and Feig, C. (2003, July 22). Delivery debate: Vaginal or C-Section? *CNN News.* Retrieved from the http://www.cnn.com/2003/HEALTH/07/22/csection.debate/index.html

Connell, R. W. (2000). *The men and the boys.* San Francisco, CA: University of California Press.

Collins, P. (1990). *Black feminist thought.* Cambridge: Unwin Hyman.

————. (2004). *Black sexual politics: African Americans, gender, and the new racism.* New York: Routledge.

Congdon, K. G. (2005). What I have learned from "other" art educators. *Studies in Art Education. 46*(2), 138–149.

Connell, R.W. (1995). *Masculinities.* California: California University Press.

————. (2002). *Gender: Short introductions.* Cambridge: Polity Press.

Conquergood, D. (2003). Rethinking ethnography: Towards a critical cultural politics. In Y. S. Lincoln and N. K. Denzin (Eds.), *Turning points in qualitative research: Tying knots in a handkerchief* (pp. 351–374). Walnut Creek, CA: AltaMira Press.

Conrad, D. L. (2002). Engagement, excitement, anxiety, and fear: Learners' experiences of starting an online course. *The American Journal of Distance Education, 16*(4), 205–226.

Cooke, M. (2001). *Women claim Islam.* London and New York: Routledge.

Coombs, N., and Banks, R. (2000). *Distance learning and students with disabilities: Easy tips for teachers.* Retrieved December 12, 2004, from http://www.csun.edu/cod/conf/2000/proceedings/0119Coombs.htm.

Cox, C. (2004, October 7). By the way, word to your mother: "Bootylicious" gets in the dictionary. *The Boston Herald,* p. 50.

Crane, D. (2000). *Fashion and its social agendas.* Chicago: The University of Chicago Press.

Crease, R. J. (1993). The play of nature: Experimentation as performance. Bloomington, IN: Indiana University Press.

Cronin, M. (2000). Schooling the revolution: Sport and education in the Irish Independence Movement 1912–22. In A. Kruger and E. Trangback (Eds.), *The History of Physical Education and Sport from European Perspectives.* Copenhagen: Institute of Exercise and

Sports Science University of Copenhagen.

Cunningham, P. A., and Lab, S. V. (1991). *Dress and popular culture*. Bowling Green, OH: State University Popular Press.

Curley, E. (Ed. and Trans.). (1994). *A Spinoza reader: The ethics and other works by Benedict de Spinoza*. Princeton, NJ: Princeton University Press.

D'Acci, J. (2004). Television, representation and gender. In R. Allen and A. Hill (Eds.), *The television reader* (pp. 373–388). New York: Routledge.

Damhorst, M. L., Miller-Spillman, K. A., and Michelman, S. O. (2005). *The meanings of dress*. New York: Fairchild Publications.

Daspit, T. (2000). Rap pedagogies: "Bring(ing) the noise" of "Knowledge born on the microphone" to radical education. In Daspit, T. and Weaver, J. (Eds.), *Popular culture and critical pedagogy: Reading, constructing, connecting* (pp. 163-182). New York: Garland Publishing, Inc.

Daspit, T., and Weaver, J. (2000). *Popular culture and critical pedagogy: Reading, constructing, connecting*. New York: Garland Publishing, Inc.

Davis, L. (1995). *Enforcing normalcy: Disability, deafness and the body*. London: Verso.

———. (2002). *Bending over backwards: Disability, dismodernism, and other difficult positions*. New York: New York University Press.

Davis, M., and Weitz, S. (1981). Sex differences in body movements and positions. In C. Mayo and N. Henley (Eds.), *Gender and nonverbal behaviour*. New York: Springer-Verlag.

Davis-Floyd, R., and Sargent, C. (1997). Introduction: The anthropology of birth. In R. Davis-Floyd and C. Sargent (Eds.), *Childbirth and authoritative knowledge: Cross-cultural perspectives*. Berkeley: University of California Press.

deBeauvier, S. (1970). *The second sex*. (1952, reprinted) New York: Bantam.

Debord, G. (2006). *Report on the construction of situations and on the international situationist tendency's conditions of organisation and action*. Retrieved January 3, 2006, from http://www.mediaartnet.org/source-text/53 (Original work published 1957).

Delaney, S. R. (1988). *The motion of light in water: Sex and science fiction writing in the East Village, 1957–1965*. New York: Arbor House/W. Morrow.

Deleuze, G. (1986). *Cinema 1: The movement-image* (H. Tomlinson and B. Habberjam, Trans.). Minneapolis: University of Minnesota Press.

———. (1989). *Cinema 2: The time-image* (H. Tomlinson and B. Habberjam, Trans.). Minneapolis: University of Minnesota Press.

Deleuze, G., and Guattari, F. (1987). *A thousand plateaus: Capitalism and schizophrenia* (B. Massumi, Trans.). Minneapolis: University of Minnesota.

Delpit, L. (1988). The silenced dialogue: Power and pedagogy in educating other people's children. *Harvard Educational Review, 58*(3), 280–298.

Denscombe, M. (1985). *Classroom control: A sociological perspective*. London: Allen & Unwin.

Denzin, N. K., and Lincoln, Y. (2005). Locating the field. In N. K. Denzin and Y.S. Lincoln (Eds.), *Handbook of Qualitative Research* (pp. 33–41). Thousand Oaks, CA: Sage.

Department of Education. (1933). *Annual Report* (1931–1932). Dublin Stationary Office.

Derrida, J. (1985). *The ear of the other: Otobiography, transference, translation*. New York:

Schocken Books.

———. (1997). The Villanova Roundtable: A conversation with Jacques Derrida. In J. D. Caputo (Ed.), *Deconstruction in a nutshell: A conversation with Jacques Derrida* (pp. 1–28). New York: Fordham University Press.

Dow, B. (1996). *Prime-time feminism: Television, media culture, and the women's movement since 1970*. Philadelphia: University of Pennsylvania Press.

Dowling, P.C. (1998). *The sociology of mathematics education: Mathematical myths/pedagogic texts*. London: Falmer.

Dowling, P. (2001). Mathematics in late modernity: Beyond myths and fragmentation. In B. Atweh, H. Forgasz, and B. Nebres (Eds.), *Sociocultural research on mathematics education: An international perspective* (pp. 19-36). Mahwah, NJ: Lawrence Erlbaum Associates.

Driver, T. F. (1997). *Liberating rites: Understanding the transformative power of ritual*. Boulder, CO: Westview Press.

Duncum, P. (2004). Visual culture isn't just visual: Multiliteracy, multimodality and meaning. *Studies in Art Education, 45*(3), 252–264.

Durham, A. (2003). Holloween: The morning-after poem. *Qualitative Inquiry, 9*(2), 300–302.

———. (2005). *From hip-hop queen to Hollywood's hot mama Morton(s): Latifah as the sexual un/desirable*. Paper presented at the International Communications Association Conference, New York, NY.

Durham, M. G. (2004). Constructing the "new ethnicities": Media, sexuality, and diaspora identity in the lives of South Asian immigrant girls. *Critical Studies in Media Communications, 21*(2), 140–161.

During, S. (1999). Popular culture on a global scale. In H. Mackay and T. O'Sullivan (Eds.), *The media reader: Continuity and transformation* (pp. 211–222). London: Sage in association with The Open University.

Dusek, V. (2006). *Philosophy of technology: An introduction*. Malden, MA: Blackwell Publishing.

Dyer, R. (1992). *Only entertainment*. New York, Routledge.

Eddy, C. (2006, June). *Performing the corpse: Bodily inscriptions and gender in Gunther Von Hagens' Body Worlds II*. Paper presented at the Canadian Women's Studies Association Conference, Toronto, ON.

Eisner, E. W. (2002). *The arts and the creation of the mind*. New Haven, CT: Yale University Press.

El Guindi, F. (1999). *Veil: Modesty, privacy, and resistance*. New York: Berg.

Emig, J. (2001). Embodied learning. *English Education, 33*(4), 271–280.

Ensor, M. P. (1996). *Looking straightforwardly, looking awry: Taking a view on the subject of interviewing*. Paper presented to the Kenton Education Association Conference, Wilgerspruit, South Africa.

Entwistle, J. (2000). *The fashioned body: Fashion, dress and modern social theory*. Cambridge, UK: Polity.

Falah, G. W. (2005). The visual representation of Muslim/Arab women in daily newspapers in the United States. In G. W. Falah, and C. Nagel (Eds.), *Geographies of Muslim women: Gender, religion, and space* (pp. 300–320). New York: The Guildford Press.

Feldman, E. B. (1970). *Becoming human through art: Aesthetic experience in the schools.* Englewood Cliffs, NJ: Prentice-Hall.

Fels, L. (2003). Performance, place, and possibility: Curricular landscapes, curricular songs. In E. Hasebe-Ludt and W. Hurren (Eds.), *Curriculum intertext: Place/language/pedagogy* (pp. 171–187). New York: Peter Lang.

Ferriter, D. (2005). *The Transformation of Ireland 1900–2000.* London: Profile Books.

Finan, K. (August 22, 2004). Leading the trend: The rear view. *The Houston Chronicle, 1.*

Finkelstein, J. (1991). *The fashioned self.* Padstow, Cornwall: Polity Press.

Flugel, J. C. (1971). *The psychology of clothes.* London: The Hogarth Press.

Foti, V. (2003). *Visions invisibles: Philosophical explorations.* Albany: State University of New York Press.

Foucault, M. (1967). *Of other spaces, heterotopias [lecture].* (J. Miskowiec, Trans.). Retrieved May 18, 2006, from

http://foucault.info/documents/heteroTopia/foucault.heteroTopia. en.html

———. (1972). *The archaeology of knowledge and the discourse on language.* New York: Pantheon.

———. (1977). *Discipline and punish: The birth of the prison.* New York: Vintage.

———. (1977). *Power/knowledge: Selected interviews and other writings, 1972–1977.* G. Colin (Ed.). New York: Random House.

———. (1988). Technologies of the self. In L. H. Martin, H. Gutman, and P.H. Hutton (Eds.), *Technologies of the self: A seminar with Michel Foucault* (pp. 16–49). Amherst: University of Massachusetts Press.

———. (1990). *The history of sexuality: An introduction. Vol. 1.* New York: Vintage.

Fraser, M., and Greco, M. (2005). *The body: A reader.* New York: Routledge.

Freedman, D. P., and Stoddard Holmes, M. (Eds.). (2003). *The teacher's body: Embodiment, authority, and identity in the academy.* Albany: State University of New York Press.

Freud, S. (1963). *The uncanny: Studies in parapsychology.* New York: Collier.

Fried, S. (2003). Film, language, sexuality and the universal: A discussion of H.D.'s film criticism and Adrienne Riche's "Shooting script." In P. Schulman and F. A. Lubich (Eds.), *The marketing of eros: Performance, sexuality, consumer culture* (pp. 151–159). Essen, Germany: Verlag Die Blaue Eule.

Frueh, J. (1989). *Hannah Wilke: A retrospective.* Columbia: University of Missouri Press.

Fuller, N. (2004). *Irish Catholicism since 1950: The undoing of a culture.* Dublin: Gil and Macmillan.

Fusco, C. (1995). *English is broken here: Notes on cultural fusion in the Americas.* New York: The New Press.

GadgetGrocer.com. (2006, February 28). *Author invents book-signing gadget.* Retrieved March 6, 2006, from http://www.gadgetgrocer.com/content/view/22/2

Garoian, C.R. (1999). *Performing pedagogy.* New York: SUNY Press.

Garoian, C. and Gaudelius, Y. (2001). Cyborg pedagogy: Performing resistance in the digital age. *Studies in Art Education, 42*(4), 333–347.

Gatens, M. (1996). *Imaginary bodies: Ethics, power and corporeality.* New York: Routledge.

Gatens, M. (2003). Epilogue to Imaginary bodies: Ethics, power and corporeality. In A. Jones

(Ed.), *The feminist visual culture reader* (pp. 466–470). New York: Routledge..

Gemeinböck, P. (2004). Negotiating the in-between: Space, body and the condition of the virtual. *Crossings: eJournal of Art and Technology, 4*(1), 1. Retrieved May 25, 2006, from http://crossings.tcd.ie/issues/4.1/Gemeinboeck

Gigliotti, C. (1999). The ethical life of the digital aesthetic. In P. Lunenfeld (Ed.), *The digital dialectic: New essays on new media* (pp. 47–63). Cambridge: Massachusetts Institute of Technology.

Gilman, S. L. (2003). Black bodies, White bodies: Toward an iconography of female sexuality in late nineteenth-century art, medicine, and literature. In A. Jones (Ed.), *The feminism and visual culture reader* (pp. 136–150). New York: Routledge.

Giroux, H. (2002). *Breaking into the movies: Film and the culture of politics.* Oxford, UK: Blackwell Publishers.

———. (2005). *Cultural studies in dark times: Public pedagogy and the challenge of neoliberalism.* Retrieved June, 2006, from the www.henryagiroux.com/online_articles /DarkTimes.htm

Giroux, H., and Simon, R. (1989). Popular culture as a pedagogy of pleasure and meaning. In H. Giroux and R. Simon (Eds.), *Popular Culture, Schooling, and Everyday Life* (pp. 1-31). Massachusetts: Bergin & Garvey.

Goffman, E. (1959). *The presentation of self in everyday life.* New York: Doubleday.

———. (1963). *Behavior in public places: Notes on the social organization of gatherings.* New York: Free Press of Glencoe; Collier-Macmillan.

Goldonowicz, J. (1985). Art and other subjects. *Art Education, 38*(6), 17.

Gough, N. (1993). *Laboratories in fiction: Science education and popular media.* Geelong, Australia: Deakin University Press.

Grady, D. (November 29, 2004). Trying to avoid second caesarean, many find choice isn't theirs. *New York Times.* Retrieved from the http://www.nytimes.com/2004/11/29/health/ 29birth.html

Green, R. (1998). Sites of genealogy–loophole of retreat, 1990–91. In E. Shohat (Ed.), *Talking visions: Multicultural feminism in a transnational age* (p. 26). New York: MIT Press.

Greene, M. (1995). *Releasing the imagination: Essays on education, the arts, and social change.* San Francisco, CA: Jossey-Bass.

Greene, P. (2000). Hitting the ton. In J. Conway (Ed.). *In shades like these: Irish teachers' life-histories from the Twentieth Century.* Dublin: Comhar Linn INTO Credit Union Ltd.

Grimes, R. L. (1995). *Beginnings in ritual studies.* Columbia: University of South Carolina Press.

Grossberg, L. (1993). The formations of cultural studies: An American in Birmingham. In V. Blundell, J. Shepherd, and I. Taylor (Eds.), *Relocating cultural studies: Developments in theory and research* (pp. 21–66). New York: Routledge.

Grosz, E. (1994). *Volatile bodies: Toward a corporeal feminism.* Bloomington, Indiana: University Press.

———. (1995). *Space, time, and perversion.* New York: Routledge.

———. (1999). Merleau-Ponty and Irigaray in the flesh. In D. Olkowski and J. Morley (Eds.), *Merleau-Ponty, interiority and exteriority, psychic life and the world* (pp. 145-166). New York: State University of New York Press.

Grumet, M. (1988). *Bitter milk: Women and teaching.* Amherst: The University of Massachusetts Press.

Hall, S. (1975). Introduction. In A. C. Smith, E. Immirzi, and T. Blackwell (Eds.), *Paper voices: The popular press and social change, 1935–1965* (pp. 11–24). Totowa, NJ: Rowman & Littlefield.

————. (1996a). On postmodernism and articulation: An interview with Stuart Hall (L. Grosburg, Ed.). In D. Morley and K. H. Chen (Eds.), *Stuart Hall: Critical Dialogues in Cultural Studies* (pp. 131–150). London: Routledge. Reprinted from Hall, S. (1986). *Journal of Communication Inquiry, 10*(2), 45–60.

————. (1996b). New ethnicities. In J. Houston, A. Baker, M. Diawara, and R. Lindeborg (Eds.), *Black British cultural studies: A reader.* Chicago: The University of Chicago Press.

————. (1997). *Representation: Cultural representations and signifying practices.* London: Thousand Oaks, Calif.: Sage in association with the Open University.

Hallward, P. (2001). *Absolutely postcolonial: Writing between the singular and the specific.* Manchester, UK: Manchester University Press.

Hamdani, D. (2004). *Muslim women: Beyond the perceptions. A demographic profile of Muslim women in Canada.* Retrieved October 15, 2005, from the www.ccmw.com

Hannah, M. (2004). Planned elective cesarean section: A reasonable choice for some women? *Canadian Medical Association, 170*(5), 813-814.

Hansen, M. (2000). *Embodying technesis: Technology beyond writing.* Ann Arbor: Michigan University Press.

————. (2002). Cinema beyond cybernetics, or how to frame the digital image. *Configurations, 10*(1), 51–90.

————. (2004a). *New philosophy for new media.* Cambridge, MA: MIT Press.

————. (2004b). "Realtime synthesis" and the différance of the body: Technocultural studies in the wake of deconstruction. *Culture Machine, 6,* 1–17, Retrieved 2006, from http://culture machine.tees.ac.uk.

Haraway, D. J. (1991). *Simians, cyborgs, and women: The reinvention of nature.* New York: Routledge.

————. (1997). *Modest-witness@second-millennium.femaleman-meets-oncomouse: Feminism and technoscience.* New York: Routledge.

————. (2003). *The companion species manifesto: Dogs, people, and significant otherness.* Chicago: Prickly Paradigm.

Hargreaves, J. (2000). The Muslim female heroic: Shorts or veils? In L. Richardson, V. Taylor, and N. Whittier (Eds.). (2004). *Feminist frontiers* (6th ed., pp. 373–386). New York: McGraw Hill.

Harris, R. (2005). Visual and verbal ambiguity, or why ceci was never a pipe. *Word & Image, 21*(2), 182–187.

Hay, C. (2002). Bearing witness to birth: A historical perspective. In C. Hay, A. Kehoe, K. Ratcliffe, and L. VandeVusse (Eds.), *Who's having this baby? Perspectives on birthing* (pp. 43-86). East Lansing: Michigan State Press.

Hayles, N. K. (1999a). *How we became posthuman: Virtual bodies in cybernetics, literature, and informatics.* Chicago: The University of Chicago.

———. (1999b). The condition of virtuality. In P. Lunenfeld (Ed.), *The digital dialectic: New essays on new media* (pp. 69–94). Cambridge: Massachusetts Institute of Technology.

———. (2002). Flesh and metal: Reconfiguring the mindbody in virtual environments. *Configurations, 10*(2), 297–320.

———. (2003). Virtual bodies and flickering signifiers. In A. Jones (Ed.), *The feminism and visual culture reader* (pp. 497–506). New York: Routledge.

———. (2005). *Computing the human.* Theory, Culture & Society, 22(1), 131–151.

———. (2006). *Lexicon linkmap.* Retrieved March 6, 2006, from http://mitpress.mit.edu/e-books/mediawork/titles/writing/sup/sup_index.html.

Hayles, N. K., and Gessler, N. (2004). The slipstream of mixed reality: Unstable ontologies and semiotic markers in The Thirteenth Floor, Dark City, and Mulholland Drive. *Publications of the Modern Language Association of America, 119*(3), 482–499.

Heartney, E. (2003). Thinking through the body: Women artists and the Catholic imagination. *Hypatia: A Journal of Feminist Philosophy, 18*(4), 3–22.

Hebdige, D. (1979*). Subculture: The meaning of style.* London: Methuen & Co.

Heidegger, M. (1962). *Being and time* (J. Macquarrie and E. Robinson, Trans.). Oxford: Blackwell.

———. (1971). *Poetry, language, thought* (A. Hofstadter, Trans.). New York: Harper & Row.

———. (1977). *The question concerning technology and other essays* (W. Lovitt, Trans.). New York: Harper Colophon Books.

Heinze, S., and Sleigh, M. (2003). Epidural or no epidural anaesthesia: Relationships between beliefs about childbirth and pain control choices. *Journal of Reproductive and Infant Psychology, 21*(4), 323-334.

Henley, N. M. (1977). *Body politics: Power, sex, and nonverbal communication.* Englewood Cliffs: Prentice-Hall.

Heward, C. (1988). *Making a man of him: Parents and their sons' education at an English public school 1929–50.* London: Routledge.

Hill-Collins, P. (1990). *Black feminist thought: Knowledge, consciousness, and the politics of empowerment.* New York: Routledge.

Hobson, J. (2003). The "batty" politic: Toward an aesthetic of the black female body. *Hypatia: A Journal of Feminist Philosophy, 18*(4), 87–104.

———. (2005). *Venus in the dark: Blackness and beauty in popular culture.* New York: Routledge.

Hocking, B., Haskell, J., and Linds, W. (2001). *Unfolding bodymind: Exploring possibility through education.* Rutland, VT: Foundation for Educational Renewal.

Holmes, M. S. (2003). *Fictions of affliction: Physical disability in Victorian culture.* Ann Arbor: University of Michigan Press.

Hoodfar, H. (1993). The veil in their minds and in our heads: The persistence of colonial images of Muslim women. *Resources for Feminist Research, 22*(3/4), 5–18.

hooks, b. (1984). *Feminist theory from margin to center.* Boston: Southend Press.

———. (1990). *Yearnings: Race gender and cultural politics.* Boston, MA: South End Press.

———. (1994). *Outlaw culture: Resisting representation.* New York: Routledge.

———. (1995). *Art on my mind: Visual politics.* New York: The New Press.

———. (2003). *We Real Cool: Black men and masculinity.* Routledge: New York, NY.

Houston, J. (1987). *The search for the beloved: Journeys in mythology and sacred psychology.* Los Angeles, CA: Jeremy P. Tarcher.

Huebner, D. (1999). *The lure of the transcendent: Collected essays by Dwayne E. Huebner.* Mahwah, N.J: Lawrence Erlbaum Associates.

Hussain, S. (2002, July). Voices of Muslim women: A community research project. *Canadian Council of Muslim Women.* Retrieved November 18, 2005, from http://www.ccmw.com/publications/Voices_of_Muslim_Women_full.htm

Hutcheon, L. (1985). *The theory of parody: The teachings of twentieth-century art forms.* New York: Methuen.

Illich, I. (1983). Silence is a commons. *CoEvolution Quarterly, 40,* 5–9.

Irwin, R. (1999/2000). Facing oneself: An embodied pedagogy. *Arts and Learning Research Journal, 16*(1), 82–86.

Irwin, R. L., and de Cosson, A. (2004). *A/r/t/ography: Rendering self through arts-based living inquiry.* Vancouver, BC: Pacific Educational Press.

Irigaray, L. (1985). *This sex which is not one* (C. Porter and C. Burke, Trans.). Ithaca, NY: Cornell University Press.

———. (1991). The bodily encounter with the mother. In M. Whitford (Ed.), *The Irigaray reader* (pp. 34–46). London: Blackwell.

———. (1992). *Elemental passions* (J. Collie and J. Still, Trans.). New York: Routledge. (Original work published 1982).

———. (1993). *An ethics of sexual difference.* Ithaca, NY: Cornell University Press.

———. (2004). *Key writings.* New York: Continuum.

James, I. (2006). *An Introduction to the philosophy of Jean-Luc Nancy.* Stanford, CA: Stanford University Press.

Jardine, D. (2003). The profession needs new blood. In D. W. Jardine, P. Clifford, and S. Friessen (Eds.), *Back to the basics of teaching and learning: Thinking the world together* (pp. 55–70). Mahwah, NJ: Lawrence Erlbaum Associates.

Jay, M. (1994). *Downcast eyes: The denigration of vision in twentieth-century French thought.* Berkeley: University of California.

Jenkins, H., McPherson, T., and Shattuc, J. (2002). The culture that sticks to your skin: A manifesto for a new cultural studies. In H. Jenkins, T. McPherson, and J. Shattuc (Eds.), *Hop on Pop: The politics and pleasures of popular culture.* Durham, NC: Duke University Press.

Jenks, C. (1995). The centrality of the eye in Western culture: An introduction. In C. Jenks (Ed.), *Visual culture* (pp. 1–25). New York: Routledge.

Jones, A. (1998). *Body art: Performing the subject.* Minnesota: University of Minnesota Press.

———. (2002). Performing the other as self: Cindy Sherman and Laura Aguilar pose the subject. In S. Smith and J. Watson (Eds.), *Interfaces: Women, autobiography, image, performance* (pp. 69–102). Ann Arbor: University of Michigan Press.

———. (2003). Conceiving the intersections of feminism and visual culture. In A. Jones (Ed.), *The feminism and visual culture reader* (pp. 1–7). London and New York: Routledge.

Jones, A., and Stephenson, A. (Eds.). (1999). *Performing the body/performing the text*. New York: Routledge.

Jones, A. and Warr, T. (2000). *The artist's body*. New York: Phaidon.

Jones, R. (2000, April 7). More children being born with induced labor *CNN News*. Retrieved April 28, 2006. (http://archives.cnn.com/2000/HEALTH/women/04/07/induction.health.wmd/).

Kaiser, S. B. (Ed.). (1997). *The social psychology of clothing (2nd ed.)*. New York: Fairchild Publications.

Keller, J. R. (2002). *Queer (un)friendly film and television*. Jefferson, NC: McFarland & Company.

Kellner, D. (1995). *Media culture: Cultural studies, identity and politics between the modern and the postmodern*. London: Routledge.

Khan, S. (2002). *Aversion and desire: Negotiating Muslim female identity in the diaspora*. Toronto: Women's Press.

Kilbourne, J. (1999). *Deadly persuasion: Why women and girls must fight the addictive power of advertising*. New York: Free Press.

Kimmel, M. (1994a). Masculinity as homophobia: Fear, shame, and silence in the construction of gender identity. In H. Brod and M. Kaufman (Eds.), *Theorizing Masculinities* (pp. 119–141). Thousand Oaks, CA: Sage

———. (1994b). Consuming manhood: The feminization of American culture and the recreation of the male body, 1832–1920. In L. Goldstein (Ed.), *The male body: Features, destinies, exposure* (pp. 12–42). University of Michigan Press.

Kimmel, M., and Messner, M. (2001). *Men's Lives (5th ed.)*. Boston: Allyn and Bacon.

Kirk, D. (1993). *The Body, schooling and culture*. Geelong: Deakin University Press.

Kitzinger, Sheila. (2005). *The politics ofbBirth*. London: Elsevier.

Klein, A.M. (1993). *Little big men: Bodybuilding subculture and gender construction*. Albany: State University of New York Press.

Klein, M. (2004). Quick fix culture: The cesarean-section-on-demand debate. *Birth, 31*(3), 161–164.

Kozel, S. (1996). The diabolical strategy of mimesis: Luce Irigaray's reading of Maurice Merleau-Ponty. *Hypatia: A Journal of Feminist Philosophy, 11*(3), 114–129.

Kracauer, S. (1947). *From Caligari to Hitler: A psychological history of the German film*. Princeton, NJ: Princeton University Press.

Kristeva, J. (1991). *Strangers to ourselves* (L. S. Roudiez, Trans.). New York: Columbia University Press.

Kumashiro, K. K. (Ed.). (2001). *Troubling intersections of race and sexuality: Queer students of color and anti-oppressive education*. Lanham, MD: Roman Littlefield.

Kumashiro, K. K. (2002). *Troubling education: Queer activism and antioppressive pedagogy*. New York: Routledge Falmer.

———. (2004). *Against common sense: Teaching and learning toward social justice*. New York: Routledge Falmer.

Lacan, J. (1981). *The four fundamental concepts of psycho-analysis*. New York: W. W. Norton & Company.

Lander, D. A. (2005). The consuming (no)body of online learners: Re-membering e-communities of practice. *Studies in Continuing Education, 27*(2), 155–174.

Lather, P. (2000). Drawing the line at angels: Working the ruins of feminist ethnography. In E. St. Pierre and W. S. Pillow (Eds.), *Working the ruins: Feminist poststructural theory and methods in education* (pp. 284–311). New York: Routledge.

Latour, B. (2004). How to talk about the body? The normative dimension of science studies. *Body & Society, 10*, 205–209.

———. (2005). *Reassembling the social: An introduction to actor-network-theory.* New York: Oxford University Press.

Law, J., and Hassard, J. (Eds.). (1999). *Actor network theory and after.* Malden, MA: Blackwell.

Leavitt, J. W. (1986). *Brought to bed: Childbearing in America 1750 to 1950.* New York: Oxford University Press.

Leder, D. (1990). *The absent body.* Chicago: University of Chicago.

Leeman, L. (2005). Patient-choice cesarean delivery. *American Family Physician, 72*(4), 697–705.

Lenoir, L. (2004, April 2). Beyoncé reshapes ideas of beauty. *Chicago Sun-Times*, p. 58.

Lent, M. (1999). The medical and legal risks of the electronic fetal monitor. *Stanford Law Review, 51*, 807-838.

Lesko, N (2000). *Masculinities at school.* Thousand Oaks, CA: Sage.

Letts, W. J. IV., and Sears, J. T. (Eds.). (1999). *Queering elementary education: Advancing the dialogue about sexualities and schooling.* New York: Rowman & Littlefield.

Lewis, R., & Mills, S. (2003). Introduction. In R. Lewis & S. Mills (Eds.), *Feminist postcolonial theory: A reader* (pp. 1–21). New York: Routledge.

Lummis, C. D. (1996). *Radical democracy.* Ithaca, NY: Cornell University Press.

Lurie, A. (1981). *The language of clothes.* London: Bloomsbury.

Mac an Ghaill, M. (1994). *The making of men: Masculinities, sexualities and schooling.* Buckingham, UK: Open University Press.

Mairs, N. (1990). *Carnal acts.* New York: Harper Collins.

Marcuse, H. (1972). *One dimensional man.* London: Abacus.

———. (1977). *The aesthetic dimension. Toward a critique of Marxist aesthetics.* Boston: Beacon.

Marks, L. (2002). *Touch: Sensuous theory and multisensory media.* Minneapolis: University of Minnesota.

Martin, E. (1987). *The woman in the body: A cultural analysis of reproduction.* Boston: Beacon Press.

Martin, J., Brady, H., Sutton, P., Ventura, S., Menacker, F., and Munson, M. (2005). Births: Final data for 2003. *National Vital Statistics Reports, 54*(2), 13–24.

Martino, W., and Pallotta-Chiarolli, M. (2003). *So what's a boy?* Buckingham, UK: Open University Press.

Maynard, M. (2004). *Dress and globalisation.* Manchester, UK: Manchester University Press.

Mayo, C. (2002). The bind that ties: Civility and social difference. *Educational Theory, 52*(2), 169–186.

McCoy, K. (2000). White noise-the sound of epidemic: Reading/writing a climate of intelligibility around the "crisis" of difference. In E. St Pierre and W. S. Pillow (Eds.), *Working the ruins: Feminist poststructural theory and methods in education* (pp. 237–257). New York: Routledge.

McDevitt, P. (1997). Muscular Catholicism: Nationalism, masculinity and Gaelic team sports, 1884–1916. *Gender and History, 9*(2), 262–284.

McElligott, T. J. (1986). *This teaching life: A memoir of schooldays in Ireland*. Dublin, Ireland: Wolfhound Press.

Meikle, S., Claudia, S., Jun, Z., and William, L. (2005). A national estimate of the elective primary cesarean delivery rate. *Obstetrics & Gynecology, 105*, 751–756.

Merleau-Ponty, M. (1962). *Phenomenology of perception* (C. Smith, Trans.). London: Routledge and Kegan Paul.

———. (1968). *The visible and the invisible* (A. Lingis, Trans.). Evanston, IL: Northwestern University Press.

Messner, M. (1997). *Politics of masculinities: Men in movements*. Thousand Oaks, CA: Sage.

Meyer, K. (2005). *Living inquiry a gateless gate and a beach*. Centre for Cross Faculty Inquiry. Course Syllabus for Living Inquiry. Vancouver, BC: The University of British Columbia.

Michaelson, K. (1988). Childbirth in America: A brief history and contemporary issues. In K. Michaelson (Ed.), *Childbirth in America: Anthropological perspectives*. South Hadley, MA: Bergin & Garvey.

Millea, H. (2005). Britney's big adventure. *Elle Magazine, 242*, 388–394. New York: Hachette Filipacchi Media.

Minh-ha, T. T. (1998). Other than myself/my other self. In G. Robertson, M. Mash, L. Tickner, J. Bird, B. Curtis, and T. Putnam (Eds.), *Traveler's Tales: Narratives of home and displacement* (pp. 9–26). New York: Routledge.

———. (1999). Painted power, with Homi Bhabha. In Trinh Minh-ha (Ed.), *Cinema interval* (pp. 17–31). New York: Routledge.

———. (2003). Difference: A special third world women issue. In A. Jones (Ed.), *The feminism and visual culture reader* (pp. 151–173). New York: Routledge.

———. (2005). *The digital film event*. New York: Routledge.

Mirzoeff, N. (1999). Introduction: What is visual culture? In N. Mirzoeff (Ed.), *An introduction to visual culture* (pp. 1–34). London and New York: Routledge.

Mitchell, C., and Weber, S. (1999). *Reinventing ourselves as teachers: Beyond nostalgia*. London: Falmer Press.

Mohanty, C. T. (1988). Under Western eyes: Feminist scholarship and colonial discourses. *Feminist Review, 30*, 65–88.

Molina Guzmán, I., and Valdivia, A. (2004). Brain, brow or bootie: Iconic Latinas in contemporary popular culture. *The Communication Review, 7*(2), 205–221.

Morgan, C. (1984). *The price of salt*. Tallahassee, FL: Naiad Press.

Morgan, D.H.G. (1992). *Discovering men*. London: Routledge.

Morrell, R. (1994). Boys, gangs and the making of masculinity in the white secondary schools of Natal, 1880–1930. *Masculinities, 2*(2), 56–82.

Morris, M (2005). Editor's Introduction. *Journal of Curriculum Theorizing, 21*(1).

Mulder, A., and Post, M. (2000). *Book for the electronic arts*. Amsterdam: DeBalie.

Mullen, C. (2003). Guest editor's introduction: A self-fashioned gallery of aesthetic practice. *Qualitative Inquiry, 9*(2), 165-181.

Muñoz, J. E. (2003). "The white to be angry:" Vaginal Creme Davis's terrorist drag. In A. Jones (Ed.), *The feminist and visual culture reader* (pp. 217–224). New York: Routledge.

Münsterberg, H. (1970). *The film: A psychological study.* New York: Dover Publications. (Original work published 1916)

Murray, S. O. (1996). *American gay.* Chicago: University of Chicago Press.

Nancy, J. L. (2000). *Of being singular plural.* Stanford, CA: Stanford University Press.

Negrón-Muntaner, F. (2004). *Boricua pop: Puerto Ricans and the Latinization of American culture.* New York: New York University Press.

Norden, M. (1994). *The cinema of isolation: A history of physical disabilities in the movies.* New Brunswick, NJ: Rutgers University Press.

Odeh, L. U. (1993). Post-colonial feminism and the veil: Thinking the difference. *Feminist Review, 43*, 26–37.

Olkowski, D.E. (2000). The end of phenomenology: Bergson's interval in Irigaray. *Hypatia: A Journal of Feminist Philosophy, 15*(3), 73–91.

Palmer, P. (1983). *To know as we are known: Education as a spiritual journey.* San Francisco: Harper Collins.

Panofsky, E. (1995). *Three essays on style.* Cambridge: MIT Press.

Patton, C. (1995). Performativity and spatial distinction. In A. Parker and E.K. Sedgwick (Eds.), *Performativity and performance.* New York: Routledge.

Payne, J. (2006). Period: Full stop? *Washington Post News,* Retrieved June 6, 2006 from, http://www.washingtonpost.com/wpdyn/content/article/2006/06/05/AR2006060500845.html

Perpich, D. (2005). Corpus meum: Disintegrating bodies and the ideal of integrity. *Hypatia: A Journal of Feminist Philosophy, 20*(3), 75–93.

Peters, M. (2004). Education and the philosophy of the body: Bodies of knowledge and knowledges of the body. In L. Bresler (Ed.), *Knowing bodies, moving minds: Towards embodied teaching and learning.* London: Kluwer.

Peters, M. A., and Burbules, N. C. (2004). *Poststructuralism and educational research.* Toronto: Rowman & Littlefield Publishers.

Phelan, P. (2003). Broken symmetries: Memory, sight, love. In A. Jones (Ed.), *The feminism and visual culture reader* (pp. 105–114). New York: Routledge

Pillow, W. S. (2003). Confession, catharsis, or cure? Rethinking the uses of reflexivity as methodological power in qualitative research. *Qualitative Studies in Education, 16*(2), 175–196.

Pinar, W. (2004). *What is curriculum theory?* Mahwah, NJ: Lawrence Erlbaum Associates. (Original work published 1975)

———. (Ed.). (1998). *Queer theory in education.* Mahwah, NJ: Lawrence Erlbaum Associates.

———. (2005). Presidential address: A bridge between Chinese and North American curricular studies. *Transnational Curriculum Inquiry, 2*(1), 1–12. Retrieved January 10, 2006, from http://nitinat.library.ubc.ca/ojs/index.php/tci

Pinar, W., and Irwin, R. (Eds.). (2005). *Curriculum in a new key: The collected works of Ted*

T. Aoki. Mahwah, NJ: Lawrence Erlbaum Associates.

Pinar, W. F., Reynolds, W. M., Slattery, P., and Taubman, P. M. (Eds.). (2004). *Understanding curriculum*. New York: Peter Lang. (Original work published 1995)

Piontek, T. (2006). *Queering gay and lesbian studies*. Urbana-Champagne, IL: University of Illinois Press.

Prentice, R. (2005). The anatomy of a surgical simulation: The mutual articulation of bodies in and through the machine. *Social Studies of Science, 35*(6), 837–866.

Price, J., and Shildrick, M. (1999). *Feminist theory and the body: A reader*. New York: Routledge.

Prosser, J. (2001). Skin memories. In S. Ahmed and J. Stacey (Eds.), *Thinking through skin* (pp. 52–68). London: Routledge.

Pyke, R. (1902, August). What men like in men. *Cosmopolitan*, 405–406.

Rabinow, P. (Ed.). (1984). *Foucault reader*. New York, NY: Pantheon Books.

Radicalesbians. (1970). The woman-identified woman. In M. Blasius and S. Phelan (Eds.), (1997) *We are everywhere: A historical sourcebook of Gay and Lesbian politics* (pp. 396–399). New York: Routledge.

Raffo, S. (Ed.). (1997). *Queerly classed*. Boston, MA: South End Press.

Rich, A. (1993). Compulsory heterosexuality and lesbian existence. In H. Abelove, M.

Barale, A., and Halperin, D. M. (Eds.), *The lesbian and gay studies reader* (pp. 227–254). New York: Routledge.

Rizvi, F. (2005). Representations of Islam and education for justice. In C. McCarthy, W. Crichlow, G. Dimitriadis, and N. Dolby (Eds.), *Race, identity, and representation in education* (pp. 167–178). New York: Routledge.

Rizvi, F., and Walsh, L. (1998). Difference, globalisation, and the internationalisation of curriculum. *Australian Universities' Review, 41*(2), 7.

Roach-Higgins, M. E., Eicher, J. B., and Johnson, K. P. (Eds.). (1995). *Dress and identity*. New York: Fairchild Publications.

Roberts, D. E. (1997). *Killing the black body: Race, reproduction, and the meaning of liberty (1ˢᵗ ed.)*. New York: Pantheon Books.

Rochlin, M. (1992). The heterosexual questionnaire. In M. S. Kimmel and M. A. Messner (Eds.), *Men's lives* (2ⁿᵈ ed., pp. 482–483). New York: Macmillan.

Rogoff, I. (2000). *Terra infirma: Geography's visual culture*. London: Routledge.

Rothman, B. K. (1986). *The social construction of birth. In Pamela Eakins (Ed.), The American way of birth*. Philadelphia: Temple University Press.

Rubin, R. (2005). Battle lines drawn over C-section. *USA Today*, Retrieved August 23, 2005 from, http://www.usatoday.com/news/health/2005-08-23-csection-battle_x.htm

Russo, V. (1987). *The celluloid closet: Homosexuality in the movies* (Rev. ed.). New York: Harper & Row.

Ryan, M. and Kellner, D. (1988). *Camera politica: The politics and ideology of contemporary Hollywood film*. Bloomington: Indiana University Press.

Ryokai, K., Marti, S., Ishii, H., Monzon, J., and Figueriedo, R. (2005). *iBrush*. MIT Media Lab. Retrieved February 20, 2006, from http://web.media.mit.edu/%7Ekimiko/iobrush/

Safran, S. (1998). The first century of disability portrayal in film: An analysis of the literature. *Journal of Special Education, 31*(4), 467–479.

Said, E. W. (1978). *Orientalism*. New York: Vintage Books.

———. (1981). *Covering Islam: How the media and the experts determine how we see the rest of the world*. New York: Pantheon Books.

Sandell, R. (2006). Form + theme + context: Balancing considerations for meaningful art learning. *Art Education, 59*(1), 33–37.

Sanders, J. H., III. (1999). Dissertation as performance [art script] (take three). *International Journal of Qualitative Studies in Education, 12*(5), 541–562.

———. (2000, November 12). *FOUNDERS: Exploring the social histories of a community school of visual art*. Readers Theater/Performance at the 2nd Arts-Based Education Research Conference, Balcones Springs, TX.

———. (2004). Moving beyond the binary. In A. Fariello and P. Owen (Eds.), *Objects and meaning: Readings that challenge the norm* (pp. 88–105). Lanham, MD: Scarecrow Press.

———. (2005). Exchanging fluid discourses of social dis-ease: Visual cultural studies as prophylactic praxis as rough trade. In K. Anijar and T. DaoJensen (Eds.), *Culture and the Condom: Complicated conversations* (pp. 59–76). New York, NY: Peter Lang.

Scott, L. (2004, October 28). Beckham bends it with Beyoncé. *Press Association*. Retrieved April 15, 2006, from LexisNexis Academic database.

Sedgwick, E. K. (1990). *Epistemology of the closet*. Los Angeles: University of California Press.

Seidman, S. (1993). Identity and politics in a "Postmodern" gay culture: Some historic and conceptual notes. In M. Warner (Ed.), *Fear of a queer planet: Queer politics and social theory* (pp. 105–142). Minneapolis: University of Minnesota Press.

Sellers-Young, B. (1998). Somatic processes: Convergence of theory and practice. *Theatre Topics, 8*(2), 173–187.

Senft, T. M. (Ed.). (1996). *Sexuality and cyberspace: Performing the digital body*. New York: Women & Performance Project.

Sensoy, O., and DiAngelo, R. (2006). "I wouldn't want to be a woman in the Middle East": White female student teachers and the narrative of the oppressed woman. *Radical Pedagogy, 8*(1), 1–14. Retrieved May 20, 2006, from http://radicalpedagogy.icaap.org/content/issue8_1/sensoy.html

Shaheen, J. G. (2003). Reel bad Arabs: How Hollywood vilifies a people. *The Annals of the American Academy of Political and Social Science, 588*, 171–193.

Shanahan, L. (2003). Bottom line?: Bottom's up! *Brandweek, 44*, 26. Retrieved January 30, 2006, from the Academic Search Premier database.

Shanken, E. (2000). Tele-agency: Telematics, telerobotics, and the art of meaning. *Art Journal, 59*(2), 65–77.

Shilling, C. (2003). *The body and social theory (2nd ed.)*. London: Sage.

Shirazi, F. (2001). *The veil unveiled: The hijab in modern culture*. Tampa: University Press of Florida.

Shohat, E. (1998). Introduction. In E. Shohat (Ed.), *Talking visions: Multicultural feminism in a transnational age* (pp. 1–62). New York: MIT Press.

Shorter, B. (1987). *An image darkly forming: Women and initiation*. London: Routledge and Kegan Paul.

Shotter, J. (2004). Responsive expression in living bodies. *Cultural Studies, 18*(2/3), 443–460.

Singer, L. (1993). *Erotic welfare: Sexual theory and politics in the age of epidemic.* New York: Routledge.

Slaughter, V., and Heron, M. (2004). Origins and Early Development of Human Body Knowledge. *Monographs of the Society for Research in Child Development, 69*(2), Serial No. 276. Malden, MA: Blackwell Publishing.

Smith, A., and Kozleski, E. B. (2005). Witnessing Brown: Pursuit of an equity agenda in American education. *Remedial and Special Education, 26*(5), 270–280.

Smith, D. (1987). *The everyday world as problematic: A feminist sociology.* Toronto, ON, Canada: University of Toronto Press.

Smith, D. G. (2003). Some thoughts on living in-between. In E. Habe-Ludt and W. Hurren (Eds.), *Curriculum intertext: Place/language/pedagogy* (pp. xv–xvii). New York: Peter Lang.

Smith, S. (2002). Bodies of evidence: Jenny Saville, Faith Ringgold, and Janine Antoni weigh in. In S. Smith and J. Watson (Eds.), *Interfaces: Women, autobiography, image, performance* (pp. 132–159). Ann Arbor: University of Michigan Press.

Snowber, C. (2002). Bodydance: Enfleshing soulful inquiry through improvisation. In C. Bagley and M. B. Cancienne (Eds.), *Dancing the data* (pp. 20-33). New York: Peter Lang.

———. (2004). *Embodied prayer: Toward a wholeness of body, mind, and soul.* Kelowna, BC: Northstone Publishing.

Snyder, S., and Mitchell, D. (2001). *Narrative prosthesis: Disabilities and the dependencies of discourse.* Ann Arbor: University of Michigan Press.

Sobchack, V. (1992). *The address of the eye: A phenomenology of film experience.* Princeton, NJ: Princeton University Press.

———. (2004). *Carnal thoughts: Embodiment and moving image culture.* Berkeley: University of California Press.

Sontag, S. (1966). *Against interpretation.* New York: Farrar, Strauss & Giroux.

Sorrial, S. (2004). Heidegger, Jean-Luc Nancy, and the question of Dasein's embodiment. *Philosophy Today, 48*(2), 216–230.

Springgay, S. (2003). Cloth as intercorporeality: Touch, fantasy, and performance and the construction of body knowledge. *International Journal of Education and the Arts, 4*(5). Retrieved May, 1, 2004, from http://ijea.asu.edu/v4n5/

———. (2004). *Inside the visible: Youth understanding of body knowledge through touch.* Unpublished doctoral dissertation, The University of British Columbia, Vancouver.

———. (2005a). Thinking through bodies: Bodied encounters and the process of meaning making in an email generated art project. *Studies in Art Education, 47*(1), 34–50.

———. (2005b). An intimate distance: Youth interrogations of intercorporeal cartography as visual narrative text. *Journal of the Canadian Association for Curriculum Studies, 3*(1), 107–122.

Springgay, S., Irwin, R. L., and Kind, S. (2005). A/r/tography as living inquiry through art and text. *Qualitative Inquiry, 11*(6), 892–912.

Springgay, S., and Peterat, L. (2002/2003). Touch, fantasy, and performance: Re-presenting bodies in a high school fashion show. *The Journal of Gender Issues in Art and Education*

3, 52–68.

Stankiewicz, M. A. (2004). Notions of technology and visual literacy. *Studies in Art Education, 46*(1), 88–91.

Stone, L. (Ed.). (1994). *The education feminism reader.* New York: Routledge.

Stump, J. (2002). Discriminatory portrayals of the mentally disabled in popular films: Some preliminary thoughts. *Contemporary Justice Review, 5*(2), 189–193.

Sturken, M., and Cartwright, L. (2001). *Practices of looking: An introduction to visual culture.* Oxford: Oxford University Press.

Suarez, S. H. (1993). Midwifery is not the Practice of Medicine. *Yale Journal of Law and Feminism, 5*(2), 315–364.

Sullivan, N. (2003). Being, thinking, writing "with." *Cultural Studies Review, 9*(1), 51–59.

Sullivan, S. (1997) Domination and dialogue in Merleau-Ponty's phenomenolgy of perception. *Hypatia: A Journal of Feminist Philosophy, 12*(1), 1–19.

Sumara, D. (2005). On the importance of the eccentric curriculum. *Journal of the Canadian Association for Curriculum Studies, 3*(1), iii–viii.

Suzuki, S. (1975). *Zen mind, beginner's mind.* New York: John Weatherhill.

Swanson, D. M. (2004). *Voices in the silence: Narratives of disadvantage, social context and school mathematics in post-apartheid South Africa.* Unpublished Doctoral Dissertation, University of British Columbia.

Sweetman, P. (2000). Anchoring the (postmodern) self? Body modification, fashion, and identity. In M. Featherstone (Ed.), *Body modification* (pp. 51–76). London: Sage.

Taylor, L. J. (1995). *Occasions of faith: An anthropology of Irish Catholics.* Philadelphia: University of Pennsylvania Press.

Thompson, J. (2005, April 17). This year's must-have cosmetic surgery: The Beyoncé nip and butt: There is growing demand from British women for buttock implants. *Independent*, p. 11.

Todd, S. (1997). Educating beyond tolerance: Reading media images of the hijab. In J. P. Robertson (Ed.), *Teaching for a tolerant world* (pp. 157–166). Urbana, Illinois: National Council of Teachers of English.

———. (2003). *Learning from the other: Levinas, psychoanlaysis, and ethical possibilities in education.* Albany: State University of New York Press.

Touré. (2004, March 4). A woman possessed. *Rolling Stone*, 34–44.

Troy, N. J. (2003). *Couture culture: A study in modern art and fashion.* Cambridge: Massachusetts Institute of Technology.

Tuana, N. (2004). Coming to understand: Orgasm and the epistemology of ignorance. *Hypatia: A Journal of Feminist Philosophy, 19*(1), 194–232.

Turkle, S. (1984). *The second self: Computers and the human spirit.* New York: Simon and Schuster.

Turner, B. (1996). *The body and society: Explorations in social theory.* New York: Sage.

Twenty-fourth annual report to congress on the implementation of the Individuals with Disabilities Education Act (2002). Retrieved April 1, 2006, from http://www.ed.gov/about/reports/annual/osep/2002/index.html

Valdivia, A. N. (2000). *A Latina in the land of Hollywood and other essays on media culture.* Tucson: University of Arizona Press.

Valdivia, A.N., and Projansky, S. (2006). Feminism and the media. In B. J. Dow and J.T. Wood (Eds.), *Sage handbook of gender and communication*. Thousand Oaks, CA: Sage Publications.

van Essen, M. (2000). Gender in beweging: Over pedagogiek en sekse in de Lichamelijke Opvoeding van de Twinstigste EEUW. *Tijdschrift voor Genderstudies, 3*, 25–35.

van Manen, M. (1991). *The tact of teaching: The meaning of pedagogical thoughtfulness*. Albany: State University of New York Press.

———. (2003). Researching lived experience. London, ON: The Althouse Press.

Vasseleu, C. (1998). *Textures of light: Vision and touch in Irigaray, Levinas and Merleau-Ponty*. New York: Routledge.

Wagner, M. (1994). *Pursuing the birth machine: The search for appropriate birth technology*. Camperdown, NSW Australia: ACE Graphics.

Wallace, M. (2004). *Dark designs and visual culture*. Durham: Duke University Press.

Ward, A. (2005, December 13). Pepsi's market value tops Coke after 112 years. *Financial Times*, p. 1.

Warshow, R. (2001). *The immediate experience: Movies, comics, theatre, and other aspects of popular culture*. Cambridge, MA: Harvard University Press. (Original work published 1946)

Watkins, R., and Schlosser, C. (2003). It's not about time: A fresh approach to educational equivalency. *TechTrends, 47*(3), 35–40.

Watson, S. (2004, October 21). The do-it-all diva: Records, films, clothes, accessories, fragrances--Beyoncé Knowles is one of a new breed of do-it-all divas who nurture their careers like global brands. *Townsville Bulletin/Townsville Sun*, p. 24.

Weiss, G. (1999). *Body image: Embodiment as intercoporeality*. New York: Routlege.

Wentz, L. (2003, July 7). Pepsi puts interests before ethnicity. *Advertising Age, 74*. S4–S6.

Wilbert, C. (2006, February 24). Who's no. 1? Coke, Pepsi chase boom in China. *The Atlanta Journal-Constitution*, p. E1.

Willis, G. and Schubert, W. (Eds.). (1991). *Reflections from the heart of educational inquiry*. Albany, NY: SUNY Press.

Wingard, R. G. (2004). Classroom teaching changes in web-enhanced courses: A multi-institutional study. *Educause Quarterly, 1*, 26–35.

Winograd, T. (1992). Computers and rationality: The myths and realities. In R. Morelli, W. M. Brown, D. Anselmi, K. Haberlandt, & D. Lloyd (Eds.), *Minds, brains and computers: Perspectives in cognitive science and artificial intelligence* (pp. 152-167). Norwood, NJ: Ablex.

Winzer, M. A. (1993). *The history of Special Education: From isolation to integration*. Washington, D.C.: Gallaudet University Press.

Wolford, L. (2000). *Virtual sins and public displays: Stereotyping and identity tourism in Pocha Nostra's ethno-techno art*. Paper presented at the Performative sites: Intersecting art, technology, and the body symposium, Penn State University.

Wolf, N. (2003). *Misconceptions: Truth, lies, and the unexpected on the journey to motherhood*. New York: Anchor Books.

Yep, G. A. (1997). Changing homophobic and heterosexist attitudes: An overview of persuasive communication approaches. In J. T. Sears and W. L. Williams (Eds.),

Overcoming heterosexism and homophobia: Strategies that work (pp. 49–64). New York: Columbia University Press.

Young, I.M. (1990). *Throwing like a girl and other essays in feminist philosophy and social theory*. Bloomington: Indiana University.

Yuval-Davis, N. (1997). *Gender and nation*. London: Sage.

Zigler, R. L. (1999). Tacit knowledge and spiritual pedagogy. *Journal of Beliefs and Values, 20*(2), 162–172.

Zine, J. (2003). The challenge of anti-Islamaphobia education. *Orbit, 33*(3), 39–41.

Zizek, S. (1993). *Tarrying with the negative: Kant, Hegel, and the critique of ideology*. Durham, NC: Duke University Press.

Contributors

Jillian Báez is a Ford Foundation Predoctoral Diversity Fellow conducting dissertation research in the Institute of Communications Research at the University of Illinois, Urbana-Champaign about media discourse and gendered experiences in relation to Latinidad. Her scholarship is featured in peer-reviewed publications, such as the *Journal of Popular Communication.*

Daniel T. Barney is an artist, educator, and doctoral student at the University of British Columbia in the Faculty of Education in the Department of Curriculum Studies. In addition to his personal interest in arts-based research, he has 11 years of teaching secondary art in northern Utah.

Barbara Bickel is an artist, researcher, educator, and independent curator. She is currently a PhD student at the University of British Columbia. Her research focuses on women, spiritual leadership, collaboration, and education. Barbara completed an MA in Education at the University of British Columbia in 2004. Her thesis was entitled *From Artist to A/r/tographer: An Autoethnographic Ritual Inquiry into Writing on the Body.* Her art and performance rituals have been exhibited and performed in Canada since 1991. Her art and thesis can be viewed online at http://www.barbarabickel.ca.

Tara D. Britt is a teacher of French at Statesboro High School in southeast Georgia. She is a candidate in the Doctoral Program at Georgia Southern University, mentored by Dr. John A. Weaver. Her dissertation is a phenomenological study on how the viewing of films representing teachers affects teachers' perceptions of their identities.

Aisha Durham is co-editor of *Home Girls Make Some Noise!: Hip Hop Feminism Anthology.* Durham is a former research/writer intern for *Time* magazine and assistant editor for research journals. She is a doctoral candidate at the University of Illinois, Urbana-Champaign, where she examines cultural representations, interpretive methods, and black feminism.

Debra Freedman is an Associate Professor at the Pennsylvania State University in the department of Educational Policy Studies. Her research and teaching interests include curriculum theory, cultural studies, and teacher education. She is committed to anti-oppressive education.

Charles Garoian, Director, School of Visual Arts at Penn State University, is the author of *Performing Pedagogy: Toward an Art of Politics* (1999). His scholarly articles are featured in journals on art and education, and he has performed and lectured in colleges and universities, galleries and museums nationally and internationally.

Yvonne Gaudelius is Interim Dean of the College of Arts and Architecture and a Professor of Art Education and Women's Studies at Penn State University. Her co-edited book *Contemporary Issues in Art Education* (2002) explored contemporary theoretical perspectives on art education and pedagogy. Her scholarly writings have appeared in numerous journals and books.

Natalie Jolly is a doctoral student at the Pennsylvania State University in the Departments of Women's Studies and Rural Sociology. Her research reflects on her two-year ethnography of birth and midwifery in the Amish community and explores the ways in which birth practices are shaped by social norms.

Karen Keifer-Boyd is a Professor of Art education in the School of Visual Arts at Penn State University. Her grant supported research focuses on strategies for teaching critical inquiry and creative approaches within dynamic interactive technologies. Her critically oriented work problematizes cultural inscriptions, seeks social transformation, and practices critical self-reflexivity.

Julie Garlen Maudlin, Ed.D., lives in Southeast Georgia with her husband and three children. She works in the public school system as an instructional coach at an elementary school serving fourth and fifth graders.

Cris Mayo is an Associate Professor in the Department of Educational Policy Studies and the Gender and Women's Studies Program at the University of Illinois at Urbana-Champaign. Her publications in the areas of gender and sexuality studies and philosophy of education include *Disputing the Subject of Sex: Sexuality and Public School Controversies* (Rowman and Littlefield, 2004), as well as articles in *Educational Theory, Philosophy of Education,* and *Philosophical Studies in Education.*

Donal O'Donoghue is an artist, critic, and educator. He lectures in Art and Education at Mary Immaculate College, University of Limerick, Ireland. He is a graduate of the National College of Art and Design, Dublin and in 2000 he was awarded the first PhD from the Faculty of Art Education NCAD.

James Sanders, an Assistant Professor at The Ohio State University's Cultural Policy and Administration Program, earned his Ph.D. in Education from UNC-Greensboro (1999), holds an MFA from SIU-Carbondale, has 26 years of experience in non-profit arts administration, and researches the intersections of educational policy, queer theory, and visual cultural.

Leonard Shurin has been involved in literacy and English as a second language (ESL) instruction and curriculum since 1984. As the Staff and Curriculum Developer for Appalachia Intermediate Unit 8, Leonard also serves on state level educational committees. He resides in Johnstown, Pennsylvania, with wife, Sherry, and daughters, Holly and Amy.

Stephanie Springgay is an Assistant Professor of Art Education and Women's Studies at Penn State University. Her research and artistic explorations focus on issues of relationality and an ethics of embodiment. In addition, as a multidisciplinary artist working with installation and video-based art, she investigates the relationship between artistic practices and methodologies of educational research through a/r/tography.

Iris Striedieck is a faculty member at Pennsylvania State University in the Educational Leadership Program. She coordinates their online masters degree with a teacher leadership focus and teaches various supervision and curriculum courses.

Dalene M. Swanson is a post-doctoral scholar at Simon Fraser University. Her interests span curriculum studies; arts-based research, teaching and learning; interdisciplinarity; critical theory; cultural studies; global citizenship; and social justice. She received Canadian and international awards in Qualitative Research and Curriculum Studies for her doctoral research at The University of British Columbia.

Diane Watt is a PhD candidate in the Faculty of Education at the University of Ottawa. During much of the decade of the 1990s she lived with her family in Islamabad, Damascus, and Tehran. Her research interests include curriculum inquiry, visual culture, and inter/cultural education, from postcolonial feminist perspectives.

John A. Weaver is Associate Professor of Curriculum Studies at Georgia Southern University. He has written *Rethinking Academic Politics and Popular Culture: A Primer* and edited *Science Fiction Curriculum, Cyborg Teacher*, and *Youth Cultures and Popular Culture*. His current work deals with digital images and animation.

Index

A

Actor Network Theory (ANT), 52-54
agency, xix, 8, 11, 13, 15, 16, 17, 19, 65,
159, 185, 210, 221, 224, 234
Ahmed, S., 159, 192, 198, 201
Ahmed, S., and Stacey, J., xix, xxii, xxiv,
41, 197
alterity, 7, 159
anti-homophobia education, 163, 168
Aoki, T., xx, xxi, 148, 152, 160, 161, 205
arational, 204
a/r/tography, 211-212

B

"being with", xx, xxiii, xxiv, 192, 196,
200, 201, 202
birth, 175-176, 187
body
    anonymous, 14
    body art, 192-193, 195-196, 201
    body-subject, 77
    cyborg, 4, 12
    deviant, 113, 120, 144
    disabled, xxiv, 113, 115-118, 121, 125,
    127
    disciplined, 100
    film, 22-23
    freakish, 132
    gendered, xvii, xix, 93, 110, 229
    image, 87, 113
    imaginary, xviii, xix, xxiii-xxiv
    knowledge, 52-53
    lived, 13, 87-89
    materiality, 11-18, 59
    memory/ies, 41-43, 47
    posthuman, 4, 6, 9, 23
    prosthetic, 4, 6
    queer, 222, 227
    racialized, 131, 134, 138, 144
    sexualized, 230-234

universal, 9
    writing, 138, 209-216
Bodyworlds, xvi, xvii, xviii, xix, xxiii
Boler, M., xxi, xxv, 42, 48, 151, 167, 168,
200
booty, 131-135
bootylicious, 131-132, 134-135, 145
Britzman, D., 158, 173, 221, 226
Bulter, J., 11, 13-14, 18, 193, 198, 204,
226, 228, 230

C

Cartesian/ism, xvi, xix, 4, 9, 11, 18-19,
69, 77, 88, 133, 148, 222
choice, rhetoric of, 176, 184
citationality (see performativity)
clothing
    as codes, 79, 82
    as communication, 79, 80-81
"coming out", 163-169
confession, 167-168
corporeal, xx, xxii, xxv, 8, 17, 51, 57, 65,
67, 77-78, 85, 90, 194, 196, 198, 201
curriculum
    bodied, xix, xxi, xxiii-xxvii, 51-52, 214
    currere, xxi, 208
    erotic, 219, 231-232
    of the everyday, 149
    lived, 205-207, 213-214
cesearean, 175, 177

D

Deleuze, G., 11-12, 22
Deleuze, G., and Guttari, F., 10-11, 18
différence
    construction of, 12, 64, 131, 139-140,
    143
digital aesthetics, 34-36
disability studies, 113

disembodied, 7-8, 15-17, 19, 40, 115,
121-122, 124, 154, 157-158, 218, 234
dress (*see* clothing)

E

embodiment
ethics of, 159, 265
feminist, 185-187
knowing, 6, 52-54
of film, 22
EyeToy®, 56-58

F

feedback looping, 55
flesh (enfleshment), xvi, xx-xxi, xxiii-
xxiv, 4, 13-14, 25, 34, 72, 98, 195,
197, 199, 201, 204-205, 209, 213-214

G

Gatens, M., xviii, xxiii-xxiv, 222
gaze, 7, 11-12, 29, 75, 102, 114, 127, 134,
225, 227, 230
Giroux, H., xix, xxvi, 22, 115
Grosz, E., xviii, xix, xx, xxii, xxiv, 14,
151, 196, 199, 210
Grumet, M., xxi-xxii, xxiv, 195, 200

H

Haraway, D., 7, 10-13, 53
Hayles, K., 9, 14, 42, 51, 53, 55, 57, 59
heteronormativity, 169, 171-173, 222

I

iBrush®, 58
intercorporeality, xxii-xxiv, xxvii, 159,
192, 197, 211
inter-embodiment, xx-xxvii, 192, 195-
196, 201
Irigaray, L., 11, 14, 199, 204, 207, 210,
213-214, 225

L

living inquiry, 85, 203-207, 209-210, 213

M

manliness, 103-106
Marks, L., 25, 28-29, 37
masculinity (ies), 93-96
Merleau-Ponty, M., xx-xxii, 13-14, 64,
77, 86, 88-89, 193, 196, 199
montage, 29-34
multiculturalism, 69, 134-137, 168
mutual articulation, 51-52, 56

N

normalcy, 114-115, 120-122, 127-128,
175, 180
Nancy, J. L., xxiii, 192-193, 195, 201

P

pedagogy
embodied, 6, 15, 19, 42
of accusation, 171-173
of awareness, 49
of discomfort, 168
of hope, 68
queer, 165, 221
performativity, xxvi, 18, 77-78, 170, 193
Pinar, B., xxi, 148, 152-153, 207-208,
214, 228

Q

queer
identity, 171, 217
sexuality, 171
theory, 217, 228

R

ritual, 203-214

S

sartorial, 79, 92
singularity, 193-194, 204
Springgay, S., xxii, 41, 59, 84-85, 92,
    157, 159, 207, 211
stillness, 41-43, 49

T

technology
    of the body, 10-11
    embodied, 36-38
    on-line, 40
    Todd, S., 154-155, 159-160

OMPLICATED

A BOOK SERIES OF CURRICULUM STUDIES

This series employs research completed in various disciplines to construct textbooks that will enable public school teachers to reoccupy a vacated public domain—not simply as "consumers" of knowledge, but as active participants in a "complicated conversation" that they themselves will lead. In drawing promiscuously but critically from various academic disciplines and from popular culture, this series will attempt to create a conceptual montage for the teacher who understands that positionality as aspiring to reconstruct a "public" space. *Complicated Conversation* works to resuscitate the progressive project—an educational project in which self-realization and democratization are inevitably intertwined; its task as the new century begins is nothing less than the intellectual formation of a public sphere in education.

The series editor is:

Dr. William F. Pinar
Department of Curriculum Studies
2125 Main Mall
Faculty of Education
University of British Columbia
Vancouver, British Columbia V6T 1Z4
CANADA

To order other books in this series, please contact our Customer Service Department:

(800) 770-LANG (within the U.S.)
(212) 647-7706 (outside the U.S.)
(212) 647-7707 FAX

Or browse online by series:

www.peterlang.com

The idea of curriculum as more than a course of studies is fundamental to the thinking in these pieces.

How can curriculum be re-worded to take in what's here? 'unbind' the word "curriculum" from it's K-12 connotations?